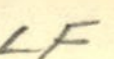

D0078537

FURIOUS FANCIES

Recent Titles in Contributions in Political Science.
Series Editor: Bernard K. Johnpoll

The Establishment in Texas Politics: The Primitive Years, 1938-1957
George Norris Green

When Europe Speaks with One Voice: The External Relations of the European Community
Phillip Taylor

Project SEARCH: The Struggle for Control of Criminal Information in America
Gordon Karl Zenk

Unequal Americans: Practices and Politics of Intergroup Relations
John Slawson

The Constitution of Silence: Essays on Generational Themes
Marvin Rintala

International Conflict in an American City: Boston's Irish, Italians, and Jews, 1935-1944
John F. Stack, Jr.

The Fall and Rise of the Pentagon: American Defense Policies in the 1970s
Lawrence J. Korb

Calling a Truce to Terror: The American Response to International Terrorism
Ernest Evans

Spain in the Twentieth Century World: Essays on Spanish Diplomacy, 1898-1978
James W. Cortada

Why the Vietcong Fought: A Study of Motivation and Control in a Modern Army in Combat
William Darryl Henderson

From Rationality to Liberation: The Evolution of Feminist Ideology
Judith A. Sabrosky

Truman's Crises: A Political Biography of Harry S. Truman
Harold F. Gosnell

"Bigotry!" Ethnic, Machine, and Sexual Politics in a Senatorial Election
Maria J. Falco

FURIOUS FANCIES

American Political Thought in the Post-Liberal Era

PHILIP ABBOTT

Contributions in Political Science, Number 35

GREENWOOD PRESS
WESTPORT, CONNECTICUT • LONDON, ENGLAND

Library of Congress Cataloging in Publication Data

Abbott, Philip.
Furious fancies.

(Contributions in political science; no. 35
ISSN 0147-1066)—
Bibliography: p.
Includes index.
1. Political science—United States.
I. Title II. Series.
JA84.U5A614 320.5'0973 79-7469
ISBN 0-313-20945-6

Library of Congress Catalog Card Number: 79-7469
ISBN: 0-313-20945-6
ISSN: 0147-1066

First published in 1980

Greenwood Press
A division of Congressional Information Service, Inc.
51 Riverside Avenue, Westport, Connecticut 06880

Printed in the United States of America

10 9 8 7 6 5 4 3 2 1

Acknowledgments

Grateful acknowledgment is made to the following publishers.

Excerpts from *The Old Regime and the French Revolution* by Alexis de Tocqueville. Translated by Stuart Gilbert. Copyright © 1955 by Doubleday & Company, Inc. Reprinted by permission of the publisher.

Excerpts from *Anarchy, State, and Utopia* by Robert Nozick, © 1974 by Basic Books, Inc., Publishers, New York.

Excerpts from *The Autonomy of Reason* by Robert Paul Wolff. Harper & Row Publishers, Inc., 1973. Reprinted by permission of the publisher.

Excerpts from *On Revolution* by Hannah Arendt. Viking Penguin, Inc., 1965. Reprinted by permission of the publisher.

Excerpts from *The Lenin Anthology* edited by Robert C. Tucker. W. W. Norton & Company, 1975. Reprinted by permission of the publisher.

Excerpts from *The Essays of William Graham Sumner* edited by Albert Galloway Keller and Maurice R. Davie. Yale University Press, 1934. Reprinted by permission of the publisher.

Excerpts from *Towards a Marxist Humanism* by Leszek Kolakowski. Translated by Jane Zielenko Peel. Grove Press, Inc., 1968. Reprinted by permission of the publisher.

Excerpts from *After the Revolution* by Robert Dahl. Yale University Press, 1970. Reprinted by permission of the publisher.

Excerpts from *A Theory of Justice* by John Rawls. Harvard University Press, 1971. Reprinted by permission of the publisher.

Excerpts from *Democratic Theory: Essays in Retrieval* by C. B. Macpherson. Oxford University Press, 1973. Reprinted by permission of the publisher.

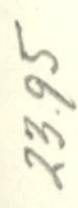

Excerpts from *Community and Power* by Robert Nisbet. Oxford University Press, 1962. Reprinted by permission of the publisher.

Excerpts from *Twilight of Authority* by Robert Nisbet. Oxford University Press, 1975. Reprinted by permission of the publisher.

Portions of Chapter 5 appeared first as a Review Article under the title "Understanding the 'New Conservatives'" in *Polity* vol. 10, no. 2 (Winter 1977), pp. 261-273.

Contents

Preface ix

1. Introduction: The Post-Liberals 3
2. With Equality and Virtue for All: John Rawls and the Liberal Tradition 28
3. Liberalism: Utopian and Scientific 55
4. Up from Pluralism 86
5. Journeymen and Pontiffs 110
6. From Liberalism to Liberation 141
7. The "Anarchist" Alternative: The Journeys of Robert Paul Wolff 163
8. The Tyranny of Fraternity in McWilliams's America 184
9. John Schaar and the Commonwealth Alternative 205
10. Conclusion: Friendship and the Liberal Society 236

Bibliography 253

Index 261

Preface

Belief systems can be studied in several ways. One is historical, including the sociology of knowledge. The history of an idea can be traced, and one learns a great deal about a belief system from a knowledge of its earlier forms and uses and its subsequent transformations. Another method is analytic. An idea is placed before an observer and is probed and dissected much like a medical student learns about anatomy from a corpse.

This book makes use of both methods. However, in its general thrust it employs a third—an attempt to determine the nature of a belief system by grasping its inner reality. Both mystification and rationalization are carefully circled. The purpose is neither to isolate the "soul" of a belief system in isolating some transrational core that is hidden behind its social use, nor to find at its center some hidden social function. In *The German Ideology* Marx complained that German philosophy attempted to move from heaven to earth. Scientific socialism would reverse the order. Here an attempt is made to move back and forth, keeping one's perspective from the last stop in order to evaluate the present one. This is an especially necessary stance when studying ideology in America, a place where heaven and earth often merge and part with dizzying speed.

Many people have read various versions and portions of this manuscript: Glenn Tinder, Richard E. Flathman, Benjamin Barber, Gordon Schochet, Michael P. Riccards, Arthur Kalleberg, Thomas Hone, Kenneth Hoover, Charles Parrish. I am very grateful for their comments. I owe a special debt to Max Mark. His views on liberal and Marxist ideologies have always fascinated me. John Rawls and Carey McWilliams have written very generous appraisals of my criticisms. Their efforts have greatly improved those portions of this book. Parts of chapters 2, 5, and 8 appeared in *Polity* and *Political Theory.* Their permission to reprint them is appreciated. One final note. A good typist is a minor blessing and I have been fortunate enough to have had two for this book: Alice Eis and Susan Meyer.

Philip Abbott
November, 1979

FURIOUS FANCIES

CHAPTER 1

Introduction: The Post-Liberals

Liberals whose hair is growing thin and the lines of whose figures are no longer what they were, are likely to find themselves today in the unhappy predicament of being treated as mourners at their own funerals. When they pluck up heart to assert that they are not yet authentic corpses, but living men with brains in their heads, they are pretty certain to be gently chided and led back to the comfortable armchair that befits senility.
—Vernon Parrington, *Main Currents in American Thought*

Parrington's own eulogy was written in 1929 before the Great Depression. It is representative of the premature death notices of liberalism displayed throughout American history. Today, another round of obituaries has been submitted. Yet, they are anything but gentle. As later chapters will point out, the critique of liberalism has been sweeping, unremitting, and, not infrequently, vengeful.

What has emerged in American political thought today is a series of attempts to bury liberalism once again. The consensus which arose in the American Academy after World War II was in part occasioned by exhaustion and, for some, after the bout with McCarthyism, a prudential retreat. But the optimism of the early 1960s seemed to invigorate the liberal consensus. The cluster of beliefs that Hartz has referred to as an unshakable "moral settlement"—individualism, progress, and an American mission in the world—were being reapplied to the incidence of racial injustice (which has always been America's equivalent to Europe's social question) and international conflict. It was less than fifteen years ago that an American philosopher could proclaim that liberalism had become the "foundation of all social morality" and the "forgotten man" of Franklin D. Roosevelt the "source of enduring strength."[1] What was once regarded a cliché would come to be treated as comic relief or even obscenity. The efforts of the early 1960s represented a pure case of reform politics in that its adherents were almost unconscious of pursuing other alternatives. But when today's intelligentsia reach to their bookshelves, it is to open what are to Americans strange and new works, not just Rousseau and Hegel but Marx, Fourier, Fanon, and Sartre.

Wartime dissent, scandal, and sabotage have produced a new sort of political philosophy in America, one which can be labeled "post-liberal." What this book attempts to do is examine the efforts toward the reconstruction of political thought in America. Each of the writers under study are fiercely independent thinkers, and they diverge at crucial points. Rawls tries to provide for a new foundation for the liberal welfare state. Nozick attempts to smash that foundation in order to return to a truncated and suspiciously simplistic interpretation of Lockean capitalism. Dahl works more closely with American politics as an operational given that must somehow be pushed in different directions. A longing for the solace of conservative order is reflected in the works of McWilliams, Schaar, Kristol, and Bell. The most shrill denunciations of liberalism are to be found in the efforts of Kariel, Zolberg, Marcuse, Macpherson, and Wolff. However, the leftism which emerges from these writers is peculiar and often puzzling.

A brief comparison with two other intellectual movements in recent history may help illuminate this description. Fritz Stern, in a study of the intellectual roots of German fascism, described the severe alienation of three nineteenth-century critics, Lagarde, Langbehn, and Moeller van den Bruck.

> Theirs was a resentment of loneliness; their one desire was for a new faith, a new community of believers...they denounced every aspect of the capitalistic society and its putative materialism. They railed against the emptiness of life in urban, commercial civilization....[2]

These men "loathed liberalism"; "everything they dreaded seemed to spring from it." Stern absolves these writers from any direct connection with Nazism. But he asks:

> ...could there have been any other "Third Reich?" Was there a safe stopping place in this wild leap from political reality? Can one abjure reason, glorify force, prophesy the age of the imperial dictator, can one condemn all existing institutions, without preparing the triumph of irresponsibility? The Germanic critics did all that, thereby demonstrating the terrible dangers of cultural despair.[3]

While some of his condemnations of liberalism are often disturbingly shrill, the American post-liberal is not a cultural prophet of the type Stern describes. The embourgeoisement of society in America is a "natural" event. Its rejection is thus at once much more difficult and more significant. This is not to say that American academia does not house anyone of that genre. Henry Kariel can be viewed not unfairly as a friendly Langbehn. Marcuse's fascination with men with "desperate laughter" is uncomfortably similar to Moeller's "mysterious" Teuton who achieves "political rebirth" from annihilation. But what is most disturbing is the frequency with which the Sorelian alternative, a direction seen at various points in history as available to the frustrated on both the right and the left, appears in American post-liberal thought. The advocacy of the primacy of the will in political action appears again and again in the most unlikely places in most of the works under review.

It finds its way not only into the theories of Kariel and Marcuse but into those of such liberal revisionists as Theodore Lowi and John Schaar. In one sense, this should not be unexpected. Much of the liberal tradition is preoccupied with the problems of founding new societies, and the assets of a strong leader are not left unexplored even in writers such as John Locke. However, the question of leadership had always been treated with ambivalence in liberalism. Moreover, and this is a point which will be explored, the Sorelian alternative attaches an existential chime to the question of beginnings, and this is quite different from the liberal's willingness to consider politics from de novo settings.

A bit closer to the mark, however, is the assessment of the "independent liberal" of the 1930s offered by R. Alan Lawson. Men such as George Soule, Stuart Chase, John Dewey, and Lewis Mumford felt the need for radical action and remained outside the New Deal while at the same time they "exercised their liberal aversion to dogma by avoiding commitments to the Marxists." Lawson contends that independent liberals fell into two groups: those who stressed "experimental reason rather than 'organic ties and historical precedents' " and those who pleaded for a society with more social cohesion as a means to preserve "the accumulated wisdom of Western civilization."[4] In Lawson's view, the effort of these independents resulted in failure: "they failed to gain power or to persuade others to enact their essential programs."[5] One point I shall argue, with the help of the "post-liberals," is that in actuality only half of the independent liberal reform failed. The "pragmatic rationalists," who called for an engineered society run by a responsible minority, have emerged again from the wreckage of the New Deal and its aftermath, fresh with new techniques, if not new arguments. The traditional liberal, often mistaken in his diagnoses and occasionally frightening even himself, lost badly. He now reappears, however, in the writings of the post-liberals ready to slay the technological dragon that he believes is coterminous with the liberal tradition.

In many ways, these men are the heirs to the traditional liberal of the 1930s. But events never precisely repeat themselves. The technological leviathan, freed if not spawned by liberalism, is now full-grown, and most of these writers do not feel they can write in the liberal tradition. Even Rawls never actually names the ideological dwelling in which he labors, feeling more comfortable citing Rousseau than Locke. Dahl begrudgingly finds some meaning in populist democracy. Kristol leans toward Aristotle; Bell presents a Schumpeterian analysis, one which is famous for accepting the conclusions although not the scenario of Marx. Wolff and Nozick retreat to analytic utopias.

One might wonder how a collection of writers of such apparent diversity can possibly be subsumed under any single category. Nozick arrives at an important part of his theory by attacking the premises of Rawls. Bell and Kristol see Rawls as the theoretical handmaiden for all that is wrong with American liberalism. Kariel is positively scornful of Dahl. As for Macpherson, these writers are bourgeois all. There will be no attempt to argue that these are simply internecine quarrels. The polemical tone waged against wayward comrades is intense and bitter, but it is based upon certain shared assumptions of substance—assumptions which opposing writers believe call for the same set of political actions.

Yet there is a different kind of comradeship among the post-liberals. It is a perception of some general and common premises about the character of American society. This does in itself not produce an intellectual movement, but, placed against the history of American political thought, it provides the basis for considering these writers as a group. Given the durability of the liberal hegemony in America one should expect a reaction of this sort. In the context of American history, the rejection or even serious revision of the liberal consensus is an event similar to the killing of one's father. In the Freudian myth, complicity in the primal crime is not necessarily objectively related to complicity in the action itself. The differences between the bravado of Kariel and the caution of Lowi are diminished by their shared participation in the death of liberalism. It matters not whether one watches the event with approval or with a certain regret. There is a hidden ambivalence in the most revengeful post-liberal and a sense of remorse in the mild opponent.

If the Hartz thesis is correct (and who can deny at least its psychic hold over the mind of the American intellectual?), it is fitting that the writers under consideration should have as their basis of comradeship complicity in the common crime, a crime that in the context of American ideas has all the force of the Freudian primal crime.

What brings these writers under the heading of post-liberal, despite the apparent differences in their politics, is a common acceptance of certain permanent inadequacies in liberalism. Sometimes, these are discovered with glee and even a little malice; more often, they are reported with frustration and despair. The belief in the failure of liberalism, however limited, rests upon four basic attitudes.

First, there is a deep-seated dissatisfaction with the ability of liberalism to deal with current problems in America. In fact, liberalism is regarded as responsible for them. The materialism and apparent lack of spiritual sources in American life obsess post-liberal thinkers. Kariel describes American society as autistic. Wolff speaks of the stupidity and viciousness of American life. McWilliams describes the loneliness of any sensitive soul in America. Bell alternately criticizes populist leveling and bourgeois acquisitiveness and the inability of liberalism to restrain either. The Europeanization of America is sometimes described with regret. But the consequence is clear. The problems that America faces as a highly industrialized society require solutions beyond the liberal tradition or with a major alteration of it.

The critiques of liberalism are based upon the belief that American society as it stands today represents the optimal range of justice that liberalism can offer. Wolff reports casually that liberalism is incapable of "utopian" criticism, that it is unable to envision a society appreciably different than what we have now. This attitude is important as a measure of post-liberal thought. For if liberalism has reached its apogee with the development of American society as it stands, even the mild reformist must search for a new ideological home. The argument that America might somehow have betrayed important parts of the liberal heritage is scrupulously avoided. Even Schaar, who finds relief in seventeenth-century republican thought, fights to avoid any implication of redemption within the broader liberal tradition. Only Dahl seems willing to pursue this direction with any fervor, and even he worries that a revitalized liberalism will not be sufficiently exciting to draw mass support.

If American society *is* liberalism in some stalled Hegelian dialectic, the images the post-liberals present of it are not pleasant. Two models appear as descriptions of America. One borrows from the liberal pluralists' view of politics. Bell describes American society as composed of groups which have "become rampant claimants in their own right."[6] What was once portrayed as a system of politics that emphasized compromise and bargaining through group competition is now described as a political system governed by principles no higher than bullying. Groups threaten and blackmail one another and occasionally stabilize at a new balance of terror. In Kariel's words, one may assume that "beyond these boundaries other things stir; that there is at least one cluster of men who are exhausted and powerless, and another cluster of men who are overbearing and decisive."[7] American society, once described by Locke as a state of nature, has again apparently partaken of its primordial history.

The other model focuses upon forces of centralization in American society.[8] Even corporate leaders and lawyers, the mainstay of the liberal substructure in America, are reported as finding that they can function quite comfortably in a new industrial state, now post-liberal, perhaps later post-constitutional. "Friendly fascism," we are told, may well be the best description of the America to come:

> ...a managed society ruled by a faceless and widely dispersed complex of warfare-welfare-industrial-communications-police-bureaucracies caught up in developing a new-style empire based on a technocratic ideology.... Under techno-urban fascism, certain elements previously regarded as inescapable earmarks of fascism would need no charismatic dictator, no one-party rule, no mass fascist party, no glorification of the state, no dissolution of legislature, no discontinuation of elections, no distrust of reason.[9]

The post-liberal searches for an alternate vision of the future in an embrace with values that he regards as neglected by liberalism: an ethics of redistribution (Rawls); drama and play (Kariel); political activism (Dahl, Schaar); utopian experimentation (Nozick); utopian criticism (Zolberg, Marcuse); fraternity (McWilliams); a sense of religion (Bell).

The post-liberal sees these alternatives with bright and excited eyes. The "new" perspectives which now seem available are often interpreted with the most casual critical scrutiny. In fact, it is the truly frenetic character of this search that places the post-liberals together despite the differences in their selection. The tenets of classical liberalism that have been subjected to ferocious examination naturally do not fare well in the comparison. Thus, the post-liberal becomes even more estranged from the liberal tradition.

In addition to these characteristics, there is a tone to post-liberal thought that is important to note. Despite the exhilaration that the post-liberal exhibits in relation to the possibilities ultimately available once the liberal consensus finally collapses, a severe pessimism affects nearly all post-liberal analysis. This produces a politics of lamentation which stands beside the recommendations the post-liberal offers.

It would be difficult, therefore, to make a case for a post-liberal enlightenment. Many of the works under consideration were written over a period which saw the headiest days of revolutionary delusion on American campuses. But Schaar complains that citizens do not need to hear his arguments and noncitizens *cannot* hear them. Kariel prefaces a book that glories in the possibilities of political action in America quietly noting that only some unforeseen catastrophe could alter the power structure. Apparently, the effects of the American consensus are so large and powerful that even beyond its grave liberalism transfixes the populations with vampirelike powers. This has led many post-liberals to begin to flirt with the idea of a basic corruption infecting the American people. Marxists have long accepted this notion with the dialectic of history acting ultimately as a redeeming force. Thus it is not surprising to find Macpherson and Marcuse voicing it. Yet Schaar, Kariel, Wolff, and Kristol, none of them Marxist or "friendly fascists," seem to revert to this kind of desperation.

However, despite the disdain and, in many instances, the hatred of liberalism, there is an untoward quality about most of post-liberal political thought. A writer with different convictions would be tempted to remind us of Marx's remark about the German "schoolboys" in the 1830s. It is true that the post-liberals do appear to be attempting to "reconcile irreconcilables" but hardly as the "petty retailers and hawkers" that Marx describes. However mightily the post-liberal seems to struggle with the basis and direction of American political thought, he seems to return rather near liberal orthodoxy. For if the effort to move beyond and discredit the liberal tradition is an identifying mark of the post-liberal, his second trait is his failure to offer plausible alternatives appreciably different from those which exist in liberal political thought itself.

No one could present a more damning account of justice based upon individual desert than Rawls, yet the result of his total effort remains very close, indeed, pathetically close, to one variety of conventional liberalism. Nozick's effort to discredit post-Millsian liberalism and replace it with a more "scientific" analysis reluctantly gives birth to a nineteenth-century utopianism. Both Rawls and Nozick, writers who stay closest to that set of beliefs that encompass a liberal consensus, are unable to present an integrated political philosophy. One will lament this fact with Rawls and glory in it with Nozick, but neither position advances the liberal dilemma. McWilliams either underestimates the concern of liberals over the problem of community or stands resigned to the fate of modernity. On either interpretation, he beds down next to the liberal, if not with him. Schaar asks radicals to remain in the fold of the American political tradition. This is conservative advice no matter what kaleidoscope one uses to view past history. Of course, Schaar's vision of republican virtue is contained within liberalism itself. Wolff's frantic journeys indicate that his break with liberalism seems to be occasioned by a deeply held skepticism, itself a product of the liberal mind. Kristol and Bell, portraying themselves as besieged liberals, offer what is essentially a holding operation and, as I shall argue, they are not sufficiently committed to manage that. The alternative offered by Kariel can probably be described best as a liberal heresy.

No doubt the reader may be annoyed at this point. The post-liberals are to be criticized for their disparagement of liberalism as well as their failure to depart far enough from it. However, the major difficulty with the post-liberals is their unwillingness to examine the complex nature of the liberal tradition. Thus they do deserve condemnation for failing to see the real nature of liberalism's faults and for failing to focus their efforts in that direction. Some remedial efforts in this regard will be made in the last chapter. The present task is to introduce the general framework within which the post-liberals can be assessed.

When any attempt at all is made to distinguish varieties of liberalism, it is usually on the basis of classical or laissez-faire versus modern or welfare liberalism. It is a matter of considerable interest that most contemporary liberals accept this distinction as well, simply arguing that different conclusions are warranted. This forms what might be called a conventional liberal account of liberalism's own history, as well as a doctrinal stance for political action. In England, Hobhouse would argue that liberal individualism "when it grapples with the facts is driven no small distance along socialist lines."[10] In America, Dewey would contend that liberalism in its modern form is simply an identical response to different conditions.[11] There was no real departure. The argument is the same, save the object of conversion is the socialist on the one hand and the capitalist on the other. A convenient and thoughtful compendium of these positions has been presented by Harry Girvetz in his *The Evolution of Liberalism.* A brief look at his account will illustrate my point. Girvetz sees in classical liberalism (which he derives chiefly from Hobbes, Locke, Smith, Bentham, and the elder Mill) a commitment to a particular "psychological creed" quite similar to Macpherson's famous description of "possessive individualism." This creed contains the following elements:

1. *Psychological egoism and psychological hedonism.* The most significant features in this belief are the assumptions that self-interest is a clear and unambiguous term, that is, rooted in human nature rather than in the changing institutional setting which constitutes our social environment.
2. *Intellectualism.* All attempts at maximizing interest are measurable and comprehensible. In Bentham's words: "When matters of pleasure and pain are at stake...who is it that does not calculate?"
3. *Quietism.* "...action must be induced, that, in the absence of the enticement provided by pleasure or advantage the organism will remain apathetic, inert, quiescent." The connection between Pope's line, "Fixed like a plant on this peculiar spot/To draw nutrition, propagate or rot," and the Lynds' reportage of the Middletown residents' belief that "Men won't work if they don't have to," provides a powerful liberal litany about indolence, incentive, and capitalism.
4. *Atomism.* Classical liberalism was a "revolt against the authority of custom and law and the claims of duty." In its stead was placed the "individual (standing) forward and apart, self-contained, atomic, bound only by the ties of interest to the society in which he lives."[12]

The fact that such descriptions of liberalism, ones so frequently taken by the post-liberals as a basis for bludgeoning individualism, are considered a reasonable picture of most of the liberal tradition illustrates the unwittingly defensive position liberalism has assumed in recent history. Girvetz, of course, performs his task. With the help of Jones, Dewey, Veblen, Homans, Mitchell, and others, he dutifully hammers away at the fallacies of classical liberalism. Egoism is incorrect or else tautological or trivial. Work can be separated from labor. Dewey's "artist, adventurer, sportsman, soldier, administrator, and speculator" needs no calculus to move him. Capitalist society has always rested upon libidinal men: "It was not as *homo economicus* that the elder Henry Ford acted when he declared that he would shut down his plant rather than deal with the union."[13]

The dichotomous accounts of classical and modern liberalism are all designed to produce some kind of conflation. All liberal theories are essentially possessive individualist, or all liberal theories are a "form of protest against established interests which balk the forces of progress" whether against a "profligate and decadent feudal aristocracy" or a "predatory capitalism."[14] It shall be argued that both conclusions miss the nature of the liberal tradition. First, all liberal theories are not based upon some sort of appetitive individualism. This point will be noted in nearly every chapter. Second, liberal theories are not always movements against established rule. While Girvetz's claim may be true in a deeper and more subtle sense, the record of liberalism as a protest ideology is quite mixed. Certainly this will be regarded as an understatement of colossal proportions by post-liberals. However, the assessment is appropriate. Liberals waged sustained assaults against privilege in the seventeenth and eighteenth centuries and still stand in opposition in regimes where the rights of speech and assembly are nonexistent. Yet, that is not really the thrust of liberalism's heritage.

Moreover, this categorization (as well as numerous variations of it) is incorrect because it is based on one of liberalism's bouts with a particular kind of challenge. On this interpretation liberals are seen as engaging in a kind of forced retreat against the attacks on capitalism. The abrasive character of a capitalist ethos is rejected in order to salvage a functioning economic order. What the conventional view misses is that capitalism and even the nature of human action associated with it are one consequence, not a basis, of the set of beliefs that form the character of liberal theory.

Chapter 2 begins to explore the incredibly difficult demands such beliefs place upon political theory. At this point, however, there is also an indication of the true nature of the liberal's (and the post-liberal's) problem.

Despite the efforts of its detractors, liberalism is not an especially cohesive political theory, and no elaborate effort will be made to ferret out common beliefs from the wide variety of writers that liberalism encompasses. As the efforts of the post-liberals are examined, the history of liberalism will gradually unravel.

Two sets of beliefs which rely upon the reader's acceptance are offered: the acceptance of perpetual human conflict and the belief in the existence and plurality of forms of the good life. Locke saw men incurably biased by "interest," "revenge," "passion," "corruption," and "partiality." James Mill saw the desire for the power to render human beings subservient to our own pleasures as a "grand governing law of human nature." Madison insisted that faction often took the form of class war but that it really was "sown in the nature of man"; "the most frivolous and fanciful distinctions have been sufficient to kindle...unfriendly passions, and excited their most violent conflict."[15] Adam Smith warned that even in times of political and economic stability men were "surrounded by unknown enemies." This belief is so prominent that Sheldon Wolin has written that liberalism is a philosophy of "sobriety."[16]

Wolin, however, misses the second portion of liberalism's heritage, what Lionel Trilling once called the belief in the primal imagination of the human spirit. The notion that persons do seek goodness, that the good is rational, and that external constraints upon the selection and pursuit of a good life are undesirable is the most bold and exhilarating feature of liberalism.

Liberalism's utopian premise is a unique one in political theory. It does share certain features common to other modern ideologies: the belief in a social order vastly different from that of the status quo and the belief that such an order can be reached without full-scale violence and a period of harsh tutelage. But it also presents a vision that no other view offers. Anyone who measures what we know about social and political life against this utopian premise should be led to consider its genuine nature. The vision of individuals freely choosing life plans appears in all liberal thought. Sometimes it is the centerpiece. Sometimes it is buried amidst concern over its consequences. Sometimes it is offered casually. Sometimes it is presented with great precision and eloquence. Here are a few samples:

Locke's analytic premise:

To understand Political Power right, and derive it from the original, we must consider what state all men are naturally in, and that is, a state of perfect Freedom to order their Actions and dispose of their Possessions, and Persons as they think fit, within the bounds of the Law of Nature, without asking leave, or depending upon the Will of any other Man.[17]

Mill's plea for "individuality":

He who lets the world, or his own portion of it, choose his plan of life for him has no need of any other faculty than the ape-like one of imitation. He who chooses his plan for himself employs all his faculties. He must use observation to see, reasoning and judgment to foresee, activity to gather materials for decision, discrimination to decide, and when he has decided, firmness and self-control to hold to his deliberate decision.... Supposing it were possible to get houses built, corn grown, battles fought, causes tried, and even churches erected and prayers said by machinery—by automatons in human form—it would be a considerable loss to exchange for these automatons even the men and women who at present inhabit the more civilized parts of the world, and who assuredly are but starved specimens of what nature can and will produce.[18]

Kant's vision of the "Kingdom of Ends":

A rational being belongs to the realm of ends as a member when he gives universal laws in it while also himself subject to these laws. He belongs to it as sovereign when he, as legislating, is subject to the will of no other. The rational being must regard himself always as legislative in a realm of ends possible through the freedom of the will, whether he belongs to it as a member or as a sovereign. He cannot maintain the latter position merely through the maximization of his will but only when he is a completely independent being without need and with power adequate to his will.[19]

Jefferson's oath:

I have sworn upon the altar of God, eternal hostility against every form of tyranny over the mind of man.[20]

Even if one leaves aside the frequency of failure in sincerely pursuing the "primal imagination," there is still the question of how liberal political theories are able to capture the belief in the plural good individually selected. By stopping for a moment to consider the implications of the set of beliefs liberalism offers, it is possible to focus upon the major problems of liberalism and thus be in a position to judge the contributions that the post-liberals attempt to make. The inexhaustible penchant of the liberal man to generate conflict makes an institution for conflict resolution in society a necessity. At the same time, however, the relative diversity of equally justifiable life plans makes the suppression of some difficult to justify. Without a belief in the primacy of seeking one good, a permanent political community appears at once excruciatingly pressing and undesirable. This explains the special attention liberalism has paid to the concept of political obligation. And yet for all the effort expended in this direction, liberalism has shown a persistent inability to provide a plausible model of political obligation once it has introduced the problem as the central task of political philosophy. Nor should it be surprising to note that this stumbling block is not an isolated instance, but symptomatic of a larger problem in liberal thought. The problem of political obligation is the result, and certainly the most prominent one, of the absence of fraternity in liberal political life. The liberal man may be freed from the tyrannies of the mind of which Jefferson spoke so eloquently and free to pursue any vision that excites his imagination, but he is a lonely man bereft of the class solidarity or comradeship that Marxism and radical democracy offer their citizens.

The solutions that liberals have offered over time to deal with this dilemma are not uniform. However, whether they are fully aware of it or not, it is in this context that the post-liberals struggle against the implications of the liberal tradition, and it will be the task of this book to assess these beliefs as well as the efforts of various writers to reject them or overcome the obstacles they present for the creation of a viable political theory.

One way in which the liberal tradition might be better approached is to take these two beliefs and see in what ways each has been defined and combined with the other. Ironically, the starting place is with Karl Marx. In his preface to the second edition of *Capital* Marx argued that liberal political economy up to Ricardo was genuinely scientific; "it investigated the real relations of production in bourgeois society."[21] Human conflict was accepted as a given and a social universe posited from it. Measured against the struggles for gain in capitalist society, liberal economies had both explanatory and predictive power. This effort became "vulgar" economy when practiced by later writers. J.S. Mill was the best representative. Scientific analysis was replaced by "bad conscience and the evil intent of apologetic." For "bourgeois daily use," Mill tried to "harmonize the political economy of capital with the claims, no longer to be ignored, of the proletariat."[22] With Ricardo, "the science of bourgeois economy had reduced the limits beyond which it could not pass."[23] The development of manifest class struggle meant that the moral values of the system could no longer be assumed and political economy left to the impartiality of scientific analysis. Another economic order could now be perceived and the capitalistic one was in need of justification. What is natural and immutable needs no moral support; liberal economics had to retreat, partially at least, to ethical philosophy.

C. B. Macpherson has contended that the same distinction can be discerned in liberal political thought:

> I think that we can say that "classical" political theory has reached, with Bentham and James Mill...the limits beyond which it could not pass. Bentham and James Mill drew out the full consequences, for the theory of government, of the "classical" postulate of possessive individualism. They were the last who could do so scientifically; critiques ranging from Carlyle's to the Christian Socialist's and the practical critiques of Chartism and other working class movements, made that evident.[24]

Vulgar political theory came to fruition with J. S. Mill, the "first serious liberal-democratic theorist." Mill attempted to infuse liberalism with "values higher than market values." "Yet in the end, Mill found himself helpless, unable to reconcile his notion of values with the political economy which he still believed in. The world's work had to go on, and he could see no way in which it could be carried on except by competitive private enterprise."[25] Mill had "exhausted himself in seeking ways to patch up the contradictions between liberalism and social democracy."[26] The last hundred years of liberal thought have been "necessarily self-deception."

This is the "left" assessment of liberalism. As a scientific theory it is hopelessly out of date. As a utopian theory it is deception or vulgarization. But perhaps it is possible to use the concepts of science and utopia in liberalism in a different fashion. The liberal's belief in the inevitability of conflict is indeed its scientific base. One can posit the modern social order based upon endemic conflict and still produce an impressive array of generalizations. To the extent to which the liberal assigns a place in his theories that corresponds to this belief, he weds himself to the current order. But what if the utopian element in liberal theory is taken seriously? It is true that this is a utopian model peculiar to liberalism; this is part of the reason Marx dismissed it. On the other hand, if these two beliefs form a definition of liberalism, the utopian element is less a response to the inadequacies of liberalism's scientific base than a separate element, one which, as has been already admitted, does not combine easily with its counterpart.

The effort is a bit more complicated, however. The scientific and utopian bases are not always given the same weight in liberal theories nor are they always defined similarly. If the scientific-utopian dimension of Marx and Macpherson is considered alongside this description of the two core beliefs of liberalism, it is possible to suggest four varieties of liberal political thought. This is not a neat, exclusive formulation. Some liberals may hold on to more than one form. For instance, J. Stuart Mill appears in each category. Moreover, variations occur within categories. However, ideologies often can be better understood when shadings are separated, solidified, and presented as identifiable alternatives. Here are the results of such a division:

Welfare liberalism. In this formulation the utopian element remains central to the theory but it is given a standardized meaning. J. S. Mill is the focal point. While Mill steered liberalism away from its utilitarian moorings and insisted upon the difficult dimension of "quality" in the consideration of the good life, he provided a foundation for theories which began to take seriously the idea that there is indeed a single model of a good life.

This form of liberalism represents something more than an attempt to come to terms with the left's claim that liberal theories do indeed rest upon some preferred personality type. The model of the good life is still presented in neutral, abstract, and universal terms. The concept of the human personality itself forms the framework.

However, any appetitive dimension is denied. If the human personality has self-regarding features they are morally acceptable ones. The pursuit of individual excellence first offered by Mill is cut off from any connotation of capitalist aggressiveness:

> I confess I am not charmed with the ideal of life held out by those who think that the normal state of human beings is that of struggling to get on; that the trampling, crushing, elbowing, and treading on each other's heels, which form the existing type of social life, are the most desirable lot of human kind, or anything but the disagreeable symptoms of one of the phases of industrial progress.[27]

The historically important feature of welfare liberalism involves the manner in which its advocates hoped to connect the good life to the political system. Mill, however, never offered a clear linkage. In fact, in many of his works he fought against this direction. But the elements of such a transition can be easily found. Mill's comments in *The Subjection of Women* are representative: "Of all the difficulties which impede the progress of thought, and the formation of well-grounded opinions on life and social arrangements, the greatest is now the unspeakable ignorance and inattention of mankind in respect to influences which form human character."[28]

In Hobhouse, Green, and Dewey there is more than an inclination to regard differences in the identification of the good life as the result of ignorance or economic deprivation. With Hegelian certainty, T. H. Green gives to the state the role of a moral teacher:

> The value then of the institutions of civil life lies in their operation as giving reality to these capacities of will and reason, and enabling them to be really exercised. In their general effect, apart from particular aberrations, they render it possible for a man to be freely determined by the idea of a possible satisfaction of himself, instead of being driven this way and that by external forces, thus they give reality to the capacity called will: and they enable him to realize his reason (i.e., his idea of self-perfection) by acting as member of a social organization in which each contributes to the better-being of all the rest.[29]

Who could deny that the utopian element in liberalism is not alive in this formulation? Dewey argued that this new liberalism was radical. His formulation of the concept could not help but bring a smile to the Marxist: "For the gulf between the future and the actual state itself is so great that it cannot be bridged by piecemeal policies undertaken ad hoc."[30]

It is true that this liberal version of praxis is still incomplete in that the welfare liberal continues to hold to his belief in the inevitability of conflict. But what are its new dimensions? Dewey would argue that the model of class struggle and revolution is now outmoded, that the real basis of conflict today lies in the "older institutions and habits" of a "pre-scientific age which stood in the way."[31] Intelligence, not force, is the appropriate method of destroying them. Conflict there will always be, but, with the proper application of intelligence and a fixed image of the ideal human personality, we shall be able to "regiment things and free people."

John Rawls's *A Theory of Justice* is an attempt to give a broader formulation to this form of liberalism. The social contract is resurrected in the form of the "veil of ignorance" and "virtue" is added to it. Rawls seeks not only to provide a deeper basis to a uniform interpretation of liberalism's utopian element but to carry this interpretation to areas of social life that liberals have not been willing to pursue. But the specter of social conflict constantly reappears in Rawls's formulation, and it shall be argued that he is not able to markedly alter the direction of welfare liberalism.

Scientific liberalism. In this form of liberalism the perceived consequences of social conflict are treated with such reverence that nearly all the energy of the liberal's imagination is devoted to finding some settlement. Conflict is seen as the result of individual differences but since life plans seem to clash so horribly, the utopian element is ignored by reducing it to simple but dangerous individual interests. Hobbes is the exemplar here: "...whatsoever is the object of any man's Appetite or Desire...he for his part calleth Good."[32] Thus men do seek the good; in fact, they seek it relentlessly. But the good has appetitive attributes. As a consequence, nature "dissociates," and men "invade and destroy one another." It is well known that Hobbes's solution to social conflict reaches beyond the liberal vision. However, if the Hobbesian alternative has not been accepted, Hobbes's view of social conflict has. Is it possible to accept his reduction of the utopian premise to interest or desire and yet avoid his own recommendations? Could Hobbes's self-proclaimed science of politics be put to use within the liberal tradition? Locke remains the pivotal writer in this tradition. While he insisted that human beings possessed rights which must not be violated, he leaves us without any doubt that the exercise of these rights breeds serious and irreversible conflict. A long list of liberals have also claimed to be able to do so: James Mill, Jeremy Bentham, Herbert Spencer, William Graham Sumner.

Each of these writers attempts to provide a "moral settlement" that does not attempt to deny Hobbesian appetites or clashes of rights but sets the arena in which they will be pursued. Richard Hofstadter has summarized this effort and the dilemma it creates with exceptional clarity in his discussion of the founding fathers:

> They thought man was a creature of rapacious self-interest, and yet they wanted him to be free—free, in essence, to contend, to engage in an inspired strife, to use property to get property. They accepted the mercantile image of life as an external battleground, and assumed the Hobbesian war of each against all; they did not propose an end to this war, but merely to stabilize it and make it less murderous. They had no hope and they offered none for any ultimate organic change in the way men conduct themselves. The result was that while they thought self-interest the most dangerous and unbrookable quality of man, they necessarily underwrote it in trying to control it.[33]

In all of these theories the concept of individualism (the key element of liberalism's utopian premise as well) is the basis of "scientific" theory. The liberal's view of human conflict derives from his individualist premises, and his "scientific" resolution is based on some theory of individual interaction, often an economically based one. However, the aim of such theories is to move beyond the perceived consequences of individualism by "purifying" individual relationships. This is why the moral settlement that these theories are designed to achieve is much more far-reaching than these liberals indicate. Thus scientific liberals seek to avoid anything resembling an ad hoc solution to human conflict. Here Marx was correct. The incidence of social conflict is seen as requiring a model with the power of high generalization, one which explains and predicts human behavior in a wide variety of settings. In this respect, the elder Mill and Bentham and the economic theorists who followed them represent the ideal type. Social Darwinism, the liberal scientific theory that most closely approaches the Hobbesian solution, fits this model as well.

Robert Nozick is the representative post-liberal theorist of scientific liberalism. Although he offers only a mutilated version of Locke, in an odd fashion the utopian element of liberalism reemerges at the close of his book.

Pluralist liberalism. This form of liberalism represents the most sustained effort to combine both utopian and scientific elements. The conflict proposition of the scientific element is openly accepted, but it is cleverly turned in upon itself in order to reform the utopianism. Group competition and conflict supervised by a limited political authority translates liberalism's philosophical problem into a sociological one. Give each individual and then each group the freedom to select the good; the conflict that emerges can be controlled by bargaining and compromise. Pluralism does not guarantee that the utopian premise will be fulfilled at any given moment for any particular group or individual, only that the system as a whole promotes such a probability. Thus while the utopian premise is toned down, the scientific one is modified as well. Bargaining replaces violence.

There are several variations in this form and an attempt to sort them out will be made in chapters 4, 5, and 9. It should be noted here, however, that one of the difficulties in capturing the pluralist alternative in an analytic framework is that in many of its forms there is a self-conscious criticism of its own solution. Pluralists often search for the possibility of community hidden beneath diversity.

The oldest version of liberal pluralism is derived from a reaction to the historical development of democracy. This is called a Whig model of politics. Both a theory of society and a set of political tactics, the Whig model incorporates conventional liberal solutions to political problems: constitutionalism, free speech, and elections. But the early Whig vision is the only version of liberalism that is willing to conceive of a hierarchically ordered society. Naturally, it sees its own social strata as the balancing force in society, a point which James Mill so successfully demolished in his famous articles in the *Westminster Review.* This Whig model did not fare well in the American setting. As Hartz notes, it died and was transmogrified in the middle of the nineteenth century. A review of these alterations will support the contention that Whiggery, again suitably transformed, has reappeared in the post-liberal era. Other post-liberals have reached back even further into the tradition of political thought in order to find an acceptable pluralism, one less harsh and more fraternal than liberalism seems able to provide. Wilson Carey McWilliams is an example.

Another form of pluralist liberalism appears with the so-called real Whigs, a remnant ideology with roots in the English Commonwealth tradition. The pluralism here is muted, and in some cases nearly submerged in an effort to find some common denominator which will unite the various elements of a "mixed" regime. This form of Whiggery freely explored the unifying forces upon which a pluralist society might draw. But the Commonwealth tradition created a conception of authority that was decidedly opposed to authority. As illogical as this appears, this peculiar conception represented a solution to liberalism's dilemma. If the common good could indeed emerge from a diverse and alert citizenry, what function did political authority perform? In Paine's words, society arises from our wants, government from our failings. Jefferson had hoped the people would be socialized to *distrust* the ambitions of their leaders.

As shall be noted, this form of pluralism could be pushed in several different directions. One of them is what has been referred to as "interest group" liberalism. The moralistic focus of the Commonwealth tradition is abandoned and self-interest is its replacement. Moral or religious motives, wrote Madison, will not restrain "impulse and opportunity." With this sort of pluralism, the scientific component has the ascendancy. What is left of utopianism is contained in the muted phrase, "enlightened self-interest." Dahl and Lowi have attempted to save what remains of the utopian element in this model.

Utopian liberalism. There have been attempts by liberals to pay serious attention to the utopian element of their tradition, as illustrated by the tendency in liberalism to emphasize the individual pursuit of the good. This is the nature of its utopianism. The more this utopianism is given an exclusive or central focus, the more it is given a hyperindividualized interpretation. The liberal finds himself both estranged from the society he set out to evaluate and skeptical of the ability of his utopianism to offer common goals.

Many liberals have found themselves in this position. J. S. Mill's value pluralism led him in this direction in *On Liberty*. Where Mill pursued the implications of such utopianism, his attacks on the current social order were the most trenchant. But elements of this thought can be plucked from Milton and Kant and Williams as well. Rarely has skepticist liberalism formed a well-developed social movement. Of all the varieties of liberalism discussed, this form has the most shadowy existence. It represents a tendency in, or an open alternative to liberal political thought. In many ways, it takes the form of a vacuum, quickly filled in with surer but more base standards. Hobbes's individualism presupposes a moral skepticism but interest immediately takes its place. In some cases the vacuum is filled with an emphasis upon a procedural interpretation of society. Here skepticism connects with constitutionalism and, in a more general way, with the scientific premise. If the utopian element of liberalism is so individualized as to prevent any value consensus, an agreement on rules can substantially reduce conflict.

It must be said, however, that the acute individualization of the utopian premise does not automatically lead to the measured order of a constitutional society. Perhaps no moral settlement should be accepted at all. Perhaps a thousand utopias ought to flourish whatever the consequences. Such talk seems very brave within the context of a liberal society. The standard of playful eccentricity is placed alongside the liberal order with its "Robert's *Rules of Order*, the Sherman Antitrust Act, the system of checks and balances, due process of law, the right to privacy" and appears to be a deadly challenge when in fact such formulations are little more than liberal heresies.[34] This is the assessment that will be offered of Henry Kariel and others with similar views.

Such a pursuit moves back toward the Hobbesian alternative in scientific liberalism. The reader who detects a perverse dialectic in this movement has made an important discovery, for the liberal utopia conceived *in extremis* ultimately flattens out individually selected goods as much as do other forms of liberalism. If all pursuits of the good are equally justifiable, provided they are individually selected, the need for some conflict-resolution agency becomes a paramount concern. To the extent that the utopian liberal is unwilling to modify his individualism, he is forced to embrace a set of principles which uniformly contains them. The dialectic is technically not quite complete since now the utopian and scientific premises stand facing one another, like two soldiers ready to do battle. But the winner in this kind of combat is obvious. The utopian premise collapses as soon as the fight begins. This whole journey is rarely clearly seen in the history of political thought, especially within the works of one writer. However, sometimes there is a purity in post-liberal thought as it considers the alternatives available for determined writers. Robert Paul Wolff provides a textbook example of the movement which has just been briefly described.

As this examination of current American political thought begins, it will become clear how trapped the post-liberals are in liberalism's tangle of science and utopia.

NOTES

1. Harry Girvetz, *The Evolution of Liberalism* (New York: Collier Books, 1963), p. 387.
2. Fritz Stern, *The Politics of Cultural Dispair* (Garden City, N.Y.: Doubleday, 1965), p. 2.
3. Ibid., p. 361.
4. R. Alan Lawson, *The Failure of Independent Liberalism* (New York: Capricorn Books, 1971), p. 13.
5. Ibid., p. 14.
6. Daniel Bell, "The Public Household," *Public Interest* 37 (Fall 1974), 53.
7. Henry Kariel, *The Premise of Politics* (Englewood Cliffs, N.J.: Prentice-Hall, 1966), p. 104.
8. The image of American society as a loose confederation of pirates is generally seen as representing a transition to radical centralization of American politics.

9. Bertram Gross, "Friendly Fascism: A Model for America," *Social Policy* (November-December 1970), 46.

10. L. T. Hobhouse, *Liberalism* (London: Oxford University Press, 1971), p. 54.

11. John Dewey, *Liberalism and Social Action* (New York: Capricorn Books, 1963), p. 53.

12. Girvetz, *The Evolution of Liberalism*, pp. 27-49.

13. Ibid., p. 172

14. Ibid., p. 385.

15. James Madison, "Federalist # 10" in the *Federalist Papers*, Clinton Rossiter, ed. (New York: Mentor, 1961), p. 79.

16. Sheldon Wolin, *Politics and Vision* (Boston: Little, Brown, 1960), p. 325.

17. John Locke, *Two Treatises on Government*, Peter Laslett, ed. Vol. II (New York: Mentor, 1960), p. 309.

18. John Stuart Mill, *On Liberty*, Gertrude Himmelfarb, ed. (Baltimore: Penguin, 1976), p. 123.

19. Immanuel Kant, *Foundations of the Metaphysics of Morals*, Lewis White Beck, trans. (Indianapolis: Library of Liberal Arts, 1959), p. 52.

20. In a letter to Benjamin Rush in *Thomas Jefferson on Democracy*, Saul K. Padover, ed. (New York: Mentor, 1939), p. 169.

21. Karl Marx, "Preface to the Second Edition," *Capital*, Lewis S. Feuer, ed. (Garden City, N.Y.: Doubleday, 1959), p. 139.

22. Ibid., p. 140.

23. Ibid., p. 139.

24. C. B. Macpherson, *Democratic Theory: Essays in Retrieval* (Oxford: Oxford University Press, 1973), p. 200.

25. Ibid., p. 201.

26. Ibid.

27. John Stuart Mill, *Principles of Political Economy* in *Collected Works*. J. M. Robson, ed. (Toronto: University of Toronto Press, 1977), p. 754.

28. John Stuart Mill, *The Subjection of Women* in John Stuart Mill and Harriet Taylor Mill, *Essays on Sex Equality*, Alice S. Rossi, ed. (Chicago: University of Chicago Press, 1970), p. 149. This side of Mill is ably presented in Shirley Robin Letwin's *The Pursuit of Certainty* (Cambridge: Cambridge University Press, 1965).

29. T. H. Green, *Lectures on the Principles of Political Obligation* (Ann Arbor: University of Michigan Press, 1967), p. 32.

30. Dewey, *Liberalism and Social Action*, p. 62.

31. Ibid., p. 76. One is reminded of an earlier American effort in this direction. Herbert Croly had argued for more power in the hands of experts in *The Promise of American Life*, pp. 427-50.

32. Thomas Hobbes, *Leviathan*, C. B. Macpherson, ed. (Baltimore: Penguin, 1968), p. 12.

33. Richard Hofstadter, *The American Political Tradition and the Men Who Made It* (New York: Vintage, 1923), p. 20. The centrality of Hobbes in American political thought is explored with considerable analytic insight by Frank M. Coleman, *Hobbes in America* (Toronto: University of Toronto Press, 1977). For a proper emphasis, however, see chap. 9.

34. Henry Kariel, "Making Scenes in a Liberal Society," *Massachusetts Review 2* (Spring 1970), 226.

CHAPTER 2

With Equality and Virtue for All: John Rawls and the Liberal Tradition

A Socialist who is convinced of the logical coherence and practical applicability of his system may dismiss (our) endeavours to harmonize divergent claims as a half-hearted and illogical series of compromises.
—L. T. Hobhouse, *Liberalism*

Numbed reviewers greeted the publication of John Rawls's *A Theory of Justice* with quiet and often begrudging praise. Then, hungry critics moved in. The majority of notices now can be described as careful and methodical, but mercilessly critical.[1] No doubt part of this calculated fury can be traced to the sheer scope of the work. For some time now political philosophers have had to content themselves with demolishing long-dead giants who answer through surrogates at other universities. It is a tantalizing experience to sink one's teeth into a product whose creator is alive and well at Harvard.

In a sense, *A Theory of Justice* may represent the last effort in liberal political philosophy, and it may be useful to begin with Rawls in order to openly judge his work against the tradition he has chosen to extend and revise.

In another sense, however, Rawls has taken upon himself the task of drawing one form of liberalism to a close. *A Theory of Justice* is designed to produce a new stability in liberal society—an inner stability, if you will—which finally strips the liberal man of envy and at the same time directs his attention toward attaining justice for all. It is in the context of the core beliefs of liberalism that *A Theory of Justice* attempts to make a contribution to political thought. However, Rawls has introduced the concepts of equality and virtue into a liberal theory of justice. Despite the absorption of many features of democratic thought into contemporary liberalism, the liberal suspicion of equality is still profound. As a result, the existence of inequalities in benefits to the citizenry is sanctioned in liberal societies. It has become almost commonplace to say that this situation has made a mockery of even the limited view of liberal justice. Similarly, the liberal insistence that virtue be rejected as a political good has contaminated and often destroyed attempts to foster this value among citizens in their private capacities. That virtue can be nourished and sustained by men without any supporting institutions is part of the submerged utopian impulse of liberalism.

Rawls's plan, then, is a daring one not because he seeks to establish a connection between virtue and justice but because he attempts to do so in a liberal context. It will be argued, however, that the attempt fails because virtue accompanied by equality nullify one another. Almost two hundred years ago, James Madison presented a picture of how American society could function when another form of liberalism was seen to have failed. His "republican principles for republican defects" was designed to produce a stable liberal order. Rawls's model is designed to remedy "defects" as well, but these are defects discovered in the age of the welfare state and, of course, in the post-liberal era. Yet an unintended effect of Rawls's work is that it prompts new consideration of the liberal vision of society along with the capacities of that society to survive in a manner different from what liberals have thought it would. This may, in the end, be the lasting historical contribution of *A Theory of Justice.*

The first step in pursuing this argument involves briefly recapitulating the manner in which Rawls introduces equality and virtue into a theory of justice. By first discussing the equality principle and then moving to an assessment of political obligation in the Rawlsian polity (much as Rawls himself proceeds), it can be shown how virtue is introduced into the system, and the problem of political obligation can be reassessed in this context.

The fount of all arguments of *A Theory of Justice* is the original position. By now, all students of political philosophy are familiar with Rawls's description. Some have contended it permits too little information to allow for an account of justice; others have argued that it permits too much to allow for the notion of fairness Rawls ascribes to it. The concern here, however, is only with the status it enjoys as a description of thinking and conduct in constructing the just society.

A good deal about such kind of thinking can be learned by the circumstances of justice, one of the few patches of knowledge permitted by the veil of ignorance. "There are objective circumstances which make human cooperation both possible and necessary."[2] Although Rawls acknowledges his debt to Hume, the description which follows is equally reminiscent of Hobbes: men's capacities are "comparable in that no one among them can dominate the rest"; all are "vulnerable to attack" and "subject to having their plans blocked by the united force of others." Men have their own plans of life which lead to "conflicting claims on natural and social resources."[3]

Rawls takes the edge off a Hobbesian version of the original position by insisting upon the mutual disinterestedness of the contracting parties. The principles of justice are derived on the supposition that envy does not exist. The parties are "not downcast by the knowledge or perception that others have a larger index of primary social goods."[4] But the justification for the extraction of envy is that it "tends to make everyone worse off" and is thus "collectively disadvantageous."[5] Later, Rawls reconsiders the problem of envy, and attention will be paid as to how and why he is able to reintroduce it at this stage. Despite this exception, Rawls, as did Hobbes before him, attempts to create justice from primordial premoral motivations. The original position is designed to elicit "widely shared and yet weak conditions."[6] There is an absence of "strong and lasting benevolent impulses."[7] Men are not "bound by previous moral ties" and try to "advance their conception of the good as best they can."[8] As a "matter of realism, there are no prior limitations on what men may desire." A conception of justice "should not presuppose...extensive ties of natural sentiment."[9] Because Rawls wishes to discover a concept of justice that is stable, both in the sense of producing similar versions from separate individuals and in the sense of eliciting general social stability, he selects a reasoning process which replaces "moral judgments by those of rational prudence" and "tries to assume as little as possible" in terms of the moral sentiments of men.

The kind of reasoning characterized by those in the original position is aptly summed up by Rawls in this fashion:

> ...the persons in the original position try to acknowledge principles which advance their system of ends as far as possible. They do this by attempting to win for themselves the highest index of primary social goods, since this enables them to promote their conception of the good most effectively whatever it turns out to be. The parties do not seek to confer benefits or impose injuries on one another; they are not moved by affection or rancor. Nor do they try to gain relative to each another; they are not envious or vain. Put in terms of a game, we might say: they strive for as high an absolute score as possible.[10]

Needless to say, these are not the sort of calculations that we normally expect from virtuous men. Here is the liberal's "scientific" element at work in full force. Presumably, the moral point of view is reflected in the desire to construct a concept of justice. Yet in the course of that task one must engage in reasoning that bears a very close resemblance to that of the egoist attempting "to win the highest index of primary social goods." It is certain, however, that the conclusions reached will produce as close a connection to the right and good as humanly possible because of the constraints of the veil of ignorance and the five "formal constraints."[11] Some may say that the principles of justice which emerge are the result of a cautious and mild egoism. This may be going a bit too far. Justice is only one of the moral virtues, and since it is the most comprehensively social one perhaps it may be fitting that it be composed of less sterner stuff than others. Moreover, the theory of justice as outlined from the vantage point of the original position is one which does not yet say how men in society actually learn its tenets. As such it is not complete.

Now the equalitarianism implied in this theory of justice does not appear to be of a radical kind. The first part of the second principle is a capsulation of the liberal shibboleth of equality of opportunity. If a position exists which confers special power or wealth, it is justifiable to the extent that everybody has a crack at it. This dimension of equality is certainly a limited one, but it was an effective argument against conferring titles by class lineage. I suspect that even today more mileage can be secured from the concept than those favoring a broader notion of equality are willing to admit. The first principle confers equal liberty of citizenship to all. These rights (which include voting, running for public office, free speech, and due process protections) have received the center of liberalism's attention since its inception. Again, it is not difficult to document the naïveté (and, in some cases, the hypocrisy) in assuming that a guarantee of political rights would produce a decent life for all citizens. However, attempts to win acceptance of these rights were bitterly contested and, by most standards, reflect at least an inch or two of historical progress. Moreover, Rawls is as insistent as the gentle nature of his writing style allows in impressing the priority of the first principle. The "limitation of liberty is justified only when it is necessary for liberty itself" or to "avoid...an even greater loss of liberty."[12] Greater economic and social benefits "are not a sufficient reason for accepting less than equal liberty."[13] Now Rawls tells us that his principles of justice and their ordering are designed to avoid the conclusions that a utilitarian often reaches in recommending economic security over liberty and that his conception best reflects intuitive sentiments on this question. In fact, of course, the first principle reflects the political sentiments of liberalism.

Up to this point nothing new, other than a clearer statement of liberal sentiment, has been uncovered. It is the second part of the second principle of justice, the difference principle, that appears to suggest a major change. The difference principle established a conception by which disparities in wealth must coincide with the needs of the least advantaged in society. Of course, those who find that the difference principle accepts the inevitability of social stratification are correct. Rawls comes from a long line of theorists who regard inequality as functionally necessary for a good society.[14] In this view, economic differentials are seen as justifiable to the extent that they contribute to social needs. Rawls is not even willing to assert that severe inequalities will not be necessary to guarantee the performance of necessary tasks. Given this conception of social theory it is not surprising that Rawls should regard the selection of a capitalist or socialist economy a minor issue—one not susceptible to philosophical resolution but rather to the historical and cultural background of a community. Socialist economies must make concessions to the market as well. Self-interest has been riveted to the conception of justice through the reasoning of the original position. While Rawls is anxious to indicate that just men in ongoing societies will act differently, he is unable to envision any other mode of economic motivation. "Some socialists have objected to all market institutions as inherently degrading" but any other system is "too dependent" on the strength of social and altruistic motivation.[15]

What Rawls has done, however, is to contend that those who breathe the fresh air at the top of the ladder of success do not morally deserve compensation for their performance. Liberals have always insisted their theories rest upon the moral worth of each individual but they have heretofore been unwilling to extend that belief into the marketplace.[16] One consequence of this reformulation is that Rawls has made income management a central part of his constitutional system. In the context of the liberal polity that is no mean achievement. Moreover, unless one wishes to abandon the principle of efficiency (at least for several generations), posit different incentives for work, or politically allocate jobs in society, it is difficult to see how much further the notion of equality can be carried. In many ways, Rawls's conception of equality, fair opportunity attached to the difference principle, is as far as liberalism can take the idea. To the extent to which it is still regarded as anemic involves less a criticism of Rawls than a wholesale rejection of the liberal creed.

However, the crucial question here, which has been overlooked in the debate over the difference principle, is how Rawls stands on the issue presenting these inequalities to the body politic. Are they to be argued out and contested by the citizenry? Or are they to be disguised and internalized? If it is the former, then there is a chance, albeit a slim one, that the difference principle can guarantee decent livelihoods for all through a rough equality of power in the political system. If it is the latter, Rawls's innovation is a description of the welfare state, American style, that is, centralized control by the powerful and privileged with occasional concessions to the citizenry who labor below. Rawls insists that his effort be judged as a whole, "of everything sitting together into a coherent view."[17] But once his account of political obligation and the concept of virtue which seals it as a complete theory is examined, I'm afraid that the critics of the left are probably right about the operative role of equality in *A Theory of Justice,* although for the wrong reasons.

After Rawls completes his principles of justice and sketches the constitutional and economic arrangements that can guarantee them, he leaves the subject of the principles of justice for institutions to take up the principles of natural duty and obligation that apply to individuals. It is precisely on this ground that liberalism has suffered its most glaring defeats, and Rawls's effort is anxiously awaited. He immediately moves beyond traditional contractarian thought by recognizing a distinction between obligations and duties. The former are principles voluntarily assumed and as such fit most neatly into the contractarian position. He asks if the parties in the original position would make the requirement to comply with just institutions conditional upon certain voluntary acts on their part such as their having accepted benefits or having promised to abide by them. Rawls admits that "offhand a principle of this kind of condition seems more in accordance with the contract idea with its emphasis upon free consent and the protection of liberty."[18] But he contends that nothing would be gained and, in fact, some risks are attendant with this position. It would be difficult to find a plausible account of voluntary acceptance to a political system into which we are born. "The public conviction that all are tied to just arrangements would be less firm" and a greater reliance on the coercive powers of the sovereign "might be necessary to achieve stability."[19] What is needed is another principle, one which defines the duties of individuals simply and clearly in order that stability of just arrangements is assured. Rawls then leaves aside obligations of any sort as an account of political obligation. The only exception is that the principle of fairness (Rawls's account of the derivation of obligations) applies to those who hold public office or who "being better situated, have advanced their aims within the system."[20] This exception is especially valuable because Rawls has, at this point at least, managed to oblige those in positions of power and authority more tightly to constitutional arrangements than average citizens. Presumably, failures on their part are to be judged more harshly than those not in positions of trust or those less advantaged by the system.

The notion of natural duties then are to be the linchpin to Rawls's account of political obligation. It is a very strong account indeed; stronger, sadly enough, than is necessary or desirable. A few words about Rawls's view of natural duties may help clarify this position. While all obligations can be accounted for by the principle of fairness, Rawls makes no attempt to bring natural duties under one principle despite the fact that "this lack of unity runs the risk of putting too much strain on priority rules."[21] When it comes to the question of duties "that hold between persons irrespective of their institutional relationships," Rawls appears to remain a confirmed intuitionist: "how are these duties to be balanced when they come into conflict, either with each other or with obligations, and with the good that can be achieved by superogatory actions? There are no obvious rules for settling these questions."[22] He is convinced that they should not be submitted to any utilitarian standard and confesses that he does not "know how this problem is to be settled, or even whether a systematic solution formulating useful and practicable rules is possible."[23] He leads us to believe, however, that there is some way out. A theory for the basic structure is "actually simpler," because "we can rely upon certain procedures of aggregation to cancel out the significance of the complicating elements of particular situations once we take the larger long-term view."[24] Rawls relies upon Ross's distinction between duties, other things being equal, and duties, all things considered, to help him over this hurdle. Since Ross is perhaps the most constructive of modern intuitionists in regard to problems of ordering, Rawls has chosen his aid well. While Rawls rejects Ross's suggestion that the duties of individuals be grouped into perfect and imperfect categories, he allows us to use the riders of *prima facie* and *all things considered* as connections between a particular judgment and the whole system of principles that defines its grounds. The important thing to note here is that examining this untidy but precious parcel of natural duties to see how they might determine our relationship to the political order could well be a delicate process. Rawls, however, makes it a good deal easier. At numerous points in the book are examples of natural duties: the duty of mutual aid, the duty of mutual respect, the duty not to harm another, the duty not to cause unnecessary suffering, the duty to support just institutions, the duty of civility. But what gives coherence to the system of natural duties is the duty to support just institutions: "From the standpoint of justice as fairness, a fundamental natural duty is the duty of justice."[25] Now Rawls points out that all the natural duties mentioned would be recognized by those in the original position.

Why, then, is the natural duty of justice the "main principle of political duty" for citizens generally? According to Rawls, other natural duties are necessary to social order as well and, in fact, they all share similar reasons to support them. All of them seem as "simple and clear" as the one natural duty of justice. None require voluntary acts to take effect. Why should not the duty of mutual aid be the "easiest and most direct" way to define our institutional ties? Certainly, it might avoid the circularity of the command: one must obey just institutions because one has a duty to support just institutions. Or more to the point: why not leave all the natural duties in a heap and tell the citizen to sort them out and arrive at a selection which, all things considered, leads him to support or resist the state in any instance? Does the natural duty of justice itself, in fact, intuitively stand out from the rest? Ask any sensitive person what his natural duties are. He probably will mention mutual respect and aid, but would he be likely to list the duty to support just institutions? That duty, at best, lives in a middle zone between duties normally recognized as owed to one another and duties that are characterized as institutional ones. Should this be interpreted as falling in the latter category, then institutional ties have been defined by institutional duties and a connection of justice to individuals remains incomplete. If this indeed should be seen as a natural duty, it deserves no precedence over others. If, in a just society, I am over paid by a bank teller at a just bank, I ought to return the money simply because it doesn't belong to me. To say that I ought to return it because I have a duty to support just institutions is needless and obscures any intuitive sense of doing right.

Rawls's special attention to the natural duty of justice leads him to confront what he denies is a paradox when he makes one of his few forays into partial compliance theory. He says that there are circumstances in which one has a natural duty of justice to obey an unjust law. Now, many writers have advanced this position and there are many cogent arguments for accepting it. The real question here is what sort and how many injustices are permitted before one is allowed to absolve himself from his duties to an institution. The problem is in many ways similar to a decision to end a friendship: how many lies, slights, and afflictions do we allow before we say we must have misjudged character in the first place or before we say that this person is no longer the same one whose company we once cherished?

Rawls contends, first of all, that the duty to obey the unjust laws of a "nearly just society" is not "much stronger than that asserting our duty to comply with just laws."[26] Moreover, "given men as they are, there will be many occasions when this duty will come into play."[27] Oddly, two additional natural duties are introduced to supplement the duty of justice in leading one to accept unjust laws. One is the duty of civility," not to invoke the faults of social arrangements as too ready an excuse for not complying with them."[28] This duty "imposes a due acceptance of the defects of institutions and a certain restraint in taking advantage of them."[29] Without it, Rawls tells us (in much the same way that Hobbes spoke of the fourth law of nature) that "mutual trust and confidence are liable to break down."[30] The second duty is the obligation of fairness one citizen owes to another. Recall Rawls's earlier insistence that the notion of voluntary acceptance be used only in conjunction with those holding political office. The citizen generally was not supposed to have any obligations to the state. Now obligations are introduced through the back door. While the concept of obligation may be inappropriate to define the relationship of the citizen to the state, it is perfectly legitimate to note that we acquire obligations to others with whom we have joined in various private associations; those who engage in political action assume obligatory ties to one another. These obligations are of "immense significance" and they "constrain in many ways what individuals can do." All this, of course, is a familiar pluralist ruse. If one cannot fully guarantee moral compliance to the state, one can speak of moral restraints among citizens. It is only incidental that these obligations be discharged through obedience to the state.

While Rawls insists that his discussion rests on the duty of justice alone a "fuller view" would note the place of these other requirements. Although none of this is meant to suggest that civility and fairness should not be considerations of the dissenter, why is there no mention of other duties, duties which might lead one to more militant rather than conciliatory action, which a "fuller view" would incorporate?

Rawls scatters his description of what he regards as a "nearly just" society throughout a number of sections. One can gain a clear idea of what it entails by presenting its characteristics in list format:

1. "There seems to be no way to characterize a feasible procedure guaranteed to lead to just legislation."[31] This imperfection holds even in full compliance theory and one suspects that it is even more marked in the nearly just society. Majorities are "bound to make mistakes" even in a just society, but we "accept the risks of suffering the defects of one another's knowledge and sense of justice in order to gain the advantages of an effective legislative procedure."[23] The aim of the Constitution is to "make sure that the self-interest of social classes does not so distort the political settlement that it is made outside the permitted limits." Is it unfair of us to suspect that in a nearly just society settlements are consistently near or outside these limits.[33]

2. "Doubtless one can manage to live with a variety of mixed and intuitionistic conceptions (of justice), and with utilitarian views when they are not too rigorously interpreted."[34] Other principles are "not unreasonable" and are "certainly adequate for many purposes." In other words, the nearly just society need not espouse the concept of justice advanced by Rawls. This is an especially magnanimous gesture on Rawls's part since the citizen is equally obligated to regimes which, if we accept Rawls's earlier arguments, do indeed show a tendency to accept immoralities. If utilitarianism can and will condone slavery, why ought I have a duty, on a par with more reliable formulations of justice, to support it? Or perhaps as some of its defenders have claimed in response to Rawls, utilitarianism only affronts our sense of justice under extremely unlikely conditions. But, surely, Rawls intends to have made a stronger case than this.

3. There may be "several" minorities who have suffered "persistent" and significant injustice and whose political appeals "have been to no avail."[35]

4. "Vindictive repression of legitimate dissent" may be "unlikely," but it is important that dissenters take note of its possibility. Like the signers of the Declaration of Independence, Rawls separates the question of the right to resist from the question of its wisdom: "There is still the question whether it is...prudent to exercise this right."[36] The difference, of course, is that Rawls advises caution not in undertaking the leap toward revolution but in the legally protected right to publicly disagree with policy.

5. There are groups in the nearly just society that are so intolerant that should they have their way they would suppress the tolerant. Rawls recog-

nizes the existence of such groups in the just society. One assumes that in a nearly just society in which the conception of justice is less widespread or only overlapping on certain issues there may be more of these groups about. Perhaps some have captured positions in the government. Although the sense of justice in the community might restrain some of these groups because it is less than perfect, some citizens can be expected to be subject to hard times at the hands of the intolerant.

This nearly just society in which one has a duty to obey can make life very difficult for some who live in it. All of this might be acceptable, however, if Rawls has reason to believe that the nearly just society shows promise of becoming a just one. Then, of course, one might be able to argue that he has a duty of justice to comply with because the polity is on the way to better things. Rawls gives no such assurance, however. In fact, the contrary may be the case. Rawls tells us that he assumes that for the most part the social system is "well-ordered." The nearly just society may be indeed in a state of stable equilibrium.

Rawls seems to present a threefold classification of political systems: nightmarish tyrannies, nearly just societies, and fully just societies. Perhaps the nearly just society represents the median between the other two. Whether the fully just society is a utopia representing the highest aspirations of humanity or simply a reasonably decent and humane regime, there is no reason, given Rawls's description of basic features of the nearly just society, to demand compliance on a par with obedience to a just society. Or, could the nearly just society be a slightly imperfect replica, not appreciably different from the fully just one? If this is true, then the suspicions of Rawls's detractors are not unfounded. The vision of the just society (and most importantly, of liberalism) is so paltry that it cannot see beyond the horizons of contemporary American politics.

Rawls makes few trips into the world that many confront daily, a world of systematic corruption, shoddy values, and intermittent brutality. One can understand his trepidation. We must learn about justice where we find it and as things stand, we can find it only in our minds. One might even say, then, that while Rawls's recommendations in the world of partial compliance theory may be misguided, the ideal theory is a separate logical entity from which different conclusions can be drawn. The fact of the matter is that while Rawls creates a theory of justice as a cautious jealous virtue, the duties that he draws from it are stern deontological ones, fitting perhaps for the rigors of personal relationships in which men can judge one another closely and daily, but far too demanding to allow for at least some measure of vigor in holding just institutions intact. The natural duty of justice does rest more comfortably with this cautious sense of justice if an additional element, the concept of virtue, is introduced into the system.

The concept of virtue does not receive much attention in contemporary ethics. In fact, the phrase "virtuous person," much less "virtuous citizen," is totally absent from ordinary discourse. No doubt, liberalism is responsible for a good deal of the disrepute or, more properly, perhaps, oversight. The early liberal virtue represented the apologia for class prerogative. Liberalism claimed a much more modest use of politics and insisted upon reserving virtue only as a private value. A historically mature liberalism would attempt to reintroduce the concept but only in this light. John Stuart Mill, for instance, argues for a liberalism that would protect the idea of excellence from the onslaught of the masses but Mill's virtue is so riddled with his own pervading skepticism that it scarcely seems capable of withstanding any political implementation. Moreover, Mill's virtue represents a retreat into the womb of conservatism as well. A dose of Coleridge could purge the democratic tendencies of Benthamite liberalism.

To look, then, at virtue as a political value, one must move beyond the liberal vision.[37] Two concepts of virtue then become evident. One is an invention of democracy and represents perhaps the most complete politization of the concept. Here, individuals throw themselves into the management of the republic and so, we are told, gain in the exhilaration of fraternity what they lose in their loss of self. The other is a much older concept and focuses upon individual excellence while insisting upon the need for considerable supporting social structures to foster the pursuit of perfection. While democratic virtue commits itself to a principled equalitarianism, the other, fashioned so carefully by Aristotle, assumes a gradation of individual potentialities.

Rawls is never really in a position to adopt a conception of democratic virtue. It is intriguing, however, that upon selecting what he calls "democratic equality" as a basis for devising the difference principle he notes in passing that the principle of fraternity does share an affinity to the difference principle.[38] Similarly, he only appears to reject a doctrine of excellence as well.[39] On closer examination, it is found that Rawls rejects out of hand only what he calls single principle perfectionist theories. Those that are more moderate in that they select perfection as but one standard among several in the context of an intuitionist theory "are not easy to argue against." Ultimately, however, Rawls finds the principle of excellence, however restricted, too imprecise to be included in a theory of social justice and insists that perfectionism be denied as a "political principle" but pursued by individuals within the limits of the principle of free association.[40]

All of this is garden-variety liberalism; many modern liberals have considered excellence as a political value and even worried a bit, as Rawls does, whether its absence results in any permanent loss. However, since there will always be citizens who pursue excellence apart from the political order, presumably enough of an example can survive for fellow citizens to emulate at their choosing. It is not until the last part of *A Theory of Justice* that virtue is reintroduced by Rawls. In many ways part III is different from the rest of the book. As Rawls notes, the "over-all direction of the exposition may seem less clear" and the crisp deductions that characterize parts I and II are absent. Instead, again in Rawls's words, "the transition from one topic to another [is] more abrupt."[41] But part III is important for more than its stylistic departures. It is in these pages that Rawls hopes to persuade us that the way men learn justice in society assures stability. And it is here that Locke exits, and Aristotle enters.

The conventional wisdom of liberalism has individual pursuits connected to political authority in the most tenuous ways, either by regarding the state as a protector or promoter of a few primary goods as does Locke or by blithely assuming a coincidence of individual and collective interests as do Smith and Bentham. Rawls means to tie the individual to the society in a much deeper and more intricate manner. Here the utopian premise of liberalism is taken in a definite direction. It is necessary, then, that apart from a few sympathetic interpretations of John Stuart Mill Rawls go beyond the liberal tradition for this task. We are given the Aristotelian principle: "other things equal, human beings enjoy the exercise of their realized capacities (their innate or trained abilities), and this enjoyment increases the more the capacity is realized, or the greater its complexity."[42] Thus, one who enjoys checkers would naturally wish to master chess or one who knew both arithmetic and algebra would prefer the latter. Since the Aristotelian principle expresses "a deep psychological fact," it is especially appropriate as a connecting link between both a moral theory and an account of political association.

Rawls is acutely aware that he is now stepping on dangerous ground, and he is anxious to show that this principle does not involve a rejection of the theory of justice and its priority rules or such a socially diluted concept of virtue as to fail to produce men with a full sense of the good. First, there are the disclaimers regarding possible illiberalism and a rejection of the utopian premise. Goodness as rationality does not suppose that individuals hold some particular role, much less that they are things to be used for some ulterior purpose. The capacity for moral personality "is not at all stringent...there is no race or recognized group of human beings that lacks this attribute."[43] Regardless of the excellence shown by persons or groups, "claims to social resources are always adjudicated by principles of mutual justice."[44] Next comes the construction of a view of society which embodies the Aristotelian principle. Closely following the works of Piaget and Kohlberg, Rawls outlines a developmental theory of the moral sentiments which indicates a progression through three moralities: authority, association, and principle. The assumption of mature moral sentiments and the workings of the Aristotelian principle mutually produce a firm sense of self-respect in individuals. Rawls assigns a central role to social and political institutions in this process. The family sets the patterns for justice and love that, in turn, are transferred to attachments to fellow citizens. Finally, the sense of justice becomes so internalized that it is acted upon by all on principle regardless of group influence. In a similar manner, the Aristotelian principle has its social dimension. No one person can do everything he might wish to do. The self-esteem engendered by the Aristotelian principle exudes a glorious afterglow when we realize that each of us shares in the results of another's pursuits:

> In a fully just society persons seek their good in ways peculiar to themselves, and they rely upon their associates to do things they could not have done, as well as things they might have done but did not.... The collective activity of society, the many associations and the public life of the largest community that regulates them, sustains our efforts and elicits our contribution. Yet the good attained from the common culture far exceeds our work in the sense that we cease to be mere fragments: that part of ourselves that we directly realize is joined to a wider and just arrangement the aims of which we affirm. The division of labor is overcome not by each becoming complete in himself, but by willing and meaningful work within a just social union of social unions in which all can freely participate as they so incline.[45]

Now this may be standard fare for those acquainted with Proudhon or Marx, but it is very heady stuff for a liberal. Rawls has come a long way from that cautious, calculating view of justice outlined in part I. Quite early in *A Theory of Justice* Rawls admonishes us for interpreting the sense of justice in terms of a genteel egoism: "The motivation of the persons in the original position must not be confused with the motivation of persons in everyday life who accept the principles of right that would be chosen and who have the corresponding sense of justice."[46] Now he presents a clear idea of the importance of justice as socialization.

Yet despite Rawls's reconstruction it must be asked if the introduction of virtue into the liberal polity sacrifices any of the genius of liberalism in the name of order and stability. Part of an answer can be found by looking at the problem of envy which Rawls postponed from the earlier sections of his book. The difference principle stated that economic inequalities were justified to the extent that they worked to the greatest benefit of the least advantaged and part of Rawls's justification of this principle rested upon the assumption that all talents were the result of a natural lottery and hence unearned. It should also be asked whether the Aristotelian principle and its "social unions" works to nullify that part of the theory of justice in any manner. Clearly it does. Rawls's master plan, the "social union of social unions," reduces "the visibility...of variations in men's prospects."[47] The various groups in society "tend to divide it into so many noncomparing groups, the discrepancies between these divisions not attracting the kind of attention which *unsettles the lives of those less well placed.*"[48] Moreover, the more advantaged will not make an "ostentatious display" of their higher estate. Men will "take little interest in their relative position" and for the most part "do what seems best to them as judged by their own plan of life without being dismayed by the greater amenities and enjoyments of others."[49]

Now, in a certain sense, all of this is quite reasonable. If I have all the primary goods requisite for the pursuit of a good life and my fellow citizens might enjoy them as well, it would be narrow and mean for me to begrudge a neighbor who had a color television set one inch larger than mine. A society that helped lead me away from such petty concerns is indeed a just one. However, the question involved is a bit different. One must ask if those political institutions which deal in distributive income shares can continue to function consistently with the sense of the difference principle when faced with a citizenry so casual about income distribution. Will the well-endowed be content with their present share when no one is likely to notice alterations because society is already divided into "so many non-comparing groups"? Should it surprise us that a society arranged in this manner has individuals engaging in bloodless but nasty office politics over small differentials between themselves and coworkers while contemplation of the life of millionaires is rare and barely raises even the most pastel shade of envy?

Rawls feels that the presence of envy may well engender jealousy and even spite. The object of envy "guards his position and begrudges [the envious] the greater advantages that would put them on a level with himself."[50] There are good reasons for one to become suspicious here. Apparently, Rawls sees envy producing jealousy in ever-increasing proportions until the sense of justice in all parties erodes and class warfare develops. That an equilibrium among classes can be lost (admittedly, more quietly and slowly) is not Rawls's concern. The contention that "excusable envy" will be rare in the just society is not really a counterargument against the cocoon Rawls has constructed against the encouragement of comparing income differentials. The issue involves a political system that allows disparities to be perceived quickly, especially since Rawls would have us believe that the difference principle may permit severe inequality. Had Rawls offered a classless society or a society less devoted to equality, all these concerns would be moot. The admission that emulative envy is not a socially undesirable emotion to express does not soften Rawls's position either. None of us would wish to regard Willy Loman as a better citizen than Eugene Debs. That, to use Rawls's phrase, would affront our intuitions.

Perhaps one must just put his faith somewhere and Rawls ought not to be chastised for selecting virtue and its accompanying structures as his talisman. It is true that the liberal has often been too willing to rely upon envy and even rancor as a means of checking the power of the state. These are not pleasant emotions and when exhibited in excess they produce ugly consequences. Remember, however, that the difference principle in Rawls's own words requires disciplined study and seasoned judgments in order to work. It seems that a pinch of envy or at least what was once referred to as "constant vigilance" would be better guarantees than reliance upon the improvements of the "conditions of civilization." But this slogan was used in times when liberalism had different demands placed upon it.

Two propositions were used to assess Rawls's effort in the context of the liberal tradition: the acceptance of perpetual conflict and the belief in the plurality of good. However, struggle as he might, Rawls could not provide a plausible political theory that captured both sentiments and yet provided a polity that gave a meaningful place for other concerns recognized as important but secondary to liberals themselves. Virtue and equality are put to ameliorative use in Rawls's framework, but they function in precisely the opposite manner. Equality is derived from Rawls's scientific premises, virtue from his utopian ones. The two concepts fly at one another; Rawls attempts to pare off the edges and refit them or else return to the original position for solace. Virtue can be redefined in light of envy and conflict, equality from a "sense of justice" derived from "everyday life" in a just society. The philosopher's query that asks why does Rawls not use some single commonsense argument, a reflective set of judgments based upon our convictions, instead of the elaborate contractual device misses the point. Rawls needs some sort of *neutral* device to begin his political theory because he works from a set of principles about conflict and the plurality of life plans that permit him no other choice. An ordinary argument will not do because it does not have enough persuasive pull. To say that the original position seems fair because it derives from "our beliefs which we have pertaining to incentive systems and the important place of liberty in society" and to ask why anyone should be so muddleheaded as to reformulate the belief into an elaborate model of imaginary persons blinded by a veil of ignorance fails to consider the arena Rawls is laboring within.[51] The original position places liberal belief in its most abstract and pure form. How much plurality can a liberal society hold, and how is justice to be construed from it? That it fails to convince nonliberals is not surprising. It never has. In fact, it infuriates them. The right is goaded by the liberal's failure to give a central place to a De Maistrean hangman. The left sees such plurality as institutionalized alienation. Alan Wolfe, for instance, rages against the universalizing claims of the liberal state:

> ...the capitalist state can be defined as the political institution which claims primary responsibility for reproducing alienated politics, that is, for maintaining a political system based upon the extraction and imposition of power from people. This is accomplished by the tendency of the capitalist state to assert that it acts in the general interest of all, its assertion of a false universality. It must do this, particularly in liberal democratic societies, in order to be able to be the specific guardian of narrower interests. The contradiction of greatest importance in the capitalist state is that, in order to be primarily responsible for the maintenance of alienated politics, it continues to exist by perpetuating alienated politics.[52]

Even Rawls's casual remark about the absence of conflict being beyond justice seems to indicate that he is at least obliquely aware of his own efforts. That it surprises the professional philosophers is indicative of their ideological virginity. Little more can be said in their favor.

The beauty of the original position, or any other device which begins a political theory on a highly abstract neutral basis, is that it provides liberal theory with some resolution to its central dilemma. By assuming a group of individuals allegedly stripped of their social bearing, the liberal is able to provide a basis for social cohesion without completely abandoning his value pluralism. Either individuals agree to forfeit some goods in the face of political conflict, or they agree to resolve disputes out of this prepolitical mentality in the marketplace of goods and/or ideas. Thus, the liberal finds his own counterpart to the Rousseauan General Will but, of course, with his own variation. The liberal General Will has all the structural elements of the democratic one: in Rousseau's vocabulary it forms its own "common ego, its life, and its will" that reaches into the psyche of the citizen, enables him to "contract with himself," and "forces him to be free."[53] And once properly instituted it is self-perpetuating. The difference, of course, is that the liberal General Will expresses a different agreement. Many writers have noted its character, but Santayana has described it well. Free cooperation would fail at once were there not a tacit common agreement that "to exploit business opportunities and organize public service useful to all" constitutes "the tasks of the good citizen." "In America there is only one way of salvation: to work and to rise by that work, adhering to a regimen not less strict than that of the monasteries, for the sake of an ill-defined but somehow better future."[54] Rousseau contrasted genuine community to a mere aggregation of people. The liberal version attempts to combine both. Individuals see each other as free agents going their own way and at the same time bounded by a social order they all accept.

The cohesion that arises from this General Will is enormously powerful (a fact only realized late in Marxist theory) and seems to be able to transcend class conflicts. The battles in society in fact proceed on Rousseauan lines. Opposition assumes the proportions of those whom Rousseau described as men of "particular will." This condition, however, only has a surface irony. While it is true that the alternate vision of society is usually based upon a Rousseauan communitarian ideal, it can effectively and with some logic be judged as a challenge to the liberal community. In this context, it is the dissident who acts like a mere man or woman and does not possess what he knows is true as a citizen. He or she is the individualist who challenges both the tacit agreement of society and the fruits it has borne. Rawls, although naturally unaware of the implications, states the liberal General Will which arises from the original position with great clarity:

> Having agreed to these principles [of justice] in view of the reasons already surveyed, it is rational to authorize the measures needed to maintain just institutions, assuming that the constraints of equal liberty and the rule of law are duly recognized. Those who find that being disposed to act justly is not good for them cannot deny these contentions. It is, of course, true that in their case joint arrangements do not fully answer to their nature, and therefore, other things equal, they will be less happy than they would be if they could affirm their sense of justice. But here one can only say: their nature is their misfortune.[55]

Could a more benevolent Rousseauanism be possible?

Yet, Rawls was unable to add to this form of liberalism. The difference principle is designed to take the anarchic edge from the liberal General Will by slipping cautiously into a more Rousseauan society and thus place an emphasis upon the bonds that tie people together rather than the nature of their formal agreement. That Rawls seeks to develop his case for equality from the enlightened self-interest of the original position illustrates his caution. Nozick uses his skill in logic sensibly when he castigates Rawls on his own terms on this point: "Rawls has not shown that the more favored man A has no grounds for complaint at being required to have less in order that another B might have more than he otherwise would."[56] But whether Rawls's difference principle is neutral enough or not, the socialization mechanisms of the ongoing system are designed to ensure that the argument from interest, whether from the "less endowed" or the "favorably endowed," is not raised too often. And to be sure that this is the case, Rawls introduces virtue to account for a hierarchy based upon personal development and direction, rather than upon interest and the power to pursue it.

In chapter 1, it was noted that many other writers in this variation of liberalism disposed altogether with the original position and began with the concept of personality itself. This approach has numerous advantages for the liberal dilemma, especially as it confronts the challenge of socialism. The human personality is an individualized approach to politics, but it is not appetitive, at least as these liberals conceive it. Composed essentially of moral elements, including such self-regarding ones as growth and excellence and the traditional ones of adaption and responsibility, the personality becomes the basis of political action. What the liberal must do is insist upon the fact that personality is created or at least molded by society itself and that it is the task of society to "hinder the hindrances," to use Hobhouse's phrase, to individual development. Dewey provides a good example: "...liberalism that takes its profession of the importance of individuality with sincerity must be deeply concerned about the structure of human association. For the latter operates to affect negatively and positively the development of individuals."[57] Liberalism is "committed to an end that is at once enduring and flexible: the liberation of individuals so that realization of their capacities may be the law of their life."[58]

It has never been entirely clear what precisely is left to the personality in an undetermined and individualistic sense if, in fact, it is so grossly dependent upon social structure for its creation and growth. However, this represents an insignificant anomaly that is gently flipped into some dark corner in this form of liberalism. What matter are the commonalities. First are the conditions for liberation: liberalism's present need is material security and the wealth of cultural resources. Second are the possibilities of the good life ahead: "Each of us know some mechanic of ordinary native capacity who is intelligent with the matters of his calling....Given a social medium in whose institutions the available knowledge, ideas and art of humanity were incarnate...the average individual would rise to undreamed heights of social and political intelligence."[59] In the meantime there is much work ahead. Liberals must assume the role of "radicals" and change social institutions. The real centralizing impulse of liberals becomes evident now. Hobhouse can openly reject Mill's self-regarding actions and reformulate Rousseau without wincing:

> I conclude that there is nothing in the doctrine of liberty to hinder the movement of general will in the sphere in which it is really efficient, and nothing in a just conception of the objects and methods of the general will to curtail liberty in the performance of the functions, social and personal, in which its value lies.[60]

Welfare liberalism in this form leaves behind the jealousy of the original position and forges ahead, removing impediment to personality in the church, in the schools, in the localities, in business, in the household, all the while providing a base of material security for the population. Values held up to halt the centralization qua liberation are derided as disguised privilege or backward folk romanticism. Opposition to busing is really racism; to sex education, "Fear of Flying"; to trustbusting, archaic capitalism; to public child care, misguided affection, to welfare, callousness.

The value of pluralism that lay at the basis of the concept of personality remains in its dusty corner nearby but forgotten. Dewey's dictum, "regiment things and free human beings," stands for the record, of course. What is especially distressing is that welfare liberalism is weak in accounting for a theory of resistance. T. H. Green's approach is the prototype despite the tinkering that has followed it:

> As a general rule, no doubt, even bad laws, laws representing the interests of classes or individuals as opposed to those of the community should be obeyed. There can be no right to disobey them, even while their repeal is urged on the ground that they violate rights, because the public interest, on which all rights are founded, is more concerned in the general obedience to law than in the exercise of those powers by individuals or classes which the objectionable laws withhold.[61]

Now Rawls would have dissident groups take turns engaging in civil disobedience so that the social order will not receive too much strain and collapse. The central bias remains the same. Yet, it is not totally the result of liberal timidity in the face of the possibility of disorder. Lurking behind the image of public order is the belief that lesser units, individuals and groups, cannot fully appreciate the truth of the liberal General Will. Hobhouse spoke of the danger of "an overtender conscience consort[ing] with an insufficient sense of social responsibility."[62] The "owner" of conscience owes a "debt to the state." "With mutual consideration, and with the development of the civic sense, conflicts between law and conscience are capable of being brought within very narrow limits, though their complete reconciliation will always remain a problem until men are generally agreed as to the fundamental conditions of social harmony."[63]

After all, the object of the state is "to secure certain conditions which it believes necessary for the welfare of its members, and can only be secured by an enforced uniformity."[64]

If the object of the state is to secure conditions for the welfare of its citizens (a reasonable enough statement taken by itself), how can conflicting ways of life and demands for control be handled? The answer has been offered by Michael Walzer: "Eventually, every anti-social act is interpreted as a demand for increased benefits."[65] But Mill formulated it much earlier in noting that the shibboleth of welfare liberalism was uniform change:

> But we are progressive as well as changeable: we continually make new inventions in mechanical things, and keep them until they are again superseded by better; we are eager for improvement in politics, in education, even in morals, though in this last our idea of improvement chiefly consists in persuading or forcing other people to be as good as ourselves. It is not progress that we object to; on the contrary, we flatter ourselves that we are the most progressive people who ever lived. It is individuality that we war against: we should think we had done wonders if we had made ourselves all alike. Forgetting that the unlikeness of one person to another is generally the first thing which draws the attention of either to the imperfection of his own type and the superiority of another, or the other possibility, by combining the advantages of both, of producing something better than either.[66]

It is important to note that even as complicated a social philosopher as John Dewey, a man who championed the union movement, condemned war hysteria, and defended Sacco and Vanzetti, simply does not have a place for resistance once the good society is reached. The good society cannot only be reached, but it is a society neatly coordinated and rationally run. Once this ideal is accepted, whether in the context of a liberal General Will (as a "social union of social unions" or "Great Society") or some Marxist ideal (as an "ensemble of social relations"), resistance is a demand either for "More!" or an irrational act of misguided individualism. Sympathy for the former is inversely related to that point at which a writer believes the system nears reality.

In the end, the welfare liberal's problems are essentially the same as the socialist's with which his theories were designed to compete.

And despite the new "stability" that Rawls attempts to fashion, he is unable to answer the question many liberals have themselves posed: how can one regiment things without regimenting human beings?

NOTES

1. See the collection and bibliography by Norman Daniels, *Reading Rawls: Critical Studies of "A Theory of Justice"* (New York: Basic Books, 1974).

2. John Rawls, *A Theory of Justice* (Cambridge, Mass.: Harvard University Press, 1971), p. 126.

3. Ibid., p. 127.

4. Ibid., p. 144.

5. Ibid.

6. Ibid., p. 129. See also p. 20.

7. Ibid., p. 14.

8. Ibid., p. 128.

9. Ibid., p. 129.

10. Ibid.

11. Ibid., pp. 130-36.

12. Ibid., p. 215.

13. Ibid., p. 207.

14. Naturally, this view admits of a wide variety of positions. Wilbert Moore traces inequality to the "unequal functional importance of positions and the unequal supply of talents for filling them." "But Some Are More Equal Than Others," *American Sociological Review* 28 (1963), 16. A different view and one that Rawls might have considered with profit, is held by Ralf Dahrendorf, "On the Origins of Social Inequality" in Peter Laslett and W. G. Runciman, eds., *Philosophy, Politics and Society,* 2d ser. (Oxford: Blackwell, 1962), pp. 88-109.

15. Ibid., p. 281.

16. Even Brian Barry, who is scathingly critical of much of *A Theory of Justice,* marvels on "how neatly and cleanly" this topic is treated. *The Liberal Theory of Justice* (Oxford: Oxford University Press, 1973), p. 155.

17. Rawls, *A Theory of Justice,* p. 578.

18. Ibid., p. 335.

19. Ibid., p. 337.

20. Ibid., p. 117.

21. Ibid., p. 114.
22. Ibid., p. 339.
23. Ibid., p. 340.
24. Ibid.
25. Ibid., p. 115.
26. Ibid., p. 355.
27. Ibid., p. 354.
28. Ibid., p. 355.
29. Ibid.
30. Ibid.
31. Ibid., p. 360.
32. Ibid.
33. Ibid.
34. Ibid., p. 353.
35. Ibid., pp. 373-74.
36. Ibid., p. 376.
37. One exception might be the concept of "republican virtue" most prominently espoused in American political thought by Jefferson and Paine. See chap. 9 for a discussion of this point.
38. Rawls, *A Theory of Justice*, p. 105.
39. Ibid., pp. 325-26.
40. Ibid., pp. 328-29.
41. Ibid., p. 395.
42. Ibid., p. 426.
43. Ibid., p. 506.
44. Ibid., p. 536.
45. Ibid., p. 529.
46. Ibid., p. 148.
47. Ibid., p. 544.
48. Ibid. Emphasis mine.
49. Ibid.
50. Ibid., p. 533.
51. Ted Hondrich, "The Use of the Basic Proposition of 'A Theory of Justice'," *Mind* 84 (January 1975), 68.
52. Alan Wolfe, "New Directions in the Marxist Theory of Politics," *Politics and Society* 4 (Winter 1974), p. 149.
53. Jean Jacques Rousseau, *On the Social Contract*, Roger Masters, ed. (New York: St. Martin's, 1978).
54. George Santayana, *Dominations and Powers* (New York: Scribner's Sons, 1951), p. 311.
55. Rawls, *A Theory of Justice*, p. 576.

56. Robert Nozick, *Anarchy, State and Utopia* (New York: Basic Books, 1974), p. 197.
57. John Dewey, *Liberalism and Social Action* (New York: Capricorn, 1935), p. 90.
58. Ibid., p. 56.
59. Ibid., p. 67.
60. L. T. Hobhouse, *Liberalism* (New York: Oxford University Press, 1964), p. 81. Originally published in 1911.
61. John Rodman, ed., *The Political Theory of T. H. Green* (New York: Appleton-Century Crifts, 1964), p. 136.
62. Hobhouse, *Liberalism*, p. 80.
63. Ibid.
64. Ibid., p. 78.
65. Michael Walzer, "Politics in the Welfare State" in *Essential Works of Socialism*, Irving Howe, ed., (New York: Bantam, 1971), p. 818.
66. John Stuart Mill, *On Liberty*, Gertrude Himmefarb, ed. (Middlesex, England: Penquin, 1974), p. 137.

CHAPTER 3

Liberalism: Utopian and Scientific

By 'freedom' is meant, under present bourgeois conditions of production, free trade, free selling and buying....
—Karl Marx and Frederick Engels, *The Communist Manifesto*

In his concern for individual development, Rawls forces men to accept a moral settlement. It should not surprise us that when American political philosophers set their pens to survey what they see as the wreckage of the twentieth century, they should place the blame upon the doctrine of individualism itself and make it a villain of the post-liberal era. Individualism has acquired a bad reputation. John Schaar writes that it is the deadly enemy of civic virtue. With the atrophy of politics comes the "cold rationality of economic domination."[1]

The movement from the focus of individualism as the source of our current discontents to the identification of philosophy that has given rise to it has been swift and firm:

> It is only when man is seen as essentially a bundle of appetites demanding satisfaction that the good society is the one which maximizes satisfactions. This view of man, dominant in Benthamism, goes back beyond the classical political economists. It is firmly embedded in the liberal tradition and has remained a considerable part of the case for the liberal-democratic society today.[2]

Santayana, speaking from different political sensibilities, had come to much the same conclusion: "...liberalism has preached religious toleration and a lay scientific education for the people, while the real interests that it furthered were free trade and the concentrated wealth that it facilitated...."[3]

These are depictions of scientific liberalism, a political theory that succumbed to the challenge of the consequences of a liberal society, one which was so awed by the specter of human conflict that it sought to transform society by giving interest its way through scientific management. Accept the primacy of interest, wrote Bentham, and no one can abjure her throne.

In this context, Robert Nozick's book hardly comes as good news to liberals. *Anarchy, State and Utopia* does not represent a simple return to one of its forms. This is not readily apparent because the most striking features of Nozick's book are its clumsiness and abstractness. It has none of the grace and eloquence of Milton or Tocqueville, or the gentility of Smith, or the wisdom of the younger Mill. Occasionally, there is evidence of the acidity of the iconoclast: "Normative sociology, the study of what the causes of problems ought to be, greatly fascinates all of us. If X is bad, and Y which also is bad, can be tied to X via a plausible story, it is very hard to resist the conclusion that one causes the others."[4] However, most attempts at humor are of the stilted, professorial sort as in chapter headings such as "State-of-Nature Theory" or "How to Back into a State without Really Trying."

What, then, can one make of this clumsy book written in that one-dimensional language that Marcuse has described, a book that is so out of touch with the movement of history? One would have expected something more moving, a last frenzied attack as is found in Burke's *Reflections on the French Revolution* in defense of an embattled ideology. Instead, the reader is treated to contemporary philosophical smugness as Nozick the magician parcels out political arguments under the guise of linguistic analysis. The state is frankly presented as a dominant insurance company for the protection of individual property rights. The market is celebrated and applied to a range of activities well beyond the vision of earlier liberals. Even blackmail is coolly discussed in terms of "productive exchange."[5] The "invisible hand" is Nozick's favorite mode of explanation; he uses it relentlessly and is puzzled that youth, with their need for a more free existence, do not find it as "satisfying" as he. Equality of opportunity, now regarded as the liberal's token concession to the democratic impulse, may *seem* fair but on closer examination dissolves into a philosophical error.

There is, then, a "revolutionary" character to Nozick's presentation. The abstract character of his arguments is designed to purify the liberal tradition. Locke is criticized for a weakness of will.[6] Conventional restrictions on market activity are the result of a failure to pursue the theoretical implications for a society of "self-interested and rational persons." What Nozick has attempted to do is sweep away even the most vigorous approaches of liberalism that attempt to manage society according to known laws of behavior. Thus, while it may appear that Nozick is calling for a return to liberalism's origins, he is in fact calling for something quite the opposite. He is attempting to find a firmer scientific base for liberalism, firmer even than Locke's contract, Bentham's calculus, Spencer's evolutionary design, indeed firmer perhaps than even Hobbes's deductive method.

One would assume that liberalism's utopian premise would finally be totally erased. However, is there a "secret" doctrine in *Anarchy, State and Utopia* that is taken for granted by liberal critics and dismissed by the left? That a plea for utopia should be born from the dreary economic rationality of the first two parts of Nozick's philosophy is a phenomenon that is most peculiar. Even Nozick, while showing signs of exhilaration, is slightly puzzled by the consequence of his own argument: "In *this* laissez faire system it could turn out that though they are permitted, there may be no functioning 'capitalist institutions'...."[7]

One wonders how the minimal state is transformed from a grand insurance company to a framework for the flowering utopia. While it would be premature to ask if liberalism can succeed in uniting utopian and scientific perspectives without the benefit of the dialectic, a more elementary question can be posed: is it really possible that liberalism has a genuinely utopian element in it at all? It is to these questions, set forth admittedly with some irony, that the remainder of this chapter is devoted. Robert Nozick's work provides a convenient test. If a plausible view can emerge here, then it is possible that it can emerge in any liberal theory. The efforts of C.

B. Macpherson, whose trenchant account of liberalism has become the basis for a new orthodoxy in academia, will form an alternate view.

The liberal baiter will find a great deal of satisfaction in Nozick's treatment of the movement of individuals to the embrace of a minimal state. There is no attempt to belittle the false sentimentality of traditional practices. No apologies, no syncretics. Hartz has claimed that the reason that America produced no Bentham was that he was superfluous. Without primogeniture, common law, and sinecure, against what was the felicific calculus to be measured? The nonliberal world is simply ignored by Nozick. If there is any antagonist at all in the early part of the book, it is a small band of libertarian anarchists whom Nozick is anxious to convert. Part II is in fact a critique of Millsian liberalism as, to use Macpherson's term, deceptive. What is presented is an account of how a disparate set of individuals who are anxious to protect rights of acquisition as efficiently as possible give support to protective associations which in turn consolidate into a dominant protection agency (ultraminimal state). Continuing to monitor the movement of "self-interested and rational actions of persons," Nozick contends that the ultraminimal state will evolve into a minimal one, that is, an agency would rationally devise a whole set of mechanisms to protect its clients from the independents (those who have chosen to remain in a state of nature, enforcing their own rights). These would include prohibition upon "unreliable risky methods" of justice along with compensation for the restrained independent. There is Hobbesian reasoning at work here. The dominant agency may even restrain persons deemed dangerous provided compensation is offered, and, surely, Nozick argues, the dominant agency may prevent independents from creating their own agency. How far removed is this position from the argument proffered to those who might refuse to create the leviathan? Hobbes tells us that "whether his consent be asked, or not, he must either submit to their decrees, or be left in the condition of war he was in before; wherein he might without injustice be destroyed by any man whatsoever."[8] Here is Nozick's view:

> Its power [the dominant protective agency] makes it the arbiter of correctness; *it* determines what, for purposes of punishment, counts as a breach of correctness. Our explanation does not assume or claim that might makes right. But might does make enforced prohibitions, even if no one thinks the mighty have a special entitlement to have realized in the world their own view of which prohibitions are correctly enforced.[9]

As with Hobbes, there is no dawdling on Nozick's part. He knows in which direction he wishes to move, and no amount of sociological reasoning is going to divert him. No matter that the fist of the state must be described as an invisible hand. As long as these political underwriters provide compensation (as they so determine) for those who refuse to be their clients it can be said that the state has no "special rights" or that "no one's rights are violated." The "principled objections of the anarchist" are "refuted" and Nozick can now use the same model to pillage the collectivists.

However, there is a good deal more wrong with the movement from state of nature to minimal state than this objection can possibly capture. Imagine a writer offering a history of the United States from the clearing of the wilderness through revolution to the Jacksonian era to the Civil War and industrial expansion through depression and World Wars solely on the basis of the "self-interested and rational actions of persons." Yet, this is precisely what Nozick does. His account of the creation of society and state is made on the basis of no cultural predispositions, no discussion of the level of technology or special local circumstances, no discussion of how individuals deal with the problems of birth, death, and sex—only how individuals might efficiently approach the problem of protecting the fruits of their appropriation. One wonders why they might be so concerned about this particular problem at all. Why not live as Stirnerite individuals, celebrating the thrill of risk and the joy of anarchist existence while taking time off now and then to forage for grubs and berries? The fact is that Nozick's theory indicates a movement to the state that is less than human, and it should not surprise us that very little can be discovered about the problems of the human condition and the task of politics and economics in relation to it.

Of course, the account offered tells a great deal about Nozick and the utility of scientific liberalism. Schumpeter once noted that the capitalist, for all his greed and morally questionable maneuvering in the marketplace, worked for the altruistic goal of his family's welfare. He wondered what sort of man capitalism would produce once the family as an institution had vanished. Perhaps a very different sort of person would replace him, and the economic system itself would be quite different as well.[10] Nozick's theory of political development gives the framework for imagining what it may be like. Consider Turnbull's description of the Ik, a mountain people displaced by war and near starvation, who find a "stable" existence based upon pure dull egoism peppered with flashes of sadism. One of the most horrific descriptions Turnbull offers is an account of mothers who chuckle when their infants toddle toward a campfire; or, to take another, of children who allow the elderly to begin to swallow a portion of the family's food and then gingerly reach down the mouths of the starving and pull out the rice before it is ingested. This activity has all the earmarks of a children's game. As with Piaget's observations on the pastime of marbles, it has rules reached through consensus and enforced by peers with standards of win and lose. In still another case, Turnbull noted that apparent vestiges of spontaneous cooperation and friendship, such as repairing a villager's hut, are done solely to create a "nyot," a bond of mutual obligation. The "recipient" of such aid hurriedly runs to the scene in order to complete the task himself so as to avoid incurring any obligation.[11]

What would Nozick's position be on the morality of these examples? What lessons would he draw? There is literally no discussion of children in *Anarchy, State and Utopia* save an analytic philosopher's folktale at the close of the book and an admonition that since parents are not morally permitted to eat their own children (could they eat someone else's if parents agreed?), perhaps animals have some claims. What are parents to teach their children? Are they to teach them anything at all? What duties, if any, do parents have to their offspring? Do children have individual rights? How are they derived? Is it permissible for parents to raise children for sale or labor?

The classical, state-of-nature theorists struggled to place the family relationship within their model. Locke, while anxious to separate paternal from political authority, warned that the Law of Nature prevents a parent from abandoning a child: "To turn him loose to unrestrain'd Liberty, before he has Reason to guide him, is not allowing him the priviledge of his Nature, to be free; but to thrust him amongst Brutes, and abandon him to a state as wretched, and as much beneath that of a Man, as theirs."[12] Now Nozick tells us that bringing a child into existence does not constitute a waiver of all rights to its existence. But what about thrusting him "amongst Brutes"? Are a child's rights violated when a parent does not teach him the dangers of fire? Or would Nozick contend that the grandparent-grandchild starvation game is morally permissible since individuals have no special or prima facie right to objects (food) that affect their interests (survival)? Or, perhaps Nozick would say that since the children appropriated the food they can put it to any use they see fit? After all, can't the elderly refuse to play this gruesome game? Perhaps they could use their right to free exchange by offering to play checkers with the children in return for a complete mouthful? Or, perhaps Nozick could use another of his bag of principles—the Lockean proviso that no one's rights are violated if the fruits of another's appropriation make no one else worse off than before the acquisition.[13] After all, the grandparent was hungry before the game and is hungry afterward. For a moment this poor soul had the expectation of nourishment and perhaps even the thrill of the game. Better to have tried to eat and lost, than simply to have starved quietly. There's still more for Nozick has many "moral" tests to apply. Perhaps the children could just revise the game a bit and agree to allow one complete ingestion every ten days. Wouldn't this make the mark? It might fit the concept of the right to "meaningful work." However, Nozick has said that meaningful work is not a plausible restriction unless it can be traded off for more efficiency or lower wages.[14] Perhaps the elderly could be required to dance a jig after a successful bite or perhaps for the next ten turns they would be required to blindfold themselves. For Nozick, the "facts of nature" do not allow for throwing out the description of an activity as "voluntary exchange". And what is a more accurate description of the facts of nature than the agility and playfulness of youth and the dependence of the old?

The moral lessons that Nozick might draw from the nyot example are less susceptible to misinterpretation. Like the Ik, Nozick sees no "free-floating debts" about him; all relationships are seen in terms of "moral borders". The degeneration of the "gift relationship" (a universal practice that can at moments make the oppressions of social life not only bearable but touching) to the most base form of egoistic interaction typifies his approach more than any other example. Compare Nozick's doctrine of justice on the basis of his presentation of individual rights to Icien life. For Nozick, justice is "from each according to what he chooses to do, to each according to what he makes for himself (perhaps with the contracted aid of others) and what others choose to do for him given previously...and haven't yet expended or transferred."[15] The Ik live by Nozick's principle and have even gone beyond the need for a minimum state. Turnbull understood: "It is certainly difficult, through a study of Icien behavior, to establish any rules of conduct that could be called social, the prime maxim of all Ik being that each man should do what he wants to do, that he should do anything else only if he is forced to."[16]

Now, certainly, Nozick will protest. His vision of human beings are not as Icien monsters. They are good, decent people who wish to live lives free from political meddling and utilitarian calculation. Nozick's men are free to set up families and love them, form bonds of genuine friendship, and treat one another as ends; he is no doubt certain that they will. In fact, in nearly all the examples Nozick offers to expose the faulty logic of the collectivists, he takes social groups as givens! One of his efforts is his case against equality of opportunity.

Nozick begins his discussion by denying the applicability of a race metaphor in describing human society: "But life is not a race in which we all compete for a prize which someone has established...."[17] So far this appears to resemble a good socialist argument against the view that a social order rests upon practices that ferret out the fit from the infirm. But Nozick goes further, much further:

> Instead, there are different persons separately giving other persons different things. Those who do the giving (each of us, at times) usually do not care about dessert or about the handicaps labored under; they care simply about what they actually get. No centralized process judges people's use of the opportunities they had; that is not what the processes of social cooperation and exchange are for.[18]

What, then, are the processes of social cooperation and exchange for? The inescapable answer is that they are not for anything at all. Maybe there is an occasional meeting of parties to trade a few commodities and go back to their respective shelters. However, if we speak of the sustained relationships of interdependence, are we not driven to a position that forces us to ask what these burdens of cooperation are all about? Sumner described industrial society this way: "It controls us all because we are all in it. It creates the conditions of our existence, sets the limits of our social relations, determines our conception of good and evil, suggests our life philosophy, molds our inherited political institutions, and reforms the oldest and toughest customs, like marriage and property."[19]

What Nozick has done is to outstrip the Social Darwinists. For all their bravado about individual liberties and the necessity of competition, they envisioned a society with a purpose. Spencer prophesized that sympathy was now "occasional and feeble but with further evolution would become habitual and strong....What now characterized the exceptionally high may be expected eventually to characterize all."[20] That which "the best human nature is capable of, is within the reach of human nature at large."[21] Now Spencer's means may have been grieviously wrong, but the utopianism in his thought foresees social interaction beyond exchange among calculating parties.

Imagine a group of amoral persons with no ties of social sentiment. Call them rogues, swashbucklers, or sociopaths. Each has a small fortune in his possession, and each wishes to take the fortunes of the others. How might they do it? The Social Darwinist argument goes something like this:

"Do not grab a gun, call yourself a state and tax away the fortunes of the rest. You may have the ability to do that (contrary to the views of Hobbes, some men have enough guile and strength to consistently overpower the rest) but instead sit down the the others, devise some game which you all think is fair with equal opportunity to win, poker perhaps. Compete for the fortunes—winner take all. This way you will eventually create the necessary conditions for the material comfort of all, establish a reign of peace, and perhaps even comradeship might arise from your efforts."

Yes, this is an unlikely scenario. But look at the one Nozick seems to offer:

"Hire protection for fear another party might take away your winnings. When this reaches a stalemate create some games, any game you like as long as it is designed to provide you with the winnings, and try to get the rest to go along. Hopefully, you can swindle somebody. If you can't, don't, whatever you do, accept some equality of opportunity arrangement. That, we all know, is a philosophical error. Instead, sit down on your fortune and wait and wait. Offer new deals, wait more. Wait. As a last resort, try this argument with the rest: 'Life is not a race for a prize with some recognized judge. No one will assess the opportunities you all have, that is not what social cooperation is for. Let's all go home, leave your fortunes here if you like. All of us have different roads to follow. It is unlikely that someone will tamper with them. Go to your families and friends, take trips, enjoy yourselves. For those of you who would like to stay—that is, if you have nothing better to do—I have this game of chance that I just invented.... Everybody blindfolds himself—you first, the dealer last. Whoever takes the blindfold off and yells foul is a 'collectivist' and automatically loses. It is to be called 'capitalism for leisure' (and under your breath, ever so softly) and—profit."

Nozick's society, therefore, *is* far from Icien individualism. Or is it?

The fault of Nozick's first argument is that it refuses to look at any relationships but economic ones. Much is said in America, and within the liberal tradition in general, about socialism's refusal to consider the need for incentive and the importance of efficiency. No one can deny the importance of these questions. However, the primacy of politics itself cannot overcome these objections. Impose a strong political order, a more than minimal state, over Nozick's human beings and one has the prophecy offered by Turnbull. The Icien system illustrates the possibility that "society is not indispensable for man's survival, that man is not the social animal he has always thought himself to be, and that he is perfectly capable of associating for purposes of survival without being social."[22] The Ik have abandoned as "useless appendages" the qualities society can offer: family, cooperation, belief, hope, love. They replaced them with a survival system. But the Ik have created an imperfect system, one which guarantees minimal survival. With our intellectual sophistication and with our advanced technology, a more perfect survival system could be assured. It is really politics that can refine Icien underdevelopment in this regard. The state, resting ever more on "both intellectual and physical violence," is the nucleus of the new system. The new task of politics is to "reduce the demands made upon us by a social system with all its necessary structural oppositions and inherent conflicts, abolishing desire and consequently that ever present and vital gap between desire and achievement, treating us, in a word, as individuals with one basic individual right, the right to survive...."[23]

If *homo economicus* of the capitalist variety is seen as the enemy, it is unlikely that replacement with a *homo politicus* will fare any better. What is so sorely needed in contemporary analysis, and Nozick's attempt is perhaps most striking only because of its naïveté, is attention to the social order. That it will somehow grow natural, luxuriant and resilient, from economic calculation *or* political management, is a common fault of both liberalism and socialism. Neither will acknowledge that social order has any roots of its own.

What is so phenomenal in Nozick's effort is that he offers a second argument for the minimal state which is designed to stand "independently" of parts I and II. The framework for utopia is designed to support the notion of a minimal state but this time it comes from "another direction." Can a writer who spends three hundred pages on dominant protection agencies and the virtues of the cash nexus now present a political theory that best realizes the utopian aspirations of "untold dreamers and visionaries"? Has Nozick in a single book captured the scientific spirit of liberalism and in part III broken beyond the liberal vision and peeked at new utopian horizons? Is the whole history of liberalism from possessive individualist as reformer, to reactionary, then as a Fourierist contained in this single book?

There are three possibilities:

1. The utopia argument convincingly establishes that Nozick, now treated by reviewers as some libertarian phoenix (or Frankenstein), has written a sly satire on the liberal idea of history.
2. The utopia argument is just another form of liberal deception.
3. The utopia argument represents a secret doctrine within the logic of liberalism that not even the most stringent individualism can completely destroy.

It is probably best to reject the satire interpretation immediately.[24] Admittedly, the stark portrayal of economic existence could be satirical, perhaps as a long *modest proposal* with dullness as the comedic weapon that replaces Swiftian bad taste. But satire must be in the mind of the creator as well as the reviewer. There is no evidence that Nozick has such an intention. Perhaps a few centuries hence some scholar will offer such an interpretation: "No intellectual existing in the second half of the twentieth century could seriously have offered the following positions...therefore *Anarchy, State and Utopia* can only be construed as a masterpiece of satirical analysis." For Nozick's contemporaries, this interpretation simply is not possible. The satire thesis must collapse into a much less interesting critique. *Anarchy, State and Utopia* is a caricature of liberal thought. It stands in relation to the *Second Treatise* as *Foundation of Leninism* does to *Theses on Feuerbach* or *Up from Liberalism* to *Appeal to Old Whigs*.

The second and third interpretations are obviously more compelling, and it is on the basis of these that the utopian argument can be considered. First, the notion that a utopian framework is an exercise in liberal deception rests upon two points: (a) the utopia argument is not appreciably different from the economic one on closer examination; that is, the appearance of separateness is a deceptive device; and (b) the utopia argument is economically and socially naïve. Beginning with (a), one finds that Nozick argues for an environment in which utopian experimentation might flourish rather than for a specific utopia on the grounds that individuals are enormously complex and that even if there were "one ideal society for everyone there is not enough known about it to even describe it."

Nozick proposes a "smorgasbord conception of utopia....an environment in which utopian experimentation may be tried out." He recommends finding utopia by using a filter device (design devices to contruct utopia). Since people do not know precisely the nature of their final product, they would use "their knowledge of specific conditions they don't want to violate in judiciously building a filter to reject the violators."[25]

Now, one who accepts the deception argument also can argue that the economic calculator model is not so subtly at work here. Nozick seems to envisage utopias as constituting a market to be packaged and sold according to supply and demand. Individuals enter existing utopias and conjure up others on the basis of advancing their marginal contribution:

> We seem to have a realization of the economist's model of a competitive market. This is most welcome, for it gives us immediate access to a powerful, elaborate, sophisticated body of theory and analysis. Many associations competing for my membership are the same structurally as many firms competing to employ me.[26]

This society of mini-utopias becomes a society of competitive firms. Critics might justly note that Nozick is silent about how individuals develop the capacities that make them employable in these "utopias." Presumably, one could refer to part II where Nozick states that a consideration of natural abilities is irrelevant to a theory of justice. Those individuals who were not sought after by existing communities could always form their own, just as Nozick contends workers can buy out the capitalists or trade off compensation for managerial control. [27] Or, perhaps by banding together they could offer attractive jobs to much-sought-after individuals. Utopian communities for the poor and unskilled could be financed on the same principle as group medical or life insurance.

Or, consider Nozick's treatment of the importance of competition among utopias. The existence of one broad community which tolerates a few experimental utopias does not violate the classical market model. Everyone might not choose to join new and small utopias; perhaps most will be content to live in a large federated community. The oligopoly justification is introduced very casually here, and Nozick's base notion of liberty returns. After all, "people are free to stagnate if they wish as well as to innovate."[28] In fact, perhaps the way of life that is assumed is utopia itself.

This is a powerful interpretation of Nozick's utopia argument, and if it is correct, *Anarchy, State and Utopia* is a vulgarization of liberal theory and does not really hide the economic bias of its tradition effectively. It is necessary now to consider the "secret doctrine" of liberalism interpretation and then return to the criticism offered in (b).

Is it possible that the vacillation of J. S. Mill, T. H. Green, and subsequent entire generations of liberals is a result of reasons other than an unwillingness or inability to abandon concepts wedded to a market society? Why had Mill, in Macpherson's words, "exhausted himself in seeking ways of patching up the contradictions between liberalism and social democracy"?[29] Why was Green, who rejected possessive individualism, "unable to see what it was that made it untenable (that is, the appearance of the possibility of a class-based social democracy)"?[30] And to turn things around a bit, why does Nozick introduce meta-utopia to the possessive individualist model? Why have these writers, and many more, been "compelled to deceive themselves"? Macpherson offers very little explanation for such massive self-deception. After all, he has left mere propagandists aside; he speaks only of great and humane thinkers. Certainly, liberals did not become Marxists simply because they could not bear to "range themselves morally against the system they knew and were strongly attached to."[31] Surely Macpherson could not be basing a theory that accounts for one hundred years of liberal political thought on the idea that liberals are simply radicals with jobs. Such a position might explain the views of the middle-class clerisy of intellectuals and bureaucrats that cluster about the liberal state, but can it seriously pretend to be an explanation of efforts of thinkers from Mill to Rawls? If this is the cause of liberal deception—and the most careful reader is not likely to find another in Macpherson's work—it is a textbook example of the crassness of Marxian reductionism. It is really astonishing that such a position could find the acceptability it has achieved. A more caustic writer might comment on the intellectual powers of the American academic left.[32]

If Macpherson's argument that the utopian element in liberalism is fraudulent lacks even minimal plausibility, how can one approach the problem of the apparent juxtaposition of science and utopia as single theories? A slightly fuller look at Nozick might help. Two points need first to be made: (1) Nozick's framework for utopia is not simply a veneer to cover the destructive nature of his economic individualism, and (2) the framework is genuinely antagonistic to the vision of social life presented in parts I and II and not, as Nozick believes, the same result argued from another perspective.

For the moment, accept Nozick's claim that a society might emerge that features numerous utopian experimental communities. There are phalanxes, kibbutzim, harmony homes, mutualist communes, places of labor, time stores, Walden IIs, IIIs, and IVs, and the like. Some are highly disciplined communitarian ventures, others are loosely organized and individualist; some are democratic, others authoritarian; some are secular, others religious. They are presided over by some federated control authority. Consider the sorts of conflicts that might arise in such an arrangement. Here are but a few cases:

1. Community A accuses community B of attempting to prey upon its members. A contends that B, which is clearly in league with the devil, is attempting to lure away members with temptations of material wealth. Community B responds by saying that if utopian experimentation is to work it must be able to present its way of life to outsiders: "Let A compete in the market place of ideas. All we want is a freedom of information act guaranteeing safe conduct and time set aside from labor for members of A to examine our community's efforts."
2. Community C and community D have a dispute over water rights.
3. A minority of community E contends that a group of apostates have gained power and, through a series of changes in the utopia's legal structure, have relegated some to unequal compensation for labor. The ruling group contends that they represent a clear majority and that the new rules are fair and nondiscriminatory, that they were intended to deal with slackers. The dissidents may change the laws through political action provided for in the group's basic law. They may leave if they wish. The minority contends that it does not wish to leave, that the basic law provides for putative rights for the minority

and that if relief is not forthcoming an appeal to heaven is the only recourse left to majority tyranny.

4. An individual in community E pleads with the federated community for mercy. He is charged with adultery, and the penalty is dismemberment. Community F replies that the basic law explicitly states such a penalty and that the individual in question was well aware of the provisions upon his entrance to the community. The whole question is beyond the jurisdiction of the federation. (Complicate the question a bit if you wish. The prisoner pleads justice and not mercy. His trial was rigged. Or, community G, devoted to the principle of free love, sees the prisoner as a martyr and convert, and threatens to intervene if "adjustments" are not made.)

Nozick is not completely oblivious to these sorts of complications. At one point he suggests that some might consider the possibility that the federal government "may pick some preferred internal structure for communities (which respects certain rights, and so on)...."[33] However, he concludes that such efforts are "unnecessary" and forages for a relevant principle in part I:

> ...to accomplish the same end individuals need only to include in the explicit terms of an agreement (contract) with any community they enter the stipulation that any member (including themselves) will be so compensated for deviations from a specified structure (which need not be society's preferred norm) in accordance with specified conditions. (One may use the compensation to finance leaving the community.)[34]

The use of the compensation principle here is certainly more appealing than in the earlier discussion of a minimal state. There Nozick considered compensation as a remedy for some "independent" who might decide to chop off one's arm. Nozick's device might provide some help in the dispute in case 3, but, if the majority regarded its interpretation of the contract as consistent with the new legislation, some political principle, despite Nozick's great reluctance, must be considered.

For the problems that arise in the other cases, Nozick assumes a style different from the rest of the book. For the first time, in the face of legitimate counterexamples, logical problems, and unpleasant consequences, Nozick invokes humility. When confronted with the likelihood of oppressive utopian regulations, he reaches for the distinction between *Gemeinschaft* and *Gesellschaft*, not as a basis for different ways of life but to suggest that a face-to-face community "can exist on land jointly owned by its members."[35] Yet he concludes wistfully that "since I do not see my way clearly through these issues, I raise them here only to leave them."[36]

The real import of Nozick's utopias lie elsewhere. However he may wish to avoid the implications, Nozick has advanced a theory which contains group duties and rights. Cases 1 and 3 involve conflict between communities. These become the units of political action. The question of whether the group is "real" and the individuals that compose it only social selves may be left aside. That individuals as well as groups have separate needs and interests and rights is illustrated by case 4. The mere fact that it is possible to raise it as a problem in the meta-utopia is indication of its recognition. What is as important is that politics emerge for the first time in Nozick's efforts. Individuals clash with groups, subgroups with groups, group with group, and groups with the state. Accommodations must be reached. Venality, goodwill, ambition, and conscience are thrown together, and one hopes that some reasonable life for all will result. As Nozick states:

> One persistent strand in utopian thinking, as we have mentioned, is the feeling that there is some set of principles obvious enough to be accepted by all men of goodwill, precise enough to give unambiguous guidance in particular situations, clear enough so that all will realize its dictates, and complete enough to cover all problems which actually will arise. Since I do not assume that there are such principles, I do not assume that the political realm will wither away. The messiness of the details of a political apparatus and the details of how *it* is to be controlled and limited do not fit easily into one's hopes for a sleek, simple utopian scheme.[37]

Individuals now can "plausibly be viewed as *owing* something to the other members of a community."[38] There are now "difficult and important problems of the controls on a central authority powerful enough to perform its appropriate functions."[39] Although Nozick still insists upon regarding government as corresponding to the minimal state, the extent of its power is problematic. Pluralism is introduced as an intrinsic value: "Many communities will achieve many different characters." Historical development is even taken seriously:

> Utopia is *not* just a society in which the framework is realized. For who could believe that ten minutes after the framework was established, we would have utopia? Things would be no different than now. It is what grows spontaneously from the individual choices of many people over a long period of time that will be worth speaking eloquently about.[40]

Locke is gone. Not the real Locke perhaps, but the bloodless, scientific, economic maximizer of parts I and II. Here enters Mill and, hard as it is to believe, Tocqueville. And here lies the secret doctrine of liberalism. Individualism involves human diversity, and, how ever one might choose to nurture it, individual diversity can only be achieved through social diversity itself. That this is a secret doctrine will surprise many students of political philosophy. It formed the basis of the liberal critique of conservatism. Here the leitmotiv was liberty, although not of the libertarian variety. Diversity could be achieved, the liberals argued, without rigid class hierarchy. Arguments over the need for spectacle and tradition were "hobgoblins." With Bentham and the elder Mill, liberty was buttressed with another argument. Societies organized on other than corporate lines were more efficient. It was an unfortunate argument from a number of perspectives, not the least of which is that an individualism which fosters diversity is inefficient from a number of vantage points. A genuinely pluralist society is a messy one. Organizations perform overlapping functions, economy of size is often violated. It is not easy to run; it forces compromises that are not morally compelling for all parties. And worst, it can get out of hand; the center may not hold. The "low-trust society" is one result:

> Every group is convinced that other groups are somehow managing to protect themselves effectively—the classic distrust situation—and precisely because it feels unable to entrust its fortunes to company or government decision-makers, feels driven to enforce its own claims by whatever means it can.[41]

But, as Macpherson predicted, something profound did happen to the liberal position as it flowed from the utilitarians. Individualism became the goal of liberal political thought itself. Diversity was shoved into the background. Benthamite men are all alike. Social Darwinists posit individuals who, in their subservience to the laws of development, behave uniformly. For Spencer, diversity is pushed somewhere into the future. Yet it does not follow, however congenial the theory was for industrial development, that such a position represents the essence of the liberal view. For as Mill and Tocqueville as well as others realized, diversity was not being served by such individualism. However, it was not necessarily served by the demand for equality either. If a Darwinist individualism produced powerlessness for the many, however well-fed they might be, equalitarianism has its own monotony. "The Chinese ideal of making people all alike" was not a remedy. A "variety of situations is a necessary condition..." of human development. It is important to "render people unlike one another."[42] Because Mill could not find a principle that could guarantee diversity with some modicum of equality does not mean that his effort was one of self-deception. It meant that he failed, that such a principle is extremely difficult to formulate, that the "secret doctrine" of the liberal is not amenable to theoretical formulation, that perhaps it is up to historical chance. But this view sees the history of post-Benthamite liberalism as a Promethean or Sisyphean one. Tragic and, perhaps, even misguided or futile, but heroic nonetheless.

It cannot be said that Nozick "exhausts himself" the way Mill did in seeking to offer an alternative to market morality. Nozick's alternate position appears effortless. What Nozick was driven to accept by the logic of individualism, Mill struggled with using the deepest perception. Nozick has not the slightest notion that the argument for the minimal state and the argument for meta-utopia do not amount to the same vision of politics and society. That both are individualist positions indicates the range of the liberal imagination. Of course, Nozick is not a Mill. Sometime Nozick may find it necessary to logically relate meta-utopia with protective agencies; then exhaustion will come soon enough.

The rebuttal offered in (b) is also an important and intriguing argument. It is contradictory to, or at least separate from (a). The position just reviewed sees liberalism as an outmoded scientific paradigm. Its utopian element is a shield for its inadequacies. Another position contends something of the opposite. Liberalism is utopian, but somehow it is invidiously utopian. The classic critique is the one Marx and Engels leveled against the "utopian socialists":

> The significance of Critical-Utopian Socialism and Communism bears an inverse relation to historical development. In proportion as the modern class struggle develops and takes definite shape, this fantastic standing apart from the contest, these fantastic attacks on it lose all practical value and all theoretical justification. Therefore, although the originators of these systems were, in many respects, revolutionary, their disciples have, in every case formed more reactionary sets. They hold just by the original views of their masters, in opposition to the progressive historical development of the proletariat....They still dream of experimental realization of the social Utopias, of founding isolated "phalanseres," of establishing "Home Colonies," of setting up a "little Icaria"—duodecimo editions of the New Jerusalem....[43]

Engels's attack was directed against socialists, but, since Nozick offers a vision of society that is designed to promote small-scale communitarianism, this argument seems relevant to an assessment of his system. In fact, experimental communitarianism does seem to partake of liberal views of reality. It emphasizes individualism and voluntarism and hopes that somehow they will remain compatible with community. John L. Thomas has noted the connection in nineteenth-century American thought:

> The communitarian experiments in effect were anti-institutional institutions. In abandoning political and religious institutions the communitarians were driven to create perfect societies of their own which conformed to their perfectionist definition of the free individual. Their communities veered erratically between the poles of anarchism and collectivism as they hunted feverishly for a way of eliminating friction without employing coercion, sure that once they had formed it, they could apply it in a federation of model societies throughout the country.[44]

Thomas refers to the doctrine that supports such thinking as "perfectionist individualism," the belief that "since social evils were simply individual acts of selfishness compounded....Americans could attempt the perfect society any time they were so inclined."[45] The teachings of Nozick may reach back to Owen and Ripley and Brisbane. The individualism is "perfectionist," not "possessive."

Here is not the place to determine how utopian this perspective is in some definitive sense. However, it can be useful to compare this view with the more popular neo-Marxist one. Again, Macpherson provides the basis for an informative comparison. One need simply ask how compelling is the location of the utopian element in each account. The contemporary critique of liberalism has been adamant on one point in its assessment. Liberalism is a reactionary ideology in that it simply cannot see beyond the horizons of current political and economic conflict. Without a notion of society without greed, opposition, and some exploitation, liberalism, at best, is to suffer the fate of Dante's Virgil, free perhaps from some of the worst pain but never able to experience the ecstasy of Heaven. Because the liberal is not really willing to accept such a broader vision, his utopias lack real determination. They are limited to "duodecimal Jerusalems," withdrawals from society.

This critique can be applied with some effectiveness to Nozick. He offers three paths to utopia: imperialistic utopianism, missionary utopianism, and existential utopianism. His framework for utopia will be acceptable to the latter two. The missionary utopians will see it as an opportunity to "convince everyone to live in one particular kind of community, but will not force them to do so." Existential utopians, whose visions are not universal, will "whole heartedly accept the framework." The imperialists, "utopians of force and dominance," will oppose the framework. Since "corrupt" persons would never choose to voluntarily live under utopia, "it will have continually and eternally, to be imposed."[46] With aplomb, Nozick says, "Well you can't satisfy everybody...." But some moments later he returns to this problem:

> Some will object to reliance on the voluntary actions of persons, holding that people are now so corrupt that they will not choose to cooperate

> voluntarily with experiments to establish justice, virtue, and the good life....So the argument continues, people must be forced to act in accordance with the good pattern; and persons trying to lead them along the bad old ways must be silenced.[47]

Nozick's answer reaches to the heart of liberalism:

> Believing with Tocqueville that it is only by being free that people will come to develop and exercise the virtues, capacities, responsibilities, and judgments appropriate to free man, that being free encourages such development, and that current people are not close to being so sunken in corruption as possibly to constitute an extreme exception to this, the voluntary framework is the appropriate one to settle upon.[48]

This position, itself, may well be genuinely utopian. The belief that major alterations in social and political life can be wrought relatively peacefully and democratically, or at least with majority support, that, in fact, a full-scale improvement in the human condition requires, with "extreme exceptions," peaceful change or majority acceptance, involves hopes that fly far above the ugly reality of the times.

To judge whether this position is a deceptive utopianism that plays into the hands of reactionary elements in society, one must compare it to the "utopianism" of Macpherson. It may be useful at this juncture to speak of three kinds of utopian premises: (a) it is possible to construct a vastly improved society; (b) it is possible to construct a society without social and political conflict; and (c) either or both (a) and (b) can be reached without both revolution and post-revolutionary terror. Nozick is utopian in respect to (a) and (c) and seems to reject (b), although he states that he "does not laugh" at those who adopt this view. Macpherson is as insistent as Nozick on (a). He is positively adamant about the possibility of (b) and ambivalent in regard to (c). It is not necessary here to review Macpherson's campaign against the capitalist welfare state and the horizons that can be reached beyond it. But the utopianism in (b) deserves more consideration. Macpherson's position is most clear in his quarrel with Isaiah Berlin's notions of positive and negative liberty. Both arguments are complicated ones and only a portion of both positions will be discussed. Berlin, in his *Two Concepts of*

Liberty, argued that negative liberty implies the absence of interference with the ability to act and that positive liberty "derives from my wish to be my own master." Berlin contends that while the two concepts appear to be "saying much the same thing" they have in fact "developed in divergent directions." The latter has led to "monstrous denials" of liberty. By positing a "higher" or "rational" or "real" self whose goals can "force individuals to be free."[49] Macpherson regards the realtionship between negative and positive liberty as a specious one and offers instead a threefold division of the latter:

1. Positive Liberty^1 (PL^1) "is...the ability to live in accordance with one's own consciousness purposes, to act and decide for oneself rather than to be acted upon and decided for by others."
2. Positive Liberty^2 (PL^2) is the "idealist or metaphysical rationalist transformation of PL^1: liberty is coercion, by the fully rational or by those who have attained self-mastery, of all the rest; coercion by those who say they know the truth, of all those who do not (yet) know it."
3. Positive Liberty^3 (PL^3) is the democratic concept of liberty as a share in controlling authority.[50]

There are a number of interesting points that can be made here even given the limited scope of this analysis. For Macpherson PL^3 is a prerequisite to PL^1, yet PL^1 does not logically lead to PL^2, nor is it even congenial to it. Macpherson is quite correct to note that the threat to negative liberty does not rest solely with PL^3. Autocracy can be as disastrous to freedom from interference as radical democracy. Yet he fails to recognize that PL^3 can be inconsistent with PL^1. What is the fate of the eccentric in democratic societies? He will insist that his way of life has been rationally selected, that he must be given the right to act according to his own conscious purposes. At this point a Rousseauan (or Marxist) weight falls down upon him, not too heavily it is hoped—censure and ostracism are more humane—but it falls nevertheless. All this is to be expected, of course. But it does help to recognize the problem and take account of it in a political theory. One can draw the line between conflicting pursuits of PL^1 wide as some liberals suggest (perhaps by using NL) or narrow. But how can we deny the clash of PL^1 and PL^3? One way to deny it is, as Berlin suggests, to contend that there is only one mode of PL^1 and those who refuse to recognize it are not exercising PL^1 at all. Thus PL^1 does lapse into PL^2. Macpherson expends a great deal of effort rejecting this claim. His arguments, however, are very weak. They seem to rest upon two points, one theoretical and one empirical. He makes a distinction between "believing that there is a pattern which fully rational men can know, and which they should impose on others" and "believing that if the chief impediments to men's developmental powers are removed....There would emerge not a pattern but a proliferation of many ways and styles of life which could not be prescribed and which would not necessarily conflict."[51] The requirements for the latter are "steep" but "not impossible" resulting in "the ending of scarcity and of class conflict." A full-blown utopianism gradually emerges. For the sake of fairness, here is Macpherson's position:

> It is true that the conflicts Berlin speaks of are not conflicts of material interests....But how many of those conflicts would remain endemic in a society without class conflict and scarcity? They are endemic in a class-divided society, and particularly in a class-divided market society which lives on the postulate of infinite desirousness. In such a society it is indeed a necessary, not a contingent, truth "that we cannot have everything." But we do not have to go to the opposite extreme of a brainwashed utopia to envisage a society where diverse genuinely human (not artificially contrived) desires can be simultaneously fulfilled.[52]

One is tempted to be flippant here. Is it possible that the elimination of scarcity and class—a very steep requirement in its own right—logically entails the absence of all conflict? When economic conflict is absent, why does it follow that conflicts born of other bases will not emerge? Macpherson's position need not be scorned. It is an assertion about the nature of society that may possibly be correct. Yet it would take an audacious writer to contend that it is more than an assertion—faith might be a more appropriate characterization. It is important to note that it is on the basis of this faith alone that Macpherson bases his rejection of Berlin and offers his case that "the monism which is the essence of PL^2 is not entailed in PL^1."[53]

The second argument that PL^1 does not lead to PL^2 rests upon a brief assessment of the causes of recent political policies that show an apparent conjunction of PL^1 and PL^2. Here Macpherson is on the weakest ground of all. Faith ceases to function as an excuse now; willful disregard for the facts is the basis for assessment. Radical adherents of PL^1 lapsed into the authoritarianism of PL^2 as a result of "finding, or assuming, that all non-authoritarian ways to the removal of those impediments are blocked, whether in theory, in practice, or in both, because of their opponents' failure to see or to acknowledge the impediments."[54] There is a great deal of difference between radicals who assumed such impediments existed and those who found them to exist. Moreover, the difference, glossed over by Macpherson, once appreciated, does little to help this position.

It is a gross moral error to place liberty in the context of PL^2 on the basis of an assumption that it is the only avenue for PL^1. If large numbers of radicals have merely assumed such impediments then there is indeed a relationship between PL^2 and PL^1. The question of whether such impediments have in fact existed raises another point. Macpherson offers the following argument: the road to PL^2 is reluctantly accepted. Macpherson's forthrightness belies his own argument. Marx "surely was not" pushed into PL^2: "the end he sought was always the leap from the realm of necessity to the realm of freedom which would enable the utmost flowering of human diversity."[55] Most PL^2 elites will subscribe to an eventual realization of PL^1. More astonishing pronouncements are yet to come. "Nor do I think Lenin could properly be described as an exponent of PL^2: he did indeed demand vanguard rule for a revolutionary transition, but vanguard rule...does not require PL^2 for its justification."[56] One quote by Lenin himself is enough of a reply. After contending that "dictatorship is iron rule" and complaining that "our government is excessively mild, very often it resembles *jelly more than iron,*" Lenin offers the following characterization. Note the demand for submission to an elite is not based upon bourgeois sabotage:

> ...concerning the significance of individual dictatorial powers from the point of view of the specific tasks of the moment, it must be said that large-scale machine industry—which is precisely the material source, the productive source, the foundation of socialism—calls for absolute and strict *unity of will,* which directs the joint labours of hundreds, thousands, and tens of thousands of people. The technical, economic and historical necessity of this is obvious, and all those who have thought about

> socialism have regarded it as one of the conditions of socialism. But how can strict unity of will be insured? By thousands subordinating their will to the will of one.
>
> Given ideal class consciousness and discipline on the part of those participating in the common work, this subordination would be something like the mild leadership of a conductor of an orchestra. It may assume the sharp forms of a dictatorship if ideal discipline and class consciousness are lacking. But be that as it may, *unquestioning subordination* to a single will is absolutely necessary for the success of processes of organization on the pattern of large-scale machine industry. On the railways it is twice and three times as necessary. In this transition from one political task to another, which *on the surface* [is] totally dissimilar to the first, lies the whole originality of the present situation. The revolution has only just smashed the oldest, strongest and heaviest of fetters, to which the people submitted under duress. That was yesterday. Today, however, the same revolution demands—precisely in the interests of socialism—that the people *unquestionably* obey the single will of the leaders of labour. Of course, such a transition cannot be made at one step. Clearly, it can be achieved only as a result of tremendous jolts, shocks, reversions to old ways, the enormous exertion of effort on the part of the proletarian vanguard, which is leading the people to the new ways.[57]

There is vanguard rule here all right, and if this is not an argument for power wielded by the more rational, then Macpherson has some definition that completely defies application.

Yet the most obvious case of the degeneration of positive liberty is dismissed in this fashion: "The transformation of radical PL^1 to PL^2, which comes with Stalin comes, it appears, only after long, continued and intensive refusal of the beneficiaries of unequal institutions, on a world-wide scale, to permit any moves to alter the institutions in the directions of more nearly equal powers."[58] It has been some time since an apology for Stalin has been offered in such a forthright manner. One could offer numerous interpretations of Stalinism: accidents of history, the absence of constitutional restraint in the early Soviet regime, the inappropriateness of the socialist experiment in Russia's stage of economic development, the ethnic heterogeneity of Russian society, Stalin's own psychological bearing. However, to contend that the destruction of the kulaks, the slave labor camps, the Moscow trials, the "Jewish doctors' plot," the nationalization of international communist parties, the secret police, and the most exhaustive and cruel censorship are all the result of the failure of those "who wield power in liberal societies to take the action required to realize PL^1," is such an extraordinary assertion that it makes Berlin's distinction between positive and negative liberty (a complicated position) and his claim that PL^1 leads to denial even more plausible.[59] What Macpherson would have us believe is that negative liberty is "the cloak for an individualist, corporate, imperial, free enterprise," PL^1 the "noblest strivings possible," and PL^2 the result not of PL^1 but of the consequences of negative liberty itself.[60] Would Macpherson tell either the inmate languishing in prison or the liberal who defends him that they are unable to judge PL^1 accurately? Do both fail to see that impediments to PL^1 are "inherent in that society," and action is "required to remove those impediments."[61]

In sum, it is at least problematic that the form of utopianism offered by Nozick, which sees the possibility of a vastly improved but not perfect society to be conceived by the people themselves, is inferior or ethically defective to the utopianism offered by Macpherson. The record of the utopian element in liberalism is anything but exemplary. However, the record of the revolutionary's sleek conflict-free utopia is hardly much of a competitor. Of course, the judgment of history is not yet in, but then it never is.

The journey from the individualism of *homo economicus* to the individualism of a humane diverse society is a complicated one and this is not reflected in *Anarchy, State and Utopia.* No claim is made here that the relationship between the two is direct or even automatic. The point is much like the old joke about the report that there are some chimpanzees who talk. The quality of their language is not the issue. What is of interest in the work of Nozick is that he could move beyond economic individualism at all. That a sketch of a more desirable society, one which moves beyond rational calculation, should emerge tells something about both the triumphs and tragedies of liberal thought and suggests that the utopian element in liberalism is a genuine one. Of course, the realtionship between its scientific element and its utopian one is often strained and muddled. It has none of the grace that Marxism possesses. However, perhaps that awkwardness can be a virtue as well as a vice.

NOTES

1. John H. Schaar, "The Case for Patriotism," *New American Review* 17 (May 1973), 88.

2. C. B. Macpherson, *Democratic Theory: Essays in Retrieval* (Oxford: Oxford University Press, 1973), p. 4.

3. George Santayana, *Dominations and Powers* (New York: Scribner's Sons, 1951) pp. 309-10.

4. Robert Nozick, *Anarchy, State and Utopia,* (New York: Basic Books, 1974), pp. 247-48.

5. Nozick rejects the legitimacy of blackmail but his view is limited: "...a seller of such silence could legitimately charge only for what he foregoes by silence. What he foregoes does not include the payment he could have received to abstain from revealing the information, though it does include the payments others would make to him to reveal the information." *Anarchy, State and Utopia,* p. 85. In other words, the maxim that price is to be determined by what the market can bear does not apply to blackmail. The duplicity of the blackmailer, the fate of the victim's reputation, and the inequality of the relationship are absent in the discussion. For a different description of the blackmailing transaction and its broader implications see my *The Shotgun Behind the Door: Liberalism and the Problem of Political Obligation* (Athens: University of Georgia Press, 1975), chap. V. It should be noted that Nozick's position is a moderate one in contemporary libertarian thought. See Murray N. Rothbard, *Man, Economy and the State,* vol. I (Princeton, N.J.: Van Nostrand, 1962), p. 443.

6. Nozick, *Anarchy, State and Utopia,* pp. 10-11.

7. Ibid., p. 321.

8. Thomas Hobbes, *Leviathan,* C. B. Macpherson, ed. (Baltimore: Penguin, 1968), p. 232.

9. Nozick, *Anarchy, State and Utopia,* pp. 118-19.

10. "As soon as men and women learn the utilitarian lesson and refuse to take for granted the traditional arrangements that their social environment makes for them, as soon as they acquire the habit of weighing the individual advantages of any prospective course of action—or, as we might also put it, as soon as they introduce into their private life a sort of inarticulate system of cost accounting—they cannot fail to become aware of the heavy

personal sacrifices that family ties and especially parenthood entail under modern conditions and of the fact that at the same time, excepting the cases of farmers and peasants, children cease to be economic assets. These sacrifices do not consist only of the items that come within the reach of the measuring rod of money but comprise in addition an indefinite amount of loss of comfort, of freedom from care, and opportunity to enjoy alternatives of increasing attractiveness and variety—alternatives to be compared with joys of parenthood that are being subjected to a critical analysis of increasing severity. The implication of this is not weakened but strengthened by the fact that the balance sheet is likely to be incomplete, perhaps even fundamentally wrong...the contribution made by parenthood...almost invariably escapes the rational searchlight of modern individuals who in private as in public life, tend to focus attention on ascertainable details of immediate utilitarian relevance and to sneer at the idea of hidden necessities of human nature or of the social organism." Joseph A. Schumpeter, *Capitalism, Socialism and Democracy* (New York: Harper, 1942), pp. 157-58. Seen from this perspective the liberation movements of the past decade are natural manifestations of the rationalizing capacity of bourgeois society rather than explicitly counter to it.

11. Colin Turnbull, *The Mountain People* (New York: Simon and Schuster, 1972), p. 181.

12. John Locke, *Two Treatises on Government*, Peter Laslett, ed., vol. 2 (New York: Mentor, 1960), p. 352.

13. Nozick, *Anarchy, State and Utopia*, pp. 175-82.

14. Ibid., pp. 246-50.

15. Ibid., p. 160.

16. Turnbull, *Mountain People*, p. 182.

17. Nozick, *Anarchy, State and Utopia*, p. 235.

18. Ibid., p. 181.

19. William Graham, *Writings of William Graham Sumner*, Albert Galloway and Maurice R. Davie, eds., vol. 1 (New Haven, Conn.: Yale University Press, 1934), p. 95. For a discussion of Sumner, see chap. 5.

20. Herbert Spencer, *Principles of Ethics*, vol. 2 (New York: Appleton & Co., 1892), p. 256.

21. Ibid.

22. Turnbull, *Mountain People*, p. 289.

23. Ibid., p. 290.

24. Brian Barry toys with this notion: "My own inclination would be to treat the book as a joke, but since it is only too clear that others are prepared to take it seriously, I shall do so as well." Book Review, *Political Theory* 3 (August 1975), 332.

25. Nozick, *Anarchy, State and Utopia,* p. 314.

26. Ibid., p. 302.

27. A plan close to the one implied by Nozick was offered by Robert Owen. He suggested that the state subsidize communes for the poor. Needless to say, the proposal contains elements that can move in unpleasant directions. However, compare this phenomenon to Kanter's discussion of "service communes." Rosabeth Moss Kanter, *Commitment and Community: Communes and Utopias in Sociological Perspective* (Cambridge, Mass.: Harvard University Press, 1972), chap. 8.

28. Nozick, *Anarchy, State and Utopia,* p. 326.

29. Macpherson, *Democratic Theory,* p. 200.

30. Ibid.

31. Ibid.

32. Could one make a similar argument about the left? Would it be possible to conclude that all socialist thought since Marx is a history of "self-deception"? By insisting upon salvaging the holy trinity of proletarian liberation, revolutionary inevitability and economic centralization, all Marxists have struggled and "exhausted" themselves over finding the plausible features of emerging industrial societies, they have been unable to accommodate substantial changes in their theories and lamely or ferociously speak of lumpen proletariats, Third World glories, and structural breakthroughs.

33. Nozick, *Anarchy, State and Utopia,* p. 324.

34. Ibid.

35. Ibid., p. 330.

36. Ibid.

37. Ibid., p. 332.

38. Ibid., p. 330.

39. Ibid.

40. Ibid., p. 332.

41. Alan Fox, "Is Equality a Necessity?", *Dissent* (Winter, 1975), 53.

42. J. S. Mill, "On Liberty," in *Essential Works of J. S. Mill,* Max Lerner, ed., (New York: Bentham, 1965), p. 320.

43. Marx and Engels, "Manifesto," in Lewis Feuer, ed., *Marx and Engels,* p. 39.

44. John L. Thomas, "Romantic Reform in America, 1815-1865," *American Quarterly,* 17 (Winter 1965), 678.

45. Ibid., p. 659.

46. Nozick, *Anarchy, State and Utopia,* pp. 319-32.

47. Ibid., p. 327.

48. Ibid., p. 328.

49. Isaiah Berlin, *Four Essays on Liberty* (Oxford: Oxford University Press, 1969), p. 18.
50. Macpherson, *Democratic Theory*, p. 109.
51. Ibid.
52. Ibid., pp. 112-13.
53. Ibid., p. 111.
54. Ibid., p. 115.
55. Ibid.
56. Ibid.
57. V. I. Lenin, "The Immediate Tasks of the Soviet Government" in Robert C. Tucker, ed., *The Lenin Anthology* (New York: Norton & Co., 1975), p. 455.
58. Macpherson, *Democratic Theory*, p. 115.
59. Ibid., p. 116.
60. Ibid.
61. Ibid.

CHAPTER 4

Up from Pluralism

In northwest Europe and the United States, the plateau of polyarchy was gained just long enough ago that the sense of triumphantly reaching new heights has turned into a feeling that we have been stuck too long on a tiresome plain. In a world distinguished by an incredible and unassimilable rate of novelty, polyarchy is inescapably old-fashioned.
—Robert A. Dahl, *After the Revolution*

The problems of constructing a liberal political theory or even a post-liberal one are not limited to the temptation to draw an account of politics from neutral elements. This is only one obstacle among many. A brief account of one of the other forms of liberalism will illustrate this point.

Pluralist liberalism, despite some modest trends in American politics at the moment, is almost totally discredited today. The experience of pluralist theory in American political science (always somewhat anomalous to the broader tradition) goes far toward explaining this state of affairs. Probably the most compelling reason, however, is the result of the demands for centralization from both radical critics and bureaucratic elites of industrial societies. The important question here, however, is how the centripetal and centrifugal positions of liberalism are combined. In pluralist liberalism is contained the most sophisticated balance available. Robert Nisbet has identified four elements of pluralist thought in general. His characterization is based on a wide reading of history; his account will be helpful:

1. *Functional autonomy.* "What characterizes the pluralist view of autonomy can best be thought of in terms of the ability of each major function in the social order to work within the maximum possible freedom to achieve its own distinctive ends."

2. *Decentralization.* "If the functional autonomy of social units is to be respected, if localism, regionalism, and the whole spirit of voluntary association is to flourish, power wielded must be distributed into as many hands as possible—not abstract, desocialized *political* hands, but those we actually see in the social order, those of workers, enterprisers, professionals, familes, and neighborhoods."
3. *Hierarchy.* "There is no form of community without some form of stratification of function and role....The value of pluralism...is rooted...in frank recognition of the value inherent in hierarchy."
4. *Tradition.* "...reliance upon, in largest possible measure, not formal law, ordinance, or administrative legislation, but use and want, and all the unaccountable means of adaptation by which human beings have proved so often to be masters of their destinies in ways governments cannot comprehend."[1]

The frankness with which Nisbet offers items 3 and 4 is noticeably lacking in liberal pluralism. Yet, what is intriguing about a pluralist society is how it attempts to capture both liberal propositions. Conflict is an accepted feature of pluralist society. Autonomous organizations, whether religious, economic, or educational, will on occasion be at cross-purposes. Moreover, they will have the strength to fight against encroachments. Conflict is not surpressed but accommodated. Presumably, the same can be said within functional units. Variety is insured by a multiplicity of units, and if a genuine pluralist tolerance in a Jamesian sense does not always emerge, at least a de facto toleration is possible. Pluralist liberalism attempts to resolve the problem of liberalism at a sociological rather than a philosophical level. A polity that directs the lives of its citizens from some central source, however benevolent and even democratic, seeks to accommodate liberal principles by a universal acceptance. By abandoning centralism, pluralism, in effect, says, "Look at this society and see if it can be said to incorporate the necessary elements." This seems to have been Tocqueville's tack. Here is a rather complicated statement from *The Old Regime and the French Revolution:*

> Some will say that a country governed by an absolute prince is a democracy because he will govern by laws and amid institutions which are favorable to the condition of the people. His government will be a democratic government. It will constitute a democratic monarchy. But the words democracy, monarchy, democratic government can only mean

> one thing, according to the true sense of the words: a government in which the people play a comparatively large role. Their meaning is closely related to the idea of political freedom. To decide a government in which political freedom is not found as democratic is to utter a palpable absurdity according to the natural sense of the words. These false or at least obscure expressions have been adopted because of (1) the desire to deceive the masses, since the word democratic always has a certain success with them; (2) the real difficulty of finding a word to express the complicated notion of an absolute government in which the people have no voice at all but in which the classes placed above them enjoy no privilege and in which the laws are designed to promote their well-being as much as possible.[2]

The distinction between political freedom and what Tocqueville called equality is an extremely subtle one, even more so because recent political thought so readily dismisses it. Contained in the concept of political freedom is the traditional liberal notion of freedom *from* interference and the now more preferred freedom *to* interfere. How is it, then, that Tocqueville could speak so eloquently of his devotion to freedom (even more so when he despaired that "no one in France sets any store in it"), yet oppose the love for equality, which he described as so "obstinate and often blind"? The answer is that contrary to a good portion of contemporary post-liberal thought, Tocqueville did not see the freedom to control one's own future as a result of equality but as a much more complicated social condition. Tocqueville himself indicates both the subtlety of this distinction and the fragility of its incorporation into society:

> On several occasions during the period extending from the outbreak of the Revolution up to our time we find the desire for freedom reviving, succumbing, then returning, only to die out once more and presently blaze up again. This presumably will be the lot for many years to come of a passion so undisciplined and untutored by experience; so easily discouraged, cowed and vanquished, so superficial and short-lived. Yet during this same period the passion for equality, first to entrench itself in the hearts of Frenchmen, has never given ground; for it links up with feelings basic to our very nature. For while the urge to freedom is forever assuming new forms, losing or gaining strength according to the march of events, our love of equality is constant and pursues the object of its

> desire with a zeal that is obstinate and often blind, ready to make every concession to those who give it satisfaction.[3]

A free nation was one which, during this period, had institutions that guaranteed civil rights and free speech and also provided a public arena for political action; one in which "every man is daily reminded of the need of meeting his fellow men, of learning what they have to say, of exchanging ideas, and coming to an agreement as to the conduct of their common interests."[4] This public sphere of action is so crucial that little can be accomplished without it:

> Only freedom is capable of tearing them away from the worship of money and from the little daily worries of their personal affairs and making them see and feel at every moment their country above and beside them; only freedom occasionally replaces the love of well-being with loftier and more energetic passions, provides ambition with higher objects than the acquisition of wealth, and creates a climate which makes it impossible to see and judge the vices and virtues of men[5]

Set against this image is the drive for equality. Tocqueville insisted that blame did not rest solely with the socialist, and he traced its influence to the physiocrats. "They attacked not only specific forms of privilege but any kind of diversity whatsoever, to their thinking all men should be equal even if equality spelled servitude...."[6] They had no concern for private rights; "only the public interest mattered." Tocqueville dismissed the physiocrats' demand for capitalism as moot; their importance lay in their failure to grasp the notion of "political liberty." The expansion of the public sphere was not, by itself, a healthy development. Tocqueville was horrified by Voltaire's statement in support of the royal abolishment of the parlements in 1771: "Since we must have a master it is better to serve a thoroughbred lion than two-hundred rats—like myself!" To Tocqueville it was this statement, so thoroughly democratic in his sense, that epitomized so much of French political thought. Only as an abstraction were the people supreme: "The nation as a whole had sovereign rights, while the individual citizen was kept in strict tutelage; the former was expected to display the sagacity and virtues of a free race, the latter to behave like an obedient servant."[7]

For Tocqueville the demand for centralization, which was a direct consequence of the desire for equality, represented neat and readily observable solutions. If equality was not forthcoming, it would seem obvious that centralization had not proceeded wide and far enough. In the pursuit of equality, few would end up in a position to finally exercise any freedom; too much would have been given up so that the game could be played:

> For in a community in which the ties of family, of caste, of class, and craft fraternities no longer exist people are far too much disposed to think exclusively of their own interests, to become self-seekers practicing a narrow individualism and caring nothing for the public good. Far from trying to counteract such tendencies despotism encourages them, depriving the governed of any sense of solidarity and interdependence, of good-neighborly feeling and a desire to further the welfare of the community at large.[8]

Thus, for Tocqueville, the road to freedom (in the positive sense) is not through the path of equality. Yet, he was no economic individualist. Tocqueville's descriptions of fearful men grasping for gain and workers' minds mutilated by division of labor in a society given over to the private virtues are equally haunting.[9] The plain fact was that freedom is "forever assuming new forms," sometimes promoted by requiring central intervention, sometimes by expanding voluntary associations.[10] Tocqueville, despite his own personal proclivities, was a great theoretician of *liberal pluralism*. The image of pluralism, from Aristotle to Burke, emphasized immobility and hierarchy. The new pluralism was different in at least two respects: diversity replaced hierarchy and constitutional democracy partially replaced custom. The blueprint, if one could call it that, for traditional pluralism rested upon a reverence for tradition and the wisdom of the ages; only through this sort of "rational irrationalism" could one hope to build up permanence and customs sufficient to defend it against tyranny. The best Burke could say was that "everything ought to be open but not indifferently to every man."[11] Liberal pluralism is more a conscious effort. Diversity is the structural feature of society; politics merely reflects, then articulates, a pluralistic universe. Ideally, justice hovers between equity and equality.[12] The formal parameters of the system are, of course, determined by constitutional restrictions on power and democratic participation. While later theorists, such as Lindbloom, would attempt to argue that the whole system was eminently rational, Eckstein may well reflect Tocqueville's subtlety when he wonders "how organized pluralism and national bargaining are to be reconciled with systems in which political equality and majority rule are major principles of legitimacy."[13] Liberal pluralism is foremost a work of art, much more complicated in its workings than the bleak mechanistic metaphor of American political scientists. That it is so singular a political system, though its form can be filled in easily enough with more base and durable matter, is obvious enough. Liberal pluralism has a most delicate efflorescence.

In fact, it is precisely this characteristic that makes liberal pluralism such an easy target for critics and such a difficult defense for its supporters. One of the most persistent questions raised by critics of pluralism involves an assessment of the causes of group formation and their subsequent effect on policy.[14]

Tocqueville, the defender of pluralism, provided the critique that is the basis of this liberal approach. In contrasting associational activity in America to that of aristocratic societies, he noted their lack of permanence and compulsion in liberal societies:

> Among democratic peoples new families continually rise from nothing while others fall, and nobody's position is quite stable. The woof of time is ever being broken and the track of past generations lost. Those who have gone before are easily forgotten, and no one gives a thought to those who follow. All a man's interests are limited to those near himself....
>
> As each class catches up with the next and gets mixed with it, its members do not care about one another and treat one another as strangers.[15]

Under these arrangements, association must rise on some basis other than the "natural" sentiments of family and class. Tocqueville hoped that enlightened self-interest would lead people away from a completely privatistic existence toward participation. While it might not "inspire great sacrifices" nor "make a man virtuous," it would produce "orderly, temperate, moderate, carefree, and self-controlled citizens."[16] They, at least, were better than none at all.

Tocqueville was careful not to correct Montesquieu, but his conclusion amounted to a significant revision: "The Americans are not a virtuous people and yet they are free."[17]

From this basis it would be possible for liberals to concentrate upon the fluidity of associational formation in society as well as the temporary character of most group alliances. Madison, of course, noted this as did Bentley, Truman, and Dahl. Little or no effort is made to assess reasons for different power among groups or the absence of certain group formations in certain policy areas, aside from the penchant of men to form factions. These questions are all solved by using that generality which has all the appearance of correctness, interest. Interests are formed and articulated; groups coalesce about them. Weak groups mean requisite "interests" are not to be had.

Tocqueville's characterization of association in America was meant to be taken as a veiled warning. In the hands of other theorists, it is offered as a given. There is, of course, a definite anticentralist bias in this form of pluralist theory, and it is much the same as Tocqueville's. Dahl's concern with "fanatics" and the peculiar suitability of pluralism for a nation of "restless and immoderate" people is testimony to this sort of sentiment. Madison's swipe at "theoristic politicians" is directed at the same point. Critics have never had much difficulty plucking statements such as these out of pluralistic texts. But what "interest group" liberalism does not possess is Tocqueville's concern for the political order as a whole.

Without a vision of citizenship in pluralist society or a sociology that goes deeper than interest formulation, American pluralists have had great difficulty in defending themselves. This is nowhere more evident than in the works of Calhoun, one of the most frustrated and sophisticated students of American pluralism. Calhoun's efforts are placed in stark relief because the pluralism he was advocating involved a defense of slavery as a "positive good." Yet, the real dilemma one finds in Calhoun's efforts to sustain a concurrent majority applies to liberal pluralism in general and especially to the American variant that extends from Madison to Dahl. Calhoun did examine the historical basis of the southern community, found it at best nonliberal, and, in order to defend it, attempted to attach to it an intricate constitutionalism. This juxtaposition of an aristocratic community overlaid with liberal pluralism simply could not stand. Hartz is correct when he notes the "weird quality" of Calhoun's writings resulting from the attempt to ground "mechanical schemes on the organic naturalism that his social defense of slavery inspired."[18]

The examination of the basis of association and associational loyalty always brings the liberal face to face with nonliberal institutions such as the church or neighborhood or institutions stripped of liberal individualism such as the county courthouse or the factory. Nisbet's point is appropriate here: "...the symbols of liberalism, like the bells of the church, depend on prejudgments and social tradition."[19] Marx could not work up much sympathy for the Indian peasant village even as it was being destroyed by the British, and it is difficult for the liberal to fight to preserve institutions without submitting them to the discerning eye of the social engineer. The conservative has no trouble with these sorts of hierarchies; the ages have created them, and, thus, they have a rationality all their own. The liberal has no such rock from which he can build his church. As Rogin suggests, liberal pluralism sees associations in terms of psychologism, dissolving the groups into "shared" individual attitudes.[20] His associations have no permanence; Tocqueville's political freedom gained by citizenship becomes a "consumer group" or a "potential group" based upon the "most widely shared attitudes" of a polity."[21] The French critics' worst fears of democratic association are confirmed. Pluralist society as art, part contrivance and part tradition, erupts into a battleground where large groups and the followers who support them for their immediate utility brutally fight one another. Or, it slips into a peaceful but ignominious death in which particular loyalties fade until all that is left is that vast tutelary power of which Tocqueville so ominously spoke. Yet, there are exits from this dilemma for liberal pluralism. They are not clear, perfect escapes; no theoretical resolution to political problems leaves its adherents unscathed. But there are proposals worth examining. One option is to give existing associations new functions and democratize them, even at the expense of an existing group elite and central authority and perhaps efficiency. The other is to expand the pluralist universe itself. By allowing new associations an easier birth, one might enliven the political arena by virtue of the new competition and resuscitate existing associations as well.

The first alternative has been suggested by Robert Dahl in his *After the Revolution: Authority in the Good Society.* That Dahl should offer a reexamination of pluralism and reach conclusions as far-reaching as he does, poses a paradox with ironic overtones in the context of recent political thought. If any single figure can be identified as the leader of pluralistic analysis in America, it is Robert Dahl. Post-liberals quite rightly have focused their critiques of pluralism upon his works. As was the case with most post-war analyses, Dahl's analysis exhibited a curious combination of smugness and anxiety. A conception of democracy based upon natural rights is dismissed as follows: "It is easy to see that such an argument inevitably involves a variety of assumptions that at best are difficult and at most impossible to prove to the satisfaction of anyone of positivist or skeptical predispositions."[22] Populist democracy, as an alternative to pluralism, "postulates only two goals to be maximized, political equality and popular sovereignty."[23] Only a "fanatic" would support such a system. "For most of us—and this may be especially true in countries that have managed to operate democracies over long periods of time—the cost of pursuing any one or two goals at the expense of others is thought to be excessive."[24] Moreover, populistic democracy is not an empirical system: "It consists only of logical relations among ethical postulates. It tells us nothing about the real world. From it we can predict no behavior whatsoever."[25] Dahl ends his *Preface to Democratic Theory* with the assurance that "with all its defects, [American democracy] does nonetheless provide a high probability that any active and legitimate group will make itself heard effectively at some stage in the process of decision."[26]

On the basis of this analysis, Dahl's position has been subjected to a sustained attack (some of it deserved and some of it unfounded), ranging from charges of elitism to a conspiracy to produce the sort of political silence that gives rise to tyranny. A span of fourteen years separates *A Preface to Democratic Theory* from *After the Revolution.* A brief comparison may be useful. There are notable similarities in Dahl's approach. The liberal firmament of pluralist values still exists but now it has more of a Whiggish tone. Authority has three dimensions: personal choice, competence, and economy. Each of these "criteria" may lead one to accept a particular decision or a practice. (Dahl still shies away from "oughts.")

The criteria of personal choice (other people exercising their choices and reaching different conclusions on policy) offers three alternatives to the problem of substantive disagreement in politics: establishment of a system of mutual guarantees restraining both majorities and determined minorities, withdrawal into a consensual association composed of like-minded people, and transference of some areas to the domain of personal choice. Now Dahl's views on these alternatives still remain essentially the same as those in his other works. His preference rests largely with the first option. "...a system of Mutual Guarantees that effectively plans some matter beyond the reach of ordinary majorities, is a characteristic of every national political system that we ordinarily call democratic."[27] Yet consensual association receives a more sympathetic treatment. Rousseau succeeded "brilliantly" yet "ambiguously" in dealing with this alternative. Dahl's interpretation of the "consensual" alternative remains characteristically liberal. It is suitable for small associations and perhaps "little city-states" voluntarily formed:

> ...if different people with different views were allowed to sort themselves out into different and entirely homogeneous and consensual associations, each of us would exist in a harmonious association where we had nothing to fear from the majority; where, as a matter of fact, any majority would express the will of all of us....[28]

Dahl now seems to recognize that the populistic model of democracy is not an empirically vacuous one. Still, he is skeptical. Autonomous communes cannot exist blissfully independent. One may plunder and exploit another, as was the case with the city-states of Greece. The need for mutual guarantees reappears at a broader level of social interaction. Dahl concluded that a "system of Mutual Guarantees does not foster homogeneous associations, but in order for homogeneous associations to exist peacefully, they must be a part of a system of Mutual Guarantees."[29]

Dahl's critique of populistic democracy becomes a more thorough one precisely because he has now granted it a stature which it could always justly claim as a theory that looked to the needs and aspirations of men in society. Yet, he is still not willing to accept these premises himself. The whole criteria of personal choice is a valid one because it is grounded on "rational self-interest." Members of consensual associations will remain in them so long as the gain exceeds some loss. And "naturally" it would be "rational to withdraw my adherence if I expect that the loss would exceed the gain."[30] Now, it would seem untoward (to say the least) for an ex-Catholic to explain leaving his church in such matter-of-fact terms. To ascribe associational loyalty and withdrawal in terms that would account for a switch to another brand of shampoo indicates the continuity in Dahl's political theory.[31] Either he recognizes the complicated nature of membership in society but feels that it can be for convenience expressed in simpler terms, or he fails to see a social order in terms other than enlightened self-interest. On the one hand his theory is incomplete; on the other, seriously wrong.

Dahl affirms his belief that the "ordinary man" is as competent as anyone else to decide when and how he will intervene on decisions that affect him. Yet, Dahl insists that the criterion of competence is still relevant, that it is a question that needs to be judged from case to case. Everyone accepts the superior confidence of others in some matters. It is not necessarily rational for you to participate in a decision that directly and seriously affects your interests. Political authority may be justified democratically, but the proper basis for authority in "any other association" may be different. Dahl does not examine social bases that give rise to centers of individuals who have accrued certain levels of competence. Nevertheless, in any society competence must remain a function of time. Even in Trotsky's utopia, an Einstein is unlikely to be able to devote enough years of his life to be a Goethe also.

The criterion of economy arises in part from this idea. Economy illustrates "that many of the things you value are scarce and that by wasting these scarce resources you reduce the total value of what you attain."[32] Dahl suggests a number of considerations that might determine the "costs" of participation: whether you enjoy taking part, whether the matters the association is concerned with are important, whether the differences at stake are great, whether the outcome is likely to turn out satisfactorily without your effort, whether you are competent to judge the issues at hand.

On the basis of this plural account of authority, Dahl states that political equality and majority rule are the most desirable forms of political authority. In fact, he is quite clear about the need for political participation: "I do not think a rational citizen weighing all these factors would be as little involved as most citizens in all countries, including our own, but I suspect a reasonable upper limit for most people would fall considerably below the political activists." As for lesser associations, "no single form of authority" is most desirable and the combinations of forms "must be nearly endless."[33]

Dahl sees three problems confronting American society. In considering each problem, it is possible to say that he moves away from a cost-benefit individuality as a basis for politics. The transition is a gradual one. It has none of the abruptness that characterizes Nozick's work and, therefore, can be easily missed (as it has by critics). Part of the reason for this is that the model of individualism offered in Dahl's theory, and in those of most American pluralists as well, is quite different from the appetitive individualism drawn so well by Nozick and also different from the individualism offered by Rawls. Dahl's citizens, as was indicated earlier, do emphasize self-interest as a basis for action, but it is a self-interest without sharp edges. Born of a fear of the consequences of intensely held beliefs about politics and society, the American pluralist is willing to rely upon self-interest as a basis for political action. Moral demands do not admit to compromise; they spiral into utopian expectations, and they spawn demagogues whose conception of self-interest is megalomanic. While polyarchy is "light years away from primary democracy it is also light years away from a truly despotic regime."[34] It is precisely this style of thought that indicates the nature of interest group liberalism. Individuals certainly eye the costs and benefits of actions. In this way they can protect their own interests and stand ready to reverse themselves if they must.

The differences between Nozick and Rawls are notable. Nozick's men see one another as vending machines with a very sturdy exterior of "rights." Dahl's individuals approach one another carefully because the other may erupt into a bundle of neurotic impulses and because each has a variety of goals to pursue. "Most of us are marginalists," Dahl tells us. We must juggle a bewildering number of goals ("leisure, privacy, consensus, stability, income, security, progress, status") and fit them all as best we can into our lives. Perhaps both models do suggest bourgeois types. Yet one fits Dickens's Mr. Gragrind and the other Cheever's Elliot Nailles. Rawls's men, on the other hand, while certainly seeking a cautious gain, engage in the exercise in order to leave it behind. The afterglow of the union of social unions, the result of a moral settlement, is more preferable to the anxieties of even a fictional marketplace.

For Nozick to move beyond his own model of human nature required an entirely separate argument, one which he conveniently gave. Dahl eases into his version of "utopian" liberalism, and, as one would expect, it does not produce towering images at either end of his journey. The first failing of American polyarchy for Dahl is its inequality of resources. While these inequalities can never be "entirely eliminated," they can be substantially reduced. The argument clearly has a prudential cast. Effective political choices cannot be made under conditions of seriously unequal resources, and political equality is impaired. Under such conditions democracy will be "rare, precarious and ephemeral." Whereas misguided moralism was the cause of Stalin and Hitler in the earlier model, extreme inequality is now the culprit. It "must beget oligarchy or despotism." "Fearful of the poor, the rich will impose oligarchy, while the poor, fearful of the rich, will be mobilized by a popular despot."[35] While Dahl contends that a characteristic of even an ill-formed polyarchy is the dispersion of resources among the population (the poor have political resources in the ballot to "acquire leverage and bargaining power"), their cumulative effect is enough to imperil even maintaining America at its current level of polyarchy. Dahl rejects compensation in forms other than income on the grounds that the result is likely to be "a patchwork of irritating regulations enforced by bureaucratic agencies." A system of welfare must be jettisoned in favor of providing income itself. Whether income maintenance can avoid expanding Tocqueville's image of a vast tutelary power in the hands of the state, as Dahl believes the present welfare system threatens to do, is an open question, but it is difficult to deny that Dahl has confronted a problem pluralism was deemed congenitally unable to pose.

The next feature of American society to come under scrutiny is the modern corporation. Dahl describes the global firm as "a new, shadowy, unregulated polity with resources greater than those of most nation states."[36] If one is to approach authority in terms of personal choice, competence, and economy, the corporation in its present form "cannot be justified." All economic enterprise is described as a "public service." Stepping swiftly now, Dahl goes on to attack the neoclassical economists. Given both the history of American pluralism and the claims of post-liberal critics, Dahl's charges are worth quoting in full:

> The neo-classical economists viewed internal controls, authority within the firm, rather as astronomers regard the gravitational force of the earth. To the astronomer, the earth's gravity is all concentrated at a theoretical point approximately at the center of the globe. From the astronomer's purely professional perspective, all the bustling life, struggle, force and drama going on at the earth's surface are matters too trivial to be noticed. A revolution, a volcano, a hurricane, an earthquake may destroy his observatory, but in principle these things do not matter. In quite the same way, the neo-classical economists reduced the firm to an infinitesmal theoretical point in space where the particularities of Mr. Gragrind or John D. Rockefeller had no more relevance than the living earth does to the astronomer. The complex government of the firm vanished and reappeared as the single rational entrepreneur pressed on by lust for profit and an inhuman capacity for responding shrewdly to the impersonal forces of the market. As a classroom exercise this provided an opportunity for the virtuoso of the blackboard, but it told nothing about how General Motors should be governed. For that matter, the effects on lung cancer of the "rational" calculations of the cigarette manufacturers are a matter for which a display of fancy cost curves hardly constitutes a satisfactory answer.

Indeed! Now, Dahl is willing to look at the internal structure of the corporation. He concludes that if one uses the principle that people ought to be permitted to participate in decisions that affect their interests, a strong prima facie case can be made for corporate citizenship for employees and customers. The key to the problem, however, is the need for structures of participation, and Dahl rejects, as any pluralist would, centralized control of the corporation by the state. Both reformist liberals and socialists saw demands for decentralization as a "mask for privilege and reaction." Yet whatever their intentions, they contributed to bureaucratic centralization. In large economic institutions, it is not desirable to regard ownership either privately or publicly. Property is a "bundle of rights." "Once the pieces in the bundle have been parceled out, nothing exactly corresponding to the conventional meaning of ownership or property remains."[38] Dahl recoils from accepting a single institution with the responsibility for discharging a universally owned enterprise precisely because his account of authority is pluralistic. He sees problems in a workers' control system, yet wonders if interest group management (shared control among union officials, consumer groups, and government) would produce "the sort of structural change that would help reduce the powerlessness of the ordinary American employee."[39] Moreover, neither interest group management or workers' control would eliminate the need for a mix of external controls in the form of governmental coordination and the market.

The third problem Dahl discusses is not limited to American society but to all modern nation-states. Mass participation in large entities must, by sheer arithmetic, be sporadic. Dahl is concerned that many find this condition a "brutal restraint" on democratic potential. Yet, there is no optimal choice. "Giant political systems are a necessity." Polyarchy is the "closest approximation we know to rule by the people." The task at hand is to resolve Goldilocks's dilemma, to find subordinate institutions that are not too big, nor too small, but just right. Two suggestions are offered: revitalize the neighborhoods as political units and seek the creation of cities of moderate size. If meaningful functions are given to both units, an approximation of primary democracy results. If every adult in a city of 200,000 belongs to a single neighborhood unit of 500 people, then every primary unit could be represented in an assembly of 200. Note that Dahl selects the neighborhood as his territorial base, a unit that is capable of producing policies based upon people's aspirations that grow out of their living together and sharing the human joys and tragedies associated with birth, growth, and death.

Dahl's efforts do not go far toward solving the intricate problems that confront American society. However, they do illustrate two important points. Pluralism, even the liberal American variant, is capable of looking at current social and political arrangements critically and even radically as well as within the resources contained in its own tradition. Second, liberal pluralism may be capable of transcending its own faults by postulating a mixture of institutions that not only avoid the peculiar centrifugal tendencies of the sort of liberalism Dahl describes but strike a balance between a society of hierarchical fiefdoms and transient "consumer communities." Yet the nagging question still remains. Can a marginalist, one who values leisure, status, progress, and privacy as well as justice, freedom, and equality, be brought into participation in the political order on the basis of "enlightened self-interest." Tocqueville described individualism apart from egoism as a "calm and considered feeling which disposes each citizen to isolate himself from the mass of his fellows and withdraw into the circle of family and friends."[40] Individualism was based on "misguided judgment rather than depraved feeling." Due more to "inadequate understanding than to perversity of heart," individualism would dam the "spring of public virtues" and finally merge with egoism.[41] Yet, self-interest seems a fragile instrument to check egoism. The liberal man is at best a two-dimensional one. He is a friend in your backyard and a utility maximizer when any meeting commences. Why the humanity and decency of the marginalist cannot readily flow of its own accord to the political arena is a puzzle.

The other alternative designed to revitalize liberal pluralism has been offered by Theodore Lowi. The notion that America represents a cramped and limited version of pluralism has long been an observation made by European writers. Tocqueville, Weber, Sombart, and Samson have all noted the peculiar nature of group formation in America. Lowi, however, has presented the argument for a wider pluralism anew and with some added conditions.

Lowi's *The End of Liberalism* was the sort of book that can hit an academic community like a thunderbolt. Combining theoretical and empirical analysis with ease and adding a fillip of openly admitted polemic, Lowi systematically attacked the liberal programs of the 1960s and concluded that liberal governments cannot plan, liberal jurisprudence was a misnomer, and liberal justice was impossible. The last chapter evoked a theme that has nearly assumed the form of a benediction in post-liberal thought: political philosophy must somehow move "beyond liberalism."[42] However, Lowi puzzled reviewers with talk of a return to "juridical democracy." He called not for revolution or even for a new militant intelligentsia:

> ...it would be wrong to leave the impression that political science created interest group liberalism or that political scientists will produce the future of theory beyond liberalism. Theories are only systematized and propagated there. In the United States the history of political theory since the founding of the Republic has resided in the Supreme Court. The future of political theory probably lies there too.[43]

The last chapter of *The End of Liberalism* was tantalizingly vague. In his next book, Lowi responded to the criticisms that juridical democracy was as formalistic as pluralism and, worse, vacuous as a political theory since it seemed to be cut adrift from actual forces in American society. In Lowi's words, "I was guilty of an unpardonable sin...I had committed a civics."[44] The dilemma that confronted Lowi was one that faces all pluralists: how can one fashion a system of uniform laws for all of society when one places his supreme value on diversity? How does one prevent the conspiratorial whisper, "What's a constitution among friends?," from becoming the political culture of a society?

In *The Politics of Disorder,* Lowi attempted to answer this question, the same question that faced Tocqueville, Madison, Truman, and Dahl. The mere attempt to deal with the question indicates Lowi's commitment to pluralism despite the fact that "interest group liberalism" is his target. There are, of course, anti-liberal musings. Lowi paints a picture of a political man, the politician of Madison, as a great immoral compromiser. "If we were all political men and the Eichmann trial had been in the United States, Eichmann's most effective defense would have been that he had not formulated extermination policy, that he took the job to keep a *real* Nazi from getting it, and that thanks to his efforts the body count was merely 6 million rather than 8 million or more."[45] Ethics recede as compromise is highly valued and institutionalized. Lowi is, of course, correct on this point. He could even have continued by noting that when compromise becomes the only value shared by all, the pluralist vision itself is dead. At that point, pluralism has been abandoned for one value, however necessary for its functioning. A sly monism has crept in. But, as with most post-liberals, ethics means drama and excitement, and one wonders if it is these values, amoral in themselves, that one yearns for even more than moral standards. Lowi's analogy to sports is instructive in this respect:

> Sports may be the only remaining mass phenomenon with a strong ethical basis. In any sports event, there is also a clear definition of defeat and victory...the biggest enemy of sports is gambling. This is not merely because some gamblers may destroy the ethics of the situation by rigging a few games and instilling doubt in all the other games.[46]

In any case, here the desire for a vitalistic political order is placed in the service of a pluralist vision. Lowi rejects the image of the republican hero who galvanizes disparate social forces into a dynamic whole. Leadership is unpredictable: "You cannot predict exactly what directions leaders will pursue, and you cannot predict exactly what impact leadership will have on the system or organization within which it emerges."[47] And for Lowi, what is most important of all is the fact that leaders require followers, not citizens. Therefore, Lowi again recommends an "anti-leadership system" of "juridical democracy" as the basis for reform. Yet, he is embarrassed at what he calls its Kantian overtones and its association with political conservatism. He realizes that constitutionalism is not synonymous with a pluralist order nor much respected by the radical left. Therefore, he must reach for some dynamic principle that somehow will break the embourgeoisment of American pluralism and yet still avoid hero worship, the "ultimate fraud of any revolutionary socialism."[48]

Lowi's answer is an extremely interesting one. Without indicating any knowledge of European syndicalism, Lowi advances what appears to be the structural alternative propounded by Proudhon.[49] He begins with a model of society offered by Kornhauser. Using two variables, accessibility of elites and availability of nonelites, Kornhauser postulated four types of societies: communal (inaccessible elites and unavailable nonelites), pluralist (accessible elites and unavailable nonelites), mass (accessible elites and available nonelites), totalitarian (inaccessible elites and available nonelites). For Kornhauser, the mass society represented something of a way station to totalitarianism.

Lowi, however, insists that pluralism is not a meaningful antidote to the problem of mass society. The pluralist society of organized groups is already mobilized and static. As such, it probably represents a modern mutation of Kornhauser's communal society. To breathe life into the pluralist society, Lowi suggests abandoning the focus on groups altogether and recommends studying social movements as "the dramatic moment in the organization of interests."[51] Using the social movement as the unit of a pluralist analysis, Lowi can show its legitimization and organization as a group, as a final stage of development.[52] The American trade union or farm bureau represents a social movement in its maturity or, if one prefers, in its senility. It follows, then, that if the social movement represents perpetual revitalization of a pluralist society (a liberal permanent revolution), any analysis must recommend ways in which it can be offered an easier birth.

Lowi's analysis is not meant to function as a new kaleidoscope but as a call to action. He recommends a rigid adherence to civil liberties to protect freedom of association. However, this is only part of the message. Social movements may be forced to compromise prematurely before the onslaught of the "political men" who run the moribund machinery of the organized group society. Thus, their contribution in terms of social innovation is never fully realized. Bureaucratization is quickly imposed upon them with the acceptance of piecemeal and symbolic reforms. Cretinlike groups ramble about the scene of American politics. Part aborted social movements and part beneficiaries of older organized interests, these groups hardly advance the needed rebirth of American pluralist politics. In this context, the leaders of social movements assume more the characteristics of public relations men than spearheads of solidified mass movements.

To counteract the premature cooptation of social movements in a pluralist society, Lowi relies upon his conception of juridical democracy. In a society in which laws must be expressly changed for alterations to occur, social movements will gain determination and strength until there is a "full coercive imposition of laws democratically arrived at."[53] In Lowi's words, "chaos is better than a bad program."[54] And for Lowi, a bad program is always an ad hoc response to an immediate demand. "A vague government response in a bad program is far worse than no government response at all."[55]

Lowi appears to have solved one of the major problems of liberal pluralism. The word "appears" is offered with caution here not to indicate that the attempt is only a superficial one but rather to suggest that the solution will always remain empirically questionable. Lowi has taken great risks in his effort to ensure a dynamic pluralistic order. A brief mention of Bertrand de Jouvenal's work on group politics can help make this point. Jouvenal has suggested that groups are the center of all politics. In fact, for him the problem of group formation and inter- and intragroup conflict takes on the same function in his theories as class does in Marx's. The history of the West is a study of the battlefields on which groups led by political entrepreneurs have fought. Class has been and will be a prime mobilization symbol for group conflict, but it is not the only one, and, for Jouvenal, it is not the basis for the problem of political order. In this light, Jouvenal's characterization of authority is much the same as Lowi's. Stability and equilibrium represent the achievements but also the shell of post-social movements.

What Jouvenal does recognize, however, is that the social movement (in Lowi's terms, the "dramatic" phase of the formation of an organized group) is formed and led by an "auctor." The new association "is really rather like a comet—a large tail of docile followers, dragged along by a small dynamic head."[56] Lowi may speak with great force about the false reliance upon leadership in government, but, by unleashing the force of social movements upon society, he is also unleashing Jouvenal's political entrepreneur. Men of great ambition and vision will make their mark upon society. The point is that these men can act to bring about a more vibrant and even just society as well as create demolition squads for a revolutionary order. Lowi's attempt to protect social movements from oppression through a firm governmental commitment to civil liberties, coupled with his attempt to protect them from early accommodation in order to solidify their internal goals, may well create the conditions for the end of a pluralist order. Lowi has not considered the nature of the demands made by social movements even in American history. What would have been the consequences for minorities of a fully protected and unaccommodated populist movement in this country? In a recent text, Lowi, himself, indicates that he has been troubled on this point. He notes the long history of rebellion as extreme responses of protest in America and reminds us of the important changes brought about by violent political action. However, rebellion, as violent action to *"change the behavior of an existing regime,"* has been dealt with by oppression or cooptation.[57] These are the alternatives Lowi is anxious to avoid. As a consequence, he explains that the rebellion model is nearly coterminous with American radicalism. Americans, unlike the French, have no Jacobin ancestry and hence no revolutionary memory. Revolution is "so far outside American experience that there is no scenario for it."[58] However, the absence of carriers of a revolutionary tradition can be explained in part by the "weak state" of American society. Radical associations need to attack a range of institutions in America beyond the political. At this point Lowi begins to wonder. If the state becomes a strong center of national life, "how far can [it] go in responding to...demands...without becoming the kind of force and symbol that confirms the revolutionary critique and converts rebellious leaders into revolutionaries?"[59] But has Lowi's social movement constitutionalism not created the very conditions for the rise of the revolutionary critique?

David Truman, the apotheosis of interest group liberalism in America, once explicitly denied the need for any public philosophy for society. All that was needed was an attachment based upon an "understanding of the system as it is, upon perception of the consequences for the system that are likely to follow from the actions of elite elements within it, and upon a willingness to act upon those perceptions in its defense."[60] Both Dahl and Lowi seem to have followed those requirements and yet still present dubious theories. All this does not mean that liberal pluralism is a bad theory, only that it is an extremely fragile one.

NOTES

1. Robert Nisbet, *Twilight of Authority* (New York: Oxford University Press, 1975), pp. 233-40.

2. Cited in Raymond Aron, *An Essay on Freedom* (New York: World Publishing, 1960), p. 11. I am indebted to Aron's discussion of Tocqueville here and in his *Main Currents in Sociological Thought,* vol. I (Garden City, N.Y.: Doubleday Anchor, 1970).

3. Alexis de Tocqueville, *The Old Regime and the French Revolution,* Stuart Gilbert, trans. (Garden City, N.Y.: Doubleday Anchor, 1955), pp. 209-10.

4. Ibid., p. xiv.

5. Ibid.

6. Ibid., p. 139.

7. Ibid., p. 167.

8. Ibid., p. xiii.

9. See especially vol. I, pt. II, Chaps. 10, 11, 13, 16, 17, 20, in *Democracy in America,* J. P. Mayer, ed. (Garden City, N.Y.: Doubleday, 1969).

10. Ibid., p. 260.

11. Cited in Nisbet, *Twilight of Authority,* p. 199.

12. On this point see John W. Chapman's masterful presentation, "The Political Theory of Pluralism" in J. Roland Pennock and John W. Chapman, eds., *Voluntary Associations* (New York: Atherton Press, 1969), esp. pp. 107-14.

13. Harry Eckstein, *Division and Cohesion in Democracy: A Study of Norway* (Princeton, N.J.: Princeton University Press, 1966), pp. 192-93.

14. William Conolly's introduction to his *The Bias of Pluralism* (New York: Atherton Press, 1969) summarizes criticism of the pluralists. It should be noted that "interest group liberalism" has invoked the ire of nearly all the academic right and left, extending from Arendt to Kariel. The most helpful balanced critique is Darryl Baskin, *American Pluralist Democracy: A Critique* (New York: Van Nostrand, 1971).

15. Tocqueville, *Democracy in America,* vol. II, pt. II, p. 507.

16. Ibid., p. 527.

17. From Tocqueville's notes, published by J. P. Mayer in *Nouvelle Revue Française* (April 1, 1959) and cited by Aron, *An Essay on Freedom,* p. 18.

18. Louis Hartz, *The Liberal Tradition in America* (New York: Harcourt Brace and World, 1955), p. 160.

19. Robert Nisbet, *Community and Power* (New York: Oxford University Press, 1962), p. 223.

20. Michael Paul Rogin, *The Intellectuals and McCarthy* (Cambridge, Mass.: M.I.T. Press, 1967), pp. 18-19.

21. Arthur F. Bentley, *The Process of Government* (Evanston, Ill.: Principia, 1949), pp. 208-09; David Truman, *The Governmental Process* (New York: Knopf, 1951), pp. 51-52.

22. Robert Dahl, *A Preface to Democratic Theory* (Chicago: University of Chicago Press, 1956), p. 45.

23. Ibid., p. 50.

24. Ibid., p. 51.

25. Ibid.

26. Ibid., p. 145.

27. Robert Dahl, *After the Revolution: Authority in the Good Society* (New Haven, Conn.: Yale University Press, 1970), p. 107.

28. Ibid., p. 18.

29. Ibid., p. 24.

30. Ibid., p. 12.

31. For example, see Murray Seidler's portrayal of the personal agony associated with the shift of American Socialist Party members to trade unionism in the context of capitalism, "The Socialist Party and American Unionism," *Midwest Journal of Political Science* (August, 1961), pp. 207-36.

32. Dahl, *After the Revolution*, p. 42.

33. Ibid., p. 52.

34. Ibid., p. 59.

35. Ibid., p. 107.

36. Ibid., p. 109.

37. Ibid., p. 116.

38. Ibid., p. 121.

39. Ibid., p. 132.

40. Tocqueville, *Democracy in America*, vol. II, p. 506.

41. Ibid., p. 507.

42. Theodore J. Lowi, *The End of Liberalism* (New York: Norton, 1969), pt. IV, pp. 287-314.

43. Ibid., p. 314.

44. Theodore Lowi, *The Politics of Disorder* (New York: Norton, 1971), p. xviii.

45. Ibid., p. xiv.

46. Ibid., p. xvi.

47. Ibid., p. 176. Comparison of Lowi to the Madison of Federalist No.

10 is not entirely whimsical. "It is in vain to say that enlightened statesmen will be able to adjust these clashing interests and render them all subservient to the public good. Enlightened statesmen will not always be at the helm. Nor, in many cases, can such an adjustment be made at all without taking into view indirect and remote considerations, which will rarely prevail over the immediate interest which one party may find in disregarding the rights of another or the good of the whole." *Federalist Papers*, Clinton Rossiter, ed., (New York: New American Library, 1961), p. 83. The premises are remarkably similar; it is the bias that is different. (Note the treatment of Madison and the question of leadership by Schaar in chap. 9.)

48. Ibid., p. 184.

49. Lowi is so firmly grounded in the liberal tradition that he never examines the bases of socialist pluralism. Treatment of the latter is beyond the scope of this book, but see Martin Buber's *Paths in Utopia* (Boston: Beacon Press, 1958). As an aside, it is interesting to note that the Proudhonian alternative based upon hatred of finance and industrial concentration, the centrality of the family, and respect for artisan capitalism has great attraction to the American mind, despite the fact that few have explored the question in the manner offered by Proudhon. (See chap. 5.)

50. William Kornhauser, *The Politics of Mass Society* (Glencoe, Ill.: Free Press, 1959) p. 41.

51. Lowi, *Politics of Disorder*, p. 36.

52. Ibid., p. 54. "A successful movement eventually is a confirmation of an iron law of decadence. But it provides the society with a great deal of energy before that effect takes place. The good democrat should try to foster new groups and should distrust old groups. The wise democrat should always expect to be betrayed by the minorities he supports."

53. Ibid., p. 56.

54. Ibid., p. 180.

55. Ibid.

56. Bertrand de Jouvenal, *Sovereignty* (Chicago: University of Chicago Press, 1957), p. 67.

57. Theodore J. Lowi, *American Government: Incomplete Conquest* (Hinsdale, III.: Dryden Press, 1976), p. 696.

58. Ibid., p. 705.

59. Ibid.

60. David Truman, "The American System in Crisis," *Political Science Quarterly* 74 (December 1959), 497.

CHAPTER **5**

Journeymen and Pontiffs

I am not asserting that the American people, at this moment, are a corrupt people—though it worries me that they are so blandly free from self-doubt about this possibility.
—Irving Kristol, *The Democratic Idea in America*

The question of the scientific and utopian elements in liberal thought was raised in earlier chapters. Science was presented as embodying a set of generalizations about the actual working of social arrangements. It is now necessary to take a slightly fuller look at the concept and its implications for a science of society. A rough distinction between two sorts of scientific enterprise can help make an important point. Some years ago, A. J. Ayer proposed a dichotomy between two approaches to philosophy.[1] One method described the philosopher as pontiff, the other as journeyman. The former approach characterized the efforts of Plato, Aquinas, and Marx—the great thinkers of Western thought—and represented the effort to create a unified system of thought. The second, which Ayer attributed to Locke and to less ambitious theorists in general, saw the task of philosophy as clearing away specific troublesome problems. Since Ayer regarded philosophy as incapable of resolving "first order" problems, he naturally preferred the journeyman approach. Many other writers accepted Ayer's sentiments in philosophy and the journeymen labored in related fields for well over a generation.

A score of other writers challenged this assertion. First, there were minor revisions. Margaret MacDonald suggested that the pontifical philosopher at his best was part poet ("Rousseau is far more like Shelley than he is like Lavoisier") and that, after all, poetry does serve a legitimate purpose, if only to "call attention in a very vivid way to facts and experiences of whose existence we all know but which, for some reason, it seems important to emphasize."[2] The difference between, say, Rousseau and Ayer lies in the method they employ to highlight philosophical problems. MacDonald is clear that what the pontiffs believe they are doing, that is, setting up a system that resolves a range of philosophical problems, is mistaken. "Metaphysical theories" are too "simple"; no "magical formula" will let us know "once and for all, almost by learning a single sentence."[3] Later, a different view of the relationship between pontiffs and journeymen is offered. Pontifical philosophy provided the framework within which journeymen worked. Sheldon Wolin applied this view very ably to political philosophy by suggesting that those writers with more modest temperaments were not working *de novo* but refining and correcting the grand efforts of others.[4] Marsilius of Padua applied Aristotelian notions of community to European feudalism; the American political scientists, for all their concern for objectivity and method, unknowingly stood in the shadow of Locke.

Behind all these discussions stands a moderate relativism. One picks his pontiff, however "poetic" he might be, and then subjects his work to precise and low-level testing. Any confirmed empirical findings can only be related to another particular pontifical philosophy with great difficulty. A Marxist analysis would, of course, challenge this assertion by noting how such efforts became increasingly troublesome as the consolidation of the industrial order proceeded. As noted in chapter 4, Marx insisted that bourgeois science was forced into moralism.

It has been suggested that part of the post-liberal critique rests upon an insistence that the liberal tradition extends from Smith, Malthus, and Ricardo to Bentham, the older Mill, and the Social Darwinists to twentieth-century positivism. Such an analysis is strained, of course, at several points. Marx regarded the assumption of appetitive individualism and class conflict, in what he took to be liberal thought, as scientific *because* it was derived from an analysis of the social order. The post-liberal critique reverses the order slightly. Scientific analysis itself, as an activity that emphasizes neutrality and the external nature of social relationships, represents an antiseptic and unreal approach to society. Science is especially suited to a liberal world view because of the latter's commitment to progress and power of rationality. Schaar attempts to make a connection between liberalism with its Faustian impulses and the technological society with its use of instrumental rationality. The bridge between post-liberal thought and the classic Marxist critique is completed with Marcuse's analysis of modern capitalist society as "biologically" preventing alternate consciousness. Thus, for Marcuse, the wildest irrational dreams are revolutionary in that they "rupture" the "continuum of aggression."

Yet, liberals who have chosen a scientific approach to society have acted as both pontiff and journeyman. The latter style, while hardly conducive to a revolutionary analysis, is quite different from the former. Its connection with producing a uniform social order is not nearly so direct, for the pontifical style emphasizes the regularity of human behavior. Random actions are cast off as anomalies, undiscovered truths, insignificant variations, or a part of conditions. The journeyman scientist, on the other hand, is suspicious of generalizations based upon externals. He prefers to emphasize the internal aspects of human behavior, especially those that defy an easy or direct correlation with action. Weber, a journeyman by temperament whose genius pushed him as far as possible into pontifical directions, struggled with ways to link them. However, both styles of social science exhibit a strong antipathy toward what they would call "moralizing." The pontifical scientist is anxious to reduce the moral sphere to his own account of society. For Marx, it was a mask for class hegemony; for Bentham, sinister interests; for Spencer, evil legislators; for Skinner, misguided humanists. A moral element slides back into all these writers' theories, of course, but it is tied to an acceptance of its own comprehensive laws that are justified independently in scientific terms. The journeyman style invariably rejects a scientific ethics as too grandiose and not plausibly related to the complexity of human action. Thus, an independent moral philosophy begins to reappear in the efforts of whatever ideological home the journeyman labors. Bernstein's socialism employs moral arguments rather than scientific ones; J. S. Mill's liberalism casts the felicific calculus off nature's throne. Yet, despite the reemergence of the autonomy of ethics in the journeyman's work, the morality that is offered is quite timid. The journeyman attacks the notion of transcendent principles whether derived from science or God, and his own ethical system is quite close to an account of systematized prudence. Weber's ethics of compromise is a fine example of the sort of moral dimension to be found in the journeyman style.

It is true, of course, that socialist journeymen never abandon ethics as neatly as their liberal counterparts. Yet, a certain blandness does take over. The Gaitskillian compromise captures much of the same spirit. However, it is the abandonment of a pontifical approach to society itself that accounts for changes in an account of morality, and this is not unique to liberalism.

A fuller exploration of the nature of scientific liberalism than an examination of Nozick would allow is necessary. Nozick's science, as dismal as it is, gave birth to liberal utopia. However, liberal political theory can move in other directions as well. Another movement can be illustrated by first showing how liberalism was able to offer a pontifical science and then by showing the nature of journeyman reaction in the post-liberal era.

First, Adam Smith will be omitted to avoid the luxury of resurrecting a model of genteel capitalism. Malthus and Ricardo can be conceded as merely gloomy technicians of the darkest day of an emerging industrial order. Even Bentham, assuming he was the fool that Marx dismisses, lashed out against sinecures and the tyranny of lawyers. This discussion shall be limited to a thoroughly discredited liberal: William Graham Sumner. Sumner is regarded by liberals themselves with the same anxiety that the left exhibits when it approaches Stalin. A liberal might exculpate Locke as abused by captains of industry. However, for the Social Darwinists excuses simply are not advanced. Irving Kristol's reaction is typical: "The fact [is] that for several decades after the Civil War, the Darwinian ethic...represents one of the most bizarre and sordid episodes in American intellectual history."[5] Clinton Rossiter shuddered at their influence and wondered if it all was not a form of "decayed conservatism."[6] Even the contemporary corporate elite finds Darwinism too harsh.

We are confronted, then, with an arrogant man relegated to the status of a third-rate political theorist who, like a prostitute, achieved momentary comfort and attention by providing services to the powers that be. But worst of all, here is a man who stood at the threshold of the industrial revolution and, as such, is stained with the blood of a nameless proletariat.

Yet even in this context, one can view Sumner, while dean of a brief but unchallengeable American capitalist enlightenment, as broodingly resigned, a Cassandra of the modern industrial order. If it is true that he and others like him held off the masses yearning to be free until the industrial revolution had become history, his efforts from the beginning were hardly more than a holding operation. Yet he faced the liberal dilemma by grabbing Nature and keeping her hostage on the side of liberalism. In many ways this was an act of cowardice that permitted the short-term luxury of letting her provide the defense of the liberal life; however, it was all done with the bravado of a pontiff.

There are really two William Graham Sumners. The reader may not care for either, but it is useful to take a brief look at both in terms of the problems symptomatic of modern liberalism. One possesses the arrogance that only one in command of a system can exhibit. Certain of the course of drama of world history, his role is to see to it its proper conclusion, pushing socialists, anarchists, and all those spouting "the gospel of gush" off the stage:

> It is evident that God alone could give distributive justice; and we find, in this world in which we are, that God has not seen fit to provide for it at all.[7]

The "peace, order, security and freedom" of modern civilized life are not the product of human resolutions: "They are at last attributable to economic forces. Our whole history must be reconstructed with a view to this fact."[8] For this Sumner, the eight-hour day is wild utopian illusion. Modernity has at last freed us from sentiment. The relationship in life which has the least bad feeling or personal bitterness is the "pure business relation":

> Where is there so much dissension and bitterness as in family matters, where people try to act by sentiment and affection? The way to improve the relation of employer and employee is not to get sentiment into it, but to get sentiment out of it.[9]

If the poor hate the rich, so be it. There have been no times in history without class hatred.

But there is another Sumner. He is the one who read Hooker with the "greatest care" and had found it "re-awakening...all my love for political science."[10] Here is a Sumner deeply troubled by modernity, who longs for a society that is aware of its new burdens so that it might find some cushions to soften its inevitable blows:

> I hold...that all the new social movements, including democratic political institutions, demand and demand especially of the masses, painstaking knowledge, philosophical power and labor far beyond what has ever hitherto been necessary. The reason for this opinion is in the fact that the latest social movements have issued an increase of social power, and that all such increase involves an alternative which can be successfully solved only by added mental and moral power, and by more work.[11]

There is something more here than a "captain of industry" speaking, exhorting his workers to greater productivity. When the peasant obtains freedom, he trades "personal discipline" for governmental compulsion. The free yeomen in America have taken up many of those burdens that were regarded as the heaviest feudal obligations. The farmers maintain roads, do police and fire duty, and maintain all public institutions "as if they lived upon a manor." Sumner is not making a case that modernity represents a complete quid pro quo. The fact that these men are "eager" to work out these burdens illustrates the wisdom of that population. But modern life does have heavy costs. Sumner is not even willing to glorify the nature of work. Labor has no dignity. In fact, the following passage could easily be applied to a Victorian's view of sex:

> It is a good safe phrase, because it sounds well, and the people for whose consumption it is provided cannot tell whether it makes any difference whether labor has dignity or not, or what would happen if it was not dignified. In truth, dignity is just what labor does not possess; for it always forces a man into strained posture, ungraceful motions, dirt, perspiration, disorder of dress and manner. It is leisure which has dignity.[12]

This is a very dark world that Sumner sees, and there is no relief to be found. Modern capitalism was, for Sumner, like a military organization. He chose to use the phrase "captains of industry" for a reason, but never with the excitement that Carlyle would attach to it. "The great leaders in the development of industrial organization need those talents of executive and administrative skill, power to command, courage and fortitude, which were formerly called for in military affairs and scarcely anywhere else. The industrial army is also as dependent on its captains as a military body is on its generals."[13] Industrial society is characterized by extreme organization:

> It controls us all because we are all in it. It creates the conditions of our existence, sets limits of our social relations, determines our conceptions of good and evil, suggests our life philosophy, molds our inherited political institutions, and reforms the oldest and toughest customs, like marriage and property.[14]

Modern capitalism, then, was pulling everything into its grasp and at the same time tearing everything asunder. Colonial methods of business were "loose and slack to an inconceivable degree." However, the gain in economic organization was won "by narrowing individual range." Our cultural and political institutions were disintegrating. Sumner was too much of a materialist to argue for attempts at their preservation. The cause of our political vitality and vigor and our social relations was economic. "We have to make up our minds to it, adjust ourselves to it, and sit down to live with it."[15] But even the most devout materialist can hope. Sumner thought, in his brighter moments, that such realism about modernity would make everyone aware that there is no liberty for the intelligent man except in "intelligent obedience to the law of right living." One must work and study. "He must not cry out that liberty is only a delusion and a puzzle; he must understand that what liberty properly means for the individual is intelligent acceptance of the conditions of earthly life, conformity to them, and manful effort to make life a success under them."[16] Esteem and dignity can proceed from a society based upon industrial virtues—"free endeavor, security of property, and repression of baser vices."

These are only occasional moments of satisfaction in an otherwise gloomy assessment, however. Capitalism's enlightenment is very short on optimism. The first to fail Sumner was the captain of industry himself. Throughout his life he insisted that expansion was always good. Concentration of wealth was necessary for growth. But what of the leaders? Apparently, they could be "idle, or silly, or vulgar." However, this was less a class fault than a defect of human nature. Perhaps the severe competition for their occupations would steel their character and "bring discipline and corrections of arrogance and masterfulness."[17] Sumner's heart was much more comfortable in praising the "forgotten man." While there is "no place for sentiment" in modern life, Sumner almost tearfully embraces the "simple, honest laborer," the "clean, quiet virtuous citizen," the "industrious self-supporting men and women who have not inherited much to make life luxurious for them."[18] Apparently, virtue came naturally, not supported by fear of a corporate proxy fight that could lead to dethronement. Were the baser instincts easily in check because there was no opportunity for the corruption attendant with luxury?

In political theory, Sumner could not bring himself to accept such a conclusion. Democracy was made possible by industrialism. Modern society freed the masses from the indolence of the will fostered by custom and tradition. But, it also raised the specter of plutocracy. No form of political power is more ill-fitted to cope with plutocracy than democracy. Democratic societies house whole sets of institutions which are extralegal. At party conventions, in primaries, in the halls of Congress, the "greed and arrogance" of plutocrats can reach out and easily corrupt the political process. For Sumner, it was a "lamentable contest" and when "last comes to last":

> ...the contest between numbers and wealth is nothing but a contest between two sets of lawyers, one drawing Acts in behalf of the state, and the other devising means of defeating those Acts in behalf of their clients. The latter set is far better paid in consideration, in security and in money.[19]

The result is the plutocrat. And what better description of the contemporary capitalist than this image offered by Sumner?

> A plutocrat is a man who, having the possession of capital, and having the power of it at his disposal, uses it, not industrially, but politically; instead of employing laborers, he enlists lobbyists. Instead of applying

> capital to land, he operates upon the market by legislation, by artificial monopoly, by legislative privileges; he creates jobs, and erects combinations, which are half political and half industrial; he practices upon the industrial cives, he makes an engine of venality, expends his ingenuity, not on the processes of production, but on "knowledge of men," and on the tactics of the lobby. The modern industrial system gives him a magnificent field, one far more profitable, very often, than that of legitimate industry.[20]

Frequently, Sumner would blame the construction of the plutocrat on those with an "impulse for legislation." Not knowing the nature of modern capitalism, reformers would only nourish the potential abuses of the new industrial system. He insisted that the great capitalist is no more necessarily a plutocrat than a great general is a tyrant. Like military enthusiasts, Sumner did not see that the seeds of corruption in these figures need only grow when fertilized by outside agencies. The turn-of-the-century capitalist saw the advantages of staffing engines of venality before reformers were accredited with awakening political lust.

In other moments Sumner would see broader causes of plutocracy. Liberal democracy is "atomistic." Individualism destroys institutions and democracy with its dream of equality, makes society the sport of new elements which combine and organize on new centers. Political interests form the basis of modern organization, and Sumner was troubled by the prospect that such powers fighting for control of the state would govern the losers like a "conquered territory." Unburdened by traditions that might cushion the effects and the desires of the victors, modern society "is sure to produce the worst exploitation of man by man which has ever existed; to live under it, and be in it, would be to suffer a tyranny such as no one has experienced yet."[21]

How are these new groups, "united by a desire for the success of the same enterprises and seeking pecuniary gain from that success," to be restrained? Sumner still remains an apologist for modernity, and such sympathies form the basis for his answer. The emancipation "from tradition, authority, caste, superstition and to a certain extent from prejudices and delusions" in today's societies may permit a release of productive energy unknown to mankind.

> Status holds down individual energy and power. If a black man is told that the only status allowed by social institutions to him is that of a slave, no black man can work out into realization the powers which he may possess. If the status of women is fixed by custom and law, no woman can show her power to do anything outside of the limits. The social arrangement which sets free individual energy is liberty; for under this each one may prove what he is by what he does and the society profits by the expansion and evolution of all the power there is in it.[22]

Aside from his earlier notions of self-discipline, Sumner suggests a way that democracy might contain within itself "the form and potency of better things." If it could only maintain a continuous and unflinching look at itself, "it might be simple-minded enough to throw off all the big dogmas of state-olatry, might be so open and visible, and might feel itself so well-known of all men, that it should laugh down all inflated theories of itself; might be so hard-headed as to treat all political mysticism with contempt; might be so practical that it would know better than to try to do too much, or to busy itself with schemes of universal happiness."[23]

But, on the brink of offering a noble though unlikely scenario for modern society, Sumner would falter. "The torments of always giving one's self a reason, satisfactory to reason and conscience, for everything one does, are a privilege of high culture." Sumner openly admires the ancient philosopher's devotion to the question: What is the highest good in life? The modern thinking world has broadened this task, and Sumner regards this as a "proud triumph." But the mass of mankind is "contented and eager to live without deliberating about it." If liberal democracy continues to place bigger and bigger demands upon the reflective power of its citizens, "it will fail to get the response which it expects." The "path of wisdom" lies in making the demands of the state as "few and simple as possible" and in "widening the automatic organs of society which are non-political." But how in this environment can society be able to "laugh down all inflated theories of itself"?[24]

On the basis of this sketch of Sumner, what can be learned about the pontifical scientific liberal? It is clear that he used the concept of nature to resolve the liberal dilemma. If conflict racked the social and political order, it could not be resolved by the establishment of proletarian hegemony. That would only elevate conflict to higher, more terrifying proportions. For Sumner it meant a ghastly plutocracy, not unlike Gross's friendly fascism described in Chapter 1. If, for just one moment, we can bite our tongues and choke back moral outrage, we can see this Darwinist did have a glimpse into the darker prospects of industrial society. However, he was a pontiff as well; in fact, it is precisely his pontifical outlook that provided him with an exit. If there were some grand design, some "finger of God" that provided an account of industrialization, perhaps he would not need to speak of justice and the public good. If there were a pattern in history, it would not be necessary to cope with the horrible moral results of industrial society. After all, the utopian image of the industrial society, a place of peace and tranquility, was just around the corner. It was even unnecessary to justify the suffering of a few generations. What other choice was available?

Of course, all of this effort was very inconsistent and, more often than not, confused. Sumner refused to resort to "moralism" when the industrial order itself tightened its grip. Instead, he pled the case for evolution. Yet he envisaged a highly anarchic individualist society at the top of the evolutionary ladder. Sumner even suggests laughing at the state. Industrial society, however, was not about to produce clusters of artisan philosophers. Sumner was especially aware of the centralizing trends in capitalism and very bravely insisted that it didn't matter after all. Industrial society hemmed us in, and the J. P. Morgans were a bargain for us all. At least there was equality of opportunity; those dreadful preindustrial prejudices at last were to crumble. Sumner made no attempt to make the robber baron into a hero. He did his job in the industrial order and received certain prerequisites in return. There is not an inkling of an attempt to envisage the captain of industry as some sort of Napoleonic leader. This would be "moralism" and Sumner would have none of it. Yet some "moralism" does creep into Sumner's system in the guise of the contribution of the forgotten man of society. However, the blue-collar functionary who paid his debts and didn't complain, no matter how technically specialized he might become, was, as Harrington has recently argued, merely the raw material for the industrial machine. Sumner knew it; his odes to the forgotten man have something of a eulogy about them:

> It is now evident that our political institutions are to be put under great strain by the attempt of the U.S. to act as governor, patron, and receiver, for the rest of America. The institutions cannot meet such a strain. They were planned for a confederation of petty agricultural republics. They might have sufficed for a republic of industrial interests and unambitious citizens. They will not suffice for an imperial world power.[25]

What alternatives were available? In the Marxist view, the rise of working-class consciousness with new sets of ideas about economics, ethics, and politics made a bourgeois science impossible. It is true, of course, that the Marxist position gains plausibility largely through the advancement of its own pontifical vision regarding the course of industrial development. Without this image of a society in a state of acute schizophrenia, one personality of which must be destroyed, any approach that encouraged indeterminancy or compromise can be regarded as "moralism." This is why Marxists are fond of searching out the most dour capitalist analysis in order to give it the compliment of honesty and consistency.

However, let us accept a unilinear interpretation for a moment. The scientific liberal was able to fashion a system out of a capitalist order because it did seem to offer a society eminently amenable to his predispositions. The market economy provided a model which permitted both a relatively peaceful arena for conflict (at least as compared to Visigothian plunder) and nonauthoritative allocation of work. The social order did not demand that one be a car salesman or a poet. Similarly, for the liberal the capitalist order with its emphasis on rationality could satisfy his lust for a scientific ordering of events. The Social Darwinist added to these attractions by positing a view of nature that exempted the social scientist from tinkering with the market to assure productive conflict and from examining the conditions that foster plurality of life choices in society. How the poet is to live except as a part-time salesman or a salesman of poetry are dilemmas that are ignored. Nature also had the advantage of assuming the proportions of a human condition. The survival of the fittest was a moral rule not because of its intrinsic quality as a desirable standard of behavior but because it was the only standard of behavior available. One worshiped it as one might some Greek deity, not because it deserved moral allegiance but because it could effectively command it. Not the least effective part of this pontifical vision is that this liberal god of Mammon had a dynamic quality as well. Forever moving ahead to new directions, selecting some to serve its grand design, it held out the image of an expanding universe of talent and result. An enormously powerful emotive element is thus built into this system. One can speak derisively of the bourgeois virtues enclosed in it, but still imagine the impact upon a perfume salesman whose worth is not determined by the aromas he offers door to door but by the function he performs in the march of nature. Add to it the motive of self-interest in the service of personal advancement, what Hartz called the charm offered by American Whiggery, and one has, for a brief moment in history, a liberal concoction of extraordinary power and social cohesion.

The market model offered a description of social society and politics that was neutral in terms of the goals of its participants. In Europe there might be talk of the special virtues of the "middling" class. But in the United States, farmer, worker, and clerk were all protocapitalists and conflict was among individuals. The scientific liberalism offered by the Darwinists greatly embellished this model. By placing individuals in the service of nature, the market became a tool of nature to be twisted, shaped, and wrested apart by those individuals who served it best. But one could not have it both ways. There was the society of Adam Smith, one that cultivated those tedious bourgeois virtues of thrift, restraint, and moderation, and the society of Sumner and Spencer, one that refused to sentimentalize the economy of size and spoke of the social bargain obtained by overlooking the lust and ostentation of the robber baron. Both capitalisms, artisan and corporate, were scientific descriptions in their day. However, these liberal pontiffs used the description of the former to justify their support of the latter. If one is fed up with the robber baron, Sumner states, one will end up making him more powerful than ever. A socialist state will offer "chances of wealth beyond the wildest dreams of avarice....Then there will indeed be a menace to social interests, and instead of industrial peace there will be such a war as no one has dreamed of yet: the war between the political ins and outs...."[26]

For Sumner, American democracy was a consequence of the industrial order of the nineteenth century. It was based on the industrial virtues of "free endeavor, security of property and the repression of baser vices." Out of it came the democratic principle that "each man shall be esteemed for his merit and worth, for just what he is, without regard to birth, wealth, rank, or other adventitious circumstances." While this principle was only "partially realizable," it was "elevating and socially progressive and profitable."[27] There was another democratic principle, however, that stated that "each one of us ought to be equal to all the others in what he gets and enjoys." It was "only a rule of division for robbers who have to divide plunder or monks who have to divide gifts."[28] But how was it possible to speak of property in the age of the holding company, or free endeavor in the age of the oligopoly and government subsidy? Sumner's system did have a scientific validity in the age of the artisan, even perhaps in the age of the robber baron, but what about the age of the Schumpeterian corporate bureaucrat? At this point Sumner and Spencer as well fall silent. A "moralism" would have been helpful because it would have at least carried the liberal image into the new era. It would have been a beaten and bruised one certainly, even perhaps a bit grotesque, but the image of "ignoring the state" by allowing sympathy to flourish would have provided a standard for judgment. Instead, we have been treated to the "free society" of Hayek and the Icien individualism of Nozick.

Where does one find the pontifical version of scientific liberalism in the second half of the twentieth century? For all practical purposes we can finally agree with Marx in a very obtuse way. It is dead. Of course, contemporary Marxists would love to have the proposition both ways. Scientific liberalism is a moribund ideology, both logically inconsistent and unable to attract support. Yet it nevertheless lives on, drawing from some enormous, residual power like some sort of great marauding vampire that debilitates its victims to such an extent that they do not quite have the strength to counterattack. American society is governed by a set of elites ("the central guidance cluster") whose purpose is immobilizational, "consciously manipulating the population away from political activity."[29] This is "not perceived" by the citizen because he "literally doesn't know what he is missing."[30] Somehow, the scientific liberal still governs by stealth. This is a neat trick indeed.

The truth is that those writers who do accept the mantle of the Social Darwinist today do so well beyond the arena of liberal doctrine. Skinner's utopias are predicated on a complete rejection of individual autonomy. While the citizens of Walden II do lead a pluralistic existence, it is hardly self-chosen. Every action is monitored by the community and submitted to the behaviorist incentive system. The technician of human life is the only "free" individual, and Skinner is not anxious to explore the complex motives that push him along in completing his tasks. Even Robert Paul Wolff, determined anti-liberal that he is, did not have the stomach for this technological elitism and retreated to a liberal doctrine for composure. The so-called futurists offer the same sort of image. For Buckminster Fuller, the computer has undermined the "Great Pirates" of capitalist development. The following passage owes much more to Bellamy than to any Social Darwinist:

> You may very appropriately want to ask me how we are going to resolve the ever-accelerating dangerous impasse of world-opposed politicians and ideological dogmas? I answer, it will be resolved by the computer; witness his unconcerned landings as airtransport passengers coming in for a landing in the combined invisibility of fog and night. While no politician or political system can ever afford to yield understandably and enthusiastically to their adversaries and opposers, all politicians can and will yield enthusiastically to the computer's safe flight-controlling capabilities in bringing all of humanity in for a happy landing.[31]

The scientific liberal as journeyman, however, lives on. In fact, the pressures of post-liberal politics have produced a new variation in what can be seen by now as the torturous history of liberalism. The journeyman's general scepticism of politics and society itself is always moderate. A brooding pervasive doubt can produce a violent rejection of existing social structures. The liberal rejection of pontifical science in general in the post-war period brought forth a philosophical conservatism quite close to the spirit of Hume. Popper attacked historicism as the belief in the predictability of future events and recommended its replacement with piecemeal engineering. Shils called for a politics of civility that recognized the "prudent exercise of authority." Weldon was so fascinated with the fact-value distinction that he could only offer his personal recommendation for democracy. But the scientific liberal as journeyman never possessed the vision held by the conservative and, as such, never presented a complete political theory. The most he could offer was a style of politics. In America, this truncated sort of political theory was never fully dominant. It quickly transformed itself in a theory of pluralism that does have a broad view of society. The American journeyman took his cues from Madison and, to a lesser extent, from Tocqueville, men who, whatever else might be said of them, were not unwilling to recommend broad political and social policies. Moreover, one could find in the American variant a dose of optimism. Lipset did say that America was the good society in operation, but *Political Man* exhibited an almost Pollyanna-like view of the general prospects for democracy and economic development.

When pluralism itself came under attack in the 1960s, it was its alleged fraudulent basis that was challenged:

> The insistence on realism, the demand for objectivity, precision, and science, and the philosophical and political refuge provided by the "real world" are too continuing and limiting in terms of both political analysis and political life.[32]

No wonder many post-liberals became entranced with the pontifical science of Marxism with its broad social categories and its insistence upon transcending reality.

Yet when the scientific liberal as journeyman approaches the problem of the post-liberal era, he must reevaluate his scepticism or turn it against different institutions. Robert Dahl's efforts in this direction have been assessed. A different group of theorists has sketched out another alternative. It is one that is almost devilish in its ingenuity. Composed of a variety of thinkers, including James Q. Wilson, Daniel Moynihan, and Nathan Glazer, they are often labeled the "new conservatives."[33] Many of them, however, insist upon the designation "liberal"; two of the most outspoken of this group are Irving Kristol, and Daniel Bell.

The best way to understand the direction of this new brand of liberalism is to review Louis Hartz's incisive discussion of the trials and triumph of Whiggery in America. The "new conservatives" represent an alternative only occasionally available to liberals in politics, one which is discernible to these writers as America comes of age in the 1980s. Hartz's analysis of Whiggery focuses upon two periods in American history, the rise of Jacksonian democracy and the industrialization after the Civil War. The first period was notable for a "massive confusion in political thought" involving "a set of victories and defeats which Americans who experienced them scarcely understood."[34] American Whiggery was smashed because it simply did not have the structural elements in society to form a power base; nor did it have a political formula relevant to the American experience. Without an aristocracy to fight, without an aristocracy to ally with, without a mob to alternately tame and denounce, the American Whig had no function in the social and political order. Its aristocrats were given over to capitalist lust. Hartz asks, "How can a wealthy middle-class ever hide the acquisitive code by which it lives?" The European peasant was transformed into a capitalist farmer and the laborer into an incipient entrepreneur. When Chancellor Kent warned of the greed of the mob, the wisdom of a MacCauleyan politics, and the virtues of a state governed by men of property and intelligence, the American democrat, great petit bourgeois giant that he was, responded by declaring, "We are all of the same estate—all commoners...."[35] The philosophy of the 1830s was smashed beyond recognition, not by a liberal reform akin to Lloyd George but by the sheer weight of the singular petit bourgeois configuration of power in America.

Hartz notes, however, that there was a limit to how many times politicians such as Weed and Webster were willing to commit suicide. Out of the agony of defeat, they "discovered the facts of American life."

> Giving up the false aristocratic frustrations of the past, and giving up as well its false proletarian fears, they embraced America's liberal unity,

> with a vengeance, and developed a philosophy of democratic capitalism. Willy-nilly, the difference between America and Europe swam into the ken of their vision, and Daniel Webster, pounding away at what he had in common with everyone else, insisted that the "visible and broad distinction" between the masses and the classes of the old countries of Europe was not to be found in the United States. Calvil Colton, also pointing to Europe, said that "every American laborer can stand up proudly, and say, I AM THE AMERICAN CAPITALIST"....Whiggery had finally hit on the secret of turning its greatest liability into its greatest advantage.[36]

The new success of American Whiggery was won for a price. The older concept of Whig politics envisioned a society of contesting units held in balance. Hierarchical social order was achieved and given some fluidity by the great achievements of Whig politics, charm, and terror. However, in America, Whiggery had been "transformed" with its success. Instead of holding society together by its political skills, it fashioned a terrible unity. The "Americanism" of the new Whig could tap the well of nationalism and frighten the American democrat who might stray to progressivism "with his own absolute liberalism." Sumner's ideas were taken over and transformed by the American Legion.

What Hartz fails to note, and what Sumner did perceive, is that American Whiggery could only keep its absolute hegemony over the American mind in periods of competition and radical growth. Horatio Alger's stories were always myths but in order for the myths to be operative they had to have some relationship to reality. Sometimes angrily, most often vaguely dispiritedly, Hartz's American democrat would perceive that his chances were not what they were supposed to be. Trusts, monopolies, and conglomerates were stealing the American dream. Even FDR, whom Hartz rightly notes actually saved Whiggery, reached back to the images of populist and progressive reform to do so:

> Just as freedom to farm has ceased, so also the opportunity in business has narrowed....The unfeeling statistics of the past three decades show that the independent businessman is running a losing race....Recently a careful study was made of the concentration of business in the United States. It showed that our economic life was dominated by some six

> hundred odd corporations....Ten million small businessmen divided the other third....Put plainly, we are steering a steady course toward economic oligarchy, if we are not there already.[37]

Hoover could preach that with a Roosevelt victory grass would grow on the streets of New York City and the power of American Whiggery would not respond to incantation. In fact, a case can be made that it has never quite recovered. As such it should not be surprising that it should take some new forms.

The journeyman spirit of the liberal remains, of course. He is suspicious of broad-scale reform, of a politics pursued at a high pitch, of basic alterations in social values. Kristol and Bell hold these sentiments.[38] The "one worst way" to cope with a crisis in values is through organized political ideological action.[39] Bell speaks of "managing" problems, insisting that they are never "solved." But what distinguishes the approach of both is not their commitment to incrementalism and a pluralism broadly defined, but their willingness to confront the economic basis of liberalism in America. Their most recent works accept the thesis that the economic, cultural, and political problems of the day are to be traced to the development of American capitalism. It is this close attention to the economic basis of the social order that places Kristol and Bell in more direct descent to Spencer and Sumner than to Dahl or Truman.

The approach of both writers, scattered as it is in articles and books, involves a searching critique of capitalism and, ultimately, a cautious but peculiarly tender defense. One can discern an examination of the ideological underpinnings of capitalism, followed by an analysis of the present crisis and, finally, proposals that, if they are not a cure, offer at least some treatment.

Kristol contends that capitalism made three promises as an economic system: continued improvement in the material conditions of its citizenry; individual freedom; and a virtuous life within a just society. The first two were delivered. The third has been continually placed into the future, and Kristol believes that, as things stand now, at least, it is not likely to be forthcoming. The reason for this is a relatively complicated one, and it shall be explored more fully. Kristol seems to place the success of the promise of justice upon the nature of the ideological system on which capitalism rests:

> People feel free when they subscribe to a prevailing social philosophy; they feel unfree when the prevailing social philosophy is unpersuasive; and the existence of constitutions or laws or judiciaries have precious little to do with these basic feelings.[40]

Four basic justifications for capitalism have been offered in this regard:

1. The Protestant ethic assumed that there was a "strong correlation between certain personal virtues—fragility, industry, sobriety, reliability, piety—and the way in which power, privileges and property were distributed." This "correlation was taken to be the sign of a just society."
2. The "Free Society" ethic argument advanced by Hayek (and by Nozick as well) severs the connection between reward and merit. In Hayek's words, "a society in which the position of the individual was made to correspond to human ideas of moral merit would therefore be the exact opposite of a free society."
3. The Darwinian ethic correlated economic success with survival instincts.
4. The technocratic ethic justifies inequality on the basis of a correlation between reward and "superior ability to achieve superior 'performance'—in economic growth, managerial efficiency, technological innovation."[41]

Kristol rejects each of these defenses. Like Sumner, his heart goes out to the older bourgeois virtues, and he laments the end of the "capitalist, republican community with shared values and a quite unambiguous claim to the title of just order." Today, the Protestant ethic is reserved only for the lower socioeconomic levels; "no one seriously claims that these traditional virtues will open the corridors of corporate power to anyone, or that the men who now occupy the executive suites are—or even aspire to be—models of bourgeois virtue."[42] The Darwinian ethic is dismissed as "bizarre" and sordid; "It could not last; and it did not." The concept of performance itself is attacked in regard to the technocratic ethic. No ruling class can really base its legitimacy on performance in any measurable sense. "If the landed gentry of Britain during those centuries of its dominance, or the business class in the United States during the first century-and-a-half of our national history, and insisted that it be judged by performance alone, it would have flunked out of history. A complete rationalization of any ruling classes' legitimacy leaves it uncomfortably vulnerable."[43] Life has too many ups and downs. Moreover, if performance is given a larger meaning, the corporate elite finds itself "passing beyond the boundaries of bourgeois propriety."[44] Macauley contended that government must rule by opinion and not the sword. Kristol, of course, accepts the adage but insists that the traditional Whig concept of opinion is not transferable to American society.

Bell's diagnosis of modern capitalism is similar to Kristol's. The crisis results from the inability of corporate capitalism to construct anything approaching a plausible justification for its own legitimacy. Bell's approach, however, emphasizes the cultural disintegration brought about by affluence. The spirit of modernism in the arts—Dionysian, vehemently anti-bourgeois, and nihilist—has grown upon the relative permissiveness of bourgeois life, and been left unchallenged by the political philosophy of liberalism. As a result, what were once bohemian enclaves in bourgeois society now permeate the entire culture. "Today, in both doctrine and life style, the anti-bourgeois have won."[45] In culture anti-nomianism and anti-institutionalism rule. Simultaneously, the inexorable pressures of corporate capitalism eroded and then smashed the Protestant ethic. Work and accumulation were rejected as ends in themselves and attached to "consumption and display." "Status and its badges, not work and the election of God, became the mark of success."[46] Work is promoted furiously, but it remains unjustified. It follows then that the corporate class had no other choice but to abdicate any role in the formation of a public philosophy.

Two points make the analysis of capitalism by Bell and Kristol so striking. One is their frankness in regard to the economic basis of liberalism in America. The term *bourgeois,* an epithet used by both the left and right and, generally, scrupulously avoided by liberals, is openly presented as the basis for liberalism. This permits Bell and Kristol to examine the foundations for liberalism in America in a manner unusual for liberal writers. However, the analysis is hardly a Marxian one. Kristol refers to the American workers as a permanent petite bourgeoisie, and Bell sees his intellectual sources in

Weber and Schumpeter. Both seem to have appreciated the class character of American post-liberal society while utilizing concepts independent of Marxism.

The advantages of this approach become evident when both present their analyses of the current crisis of the American polity. Since Bell and Kristol offer quite similar views, they will be discussed together. One of the most intriguing aspects of the new Whiggery is its willingness to jettison the image of the liberal pluralist's vision of society as a melange of shifting centers of power without permanent cohesion. The world of the Whig is a treacherous and demanding one; he is not willing to agree that the invisible hand of political balance is a reliable one. Daniel Bell has been most adamant on this point. In an argument that is certain to become a classic illustration of liberalism, he notes that the liberal image of society as composed of three sectors (the domestic household, the market economy, and the public household) has become altered in a major way. The public household is no longer limited to "public goods," at least as previously conceived. Smith's description of governmental supervision of roads, defense, and a few public works has been expanded so that the basic allocative institutions in society are no longer economic but political. The result is that an enormous, perhaps even fatal burden is placed upon the public household. Decisions are now more concentrated than before and much more visible:

> The group process—which was the vaunted discovery of the "realists" of American political science—consisted largely of economic bargaining between functional or pressure groups operating outside the formal structure of the political system. What we now find are ethnic and ascriptive groups claiming formal representation both in the formal political structure and in all institutions of the society....What we have today is a thoroughgoing politicizing of society in which not only the market is subordinated to political decision but all institutions have to bend to the demands of a political center and politicize themselves.[47]

American pluralism has not erased ethnic and racial ties, nor has it isolated them into enclaves of institutional autonomy. On the contrary, it has heightened them. Group identities have become an effective basis for political claims: crosscutting allegiances thus decline, and representation becomes based upon "primordial or biological ties." What seems to be emerging, according to Bell's analysis, is a peculiar amalgam of characteristics of premodern and industrial societies. The centrifugal forces of industrialization have had their impact: the state is the focus for the organization of society. Centripetal forces have emerged in unexpected ways. An extreme "modernism" has captured the cultural arena and a return to an ascriptive reward structure based upon sex and color appears to have reemerged. Behind these developments stands the critique of liberalism offered by both the right and left. American society is given over to a consumer ethic of frightening proportions. The claims of sisterhood and black virtue are placed in the service of material acquisition and individual success. A "revolution of rising entitlements" has become an essential feature of society. Every major group demands an expanded base of security (a minimum income, free college education, guaranteed employment) as a claim on the community at large. Yet such entitlements can be managed only by sustained economic growth, a condition threatened by the sheer size of the entitlements themselves. The result is wild and recurrent inflation that creates economic and political instability that brings calls for more entitlements.

The class dimensions of this vision of American society have been outlined by Kristol. Like Bell, Kristol is not enamored of the virtues of American pluralism. He speaks of "slovenly bureaucracies" and the lack of restraint in pluralist politics:

> ....When everyone follows the rules of the game, it can be demonstrated with all the rigor of a mathematical theorem—that it is to the self-interest of individuals or of organized factions *not* to follow the rules of the game, but simply to take advantage of the fact that the others do. That there are such individuals and factions, only too willing to draw this logical inference and to act upon it, current American events vividly remind us.[48]

However, Kristol's description of contemporary America very cleverly draws upon recent history and, with a bluntness that is characteristic of this mode of analysis, focuses upon the development of capitalism. The founding fathers "*intended* this nation to be capitalist and regarded it as the *only* set of economic arrangements consistent with the liberal democracy they had established."[49] Their commitment, however, was to an entrepreneurial capitalism of cottage industries:

> The large, publicly-owned corporation of today which strives for immortality, which is committed to no line of business but rather (like an investment banker) seeks the best return on investment, which is governed by an anonymous oligarchy—such an institution would have troubled and puzzled them....[50]

The corporate revolution was an "unpopular revolution." "No other institution in American history—not even slavery—has ever been so consistently unpopular as has the large corporation with the American public."[51] Two movements challenged the corporate revolution. The first, populism, fashioned the corporation as the center of a campaign of political paranoia. Kristol is ambivalent about the populist temper. He regards its distrust of authority and belief in the popular will as "indispensable" to any democracy. But populism does have an antinomian impulse and harbors a "Jacobin contempt for the 'mere' forms of law and order and civility." Progressivism, as a more refined protest, receives sympathetic treatment as well.

Both movements, in the main, were reformist. Populism was born from an "authentic bewilderment" and progressivism from "an adversary posture toward 'big business' specifically rather than toward capitalism in general." This is not true today. The heirs of progressivism have become anti-liberal:

> Though they continue to speak the language of "Progressive reform," in actuality they are acting upon a hidden agenda: to propel the notion from that modified version of capitalism we call "the welfare state" toward an economic system so stringently regulated in detail as to fulfill many of the traditional anti-capitalist aspirations of the left.[52]

A hidden socialist movement is in our midst. For Kristol, its power is not to be underestimated. The "New Politics" now encompasses millions of people. This "new class" of scientists, lawyers, city planners, social workers, educators, criminologists, sociologists, and public health doctors is unlike the old progressive elite. It finds its chances of success in the public sector and is not anxious to open up the economy to make more room for itself. The conflicts in American politics today reflect nothing less than the professional classes engaging "in a class struggle with the business community for status and power." Their ideological banner is equality not in the sense of opening equal power to affect decisions in society, although part of its rhetoric fits that description, but in the sense of constructing a service elite that will administer benefits more equally to the rest of the population than the business community is able to do. All the while the American working class is alternately hostile and begrudgingly supportive of this effort. It rankles at welfare and busing but the relationship with the corporation was always a marriage of convenience, and it thus accepts the progressive veneer of the "new class" that strikes out against "big business."

Thus far primarily the negative side of the new American Whiggery, what Hartz has referred to as the application of Whig terror, has been discussed. Horrors for the future have been paraded before us; resentment, the motivational underbelly of the demand for equality, has been laid bare; even the vulgarity of commercial society has been conceded. What is missing is the absence of any attempt to unleash the irrational Locke. The Europeanization of America is presented but almost as a fait accompli, not as a threat against reform. It should not be surprising, then, to find that the charm of the new Whiggery should be relatively more subdued. The Alger motif *is* used. Kristol insists that the bourgeois conception of equality is "natural" in a way that other political ideas are not. Bell envisions a just meritocracy. Neither treats the problems of the disadvantaged in terms of both access to power and self-development with aplomb. Kristol believes that the "concern and distress" of the working and lower middle class can be "coped with."[53] Bell is willing to acknowledge the "priority of the disadvantaged" as an "axiom of social policy."[54]

What emerges new to the Whig repertoire is an emphasis upon the need for traditions that emphasize the concern for the public good. Kristol is the most pessimistic but even he yearns for a return to civic virtue, "the willingness of the good democratic citizen...to transcend the historical pursuit of self-interest and devote himself directly and disinterestedly to the common good."[55] Bell calls for a reemergence of the public household in which, once again, "needs" (properly limited by resources at hand) are given priority over "unlimited appetites and wants."[56]

An unsympathetic reader might find shades of a Tory notion of labor discipline in the new Whiggery's plea for restraint and the common good. However, the transformation of American Whiggery faces deeper problems than such an analysis might suggest. The challenge facing Whiggery in general cannot be viewed simply as walking on a tightrope between the clamor of levelers on one side and captains of industry on the other. The Whig faces another danger—traversing the tightrope altogether and resting on a platform somewhere above the battle. In other words, he must stand between the contending forces of society without coming to stand above them. As such, he must remain on this metaphorical tightrope. Hartz's analysis of the first American Whigs showed them to be unable or unwilling to walk the tightrope at all, so enamored were they with dreams of European property relationships. The second Whig movement jumped on the tightrope and, so Hartz argues, because of the peculiar conditions of American development, found it anything but narrow. The Whig lost his need for balance. The movement just described, the third Whiggery to appear in America, has discovered the art of balance but does not appear to be sufficiently infatuated with the challenge of balance itself.

For the most part, Kristol and Bell seem to fulfill their duties as Whigs. Both writers are quite adept, but hardly convincing, when portraying the American corporate elite as a passive force in politics being ripped asunder by trade unions and the "new class." But their attitude toward corporate capitalism is never as alternatively bold and tortured as Sumner's. Kristol's position may not be acceptable to many but it represents a consistent view:

> One need not, therefore, be an admirer of the large corporation to be concerned about its future. One might even regard its "bureaucratic-acquisitive" ethos, in contrast to the older "bourgeois-moralistic ethos,"

> as a sign of cultural decadence—and still be concerned about its future. In our pluralistic society we frequently find ourselves defending specific concentrations of power, about which we might otherwise have the most mixed feelings, on the grounds that they contribute to a diffusion of power, a diffusion which creates the "space" in which individual liberty can survive and prosper.[57]

Thus, it is not the subdued attitude toward the corporation that indicates a fatal flaw in the new Whiggery. The beauty of all Whig political thought is its perception of the economic basis of conflict, and its willingness to appease various groups in the service of a vision of a loosely hierarchical order. In this context, what is so puzzling is the length to which the new Whiggery will go to point out the bourgeois basis of liberalism. What might be called the liberal values of Western society, with due note to the role of the middle classes in fostering these values at certain periods, is referred to as "bourgeois civilization." Bell might note the elegance in liberal thought, but he insists upon reducing it to its origins. Thus within a few pages he can tell us how liberalism emphasizes the diversity of *all individuals* and how it *is bourgeois* society that takes the individual as the primary unit for society.

There are three broad positions one can assume on this question: (a) liberalism is a class ideology in that it arose as a legitimizing device for the interests of a particular class and still functions solely to protect those interests; (b) liberalism represents a historically transcendent set of values useful, even essential, to the good life; and (c) liberalism has or does reflect a class bias but its formulation has provided standards that can benefit all of society. Curiously, Kristol and Bell seem to take the first position. Obviously, neither writer is crypto-Marxist. It is, I think, an aristocratic inclination that seems to lead them to come so close to the first position. When Kristol asks "how...a bourgeois society [can] survive in a cultural ambiance which derides every traditional bourgeois virtue and celebrates promiscuity, homosexuality, drugs, political terrorism—anything, in short, that is in bourgeois eyes perverse," he is clearly not celebrating the end of the liberal epoch.[58] However, he is blaming liberalism for its material vulgarity and its lack of nobility. It is the "middling" nature of bourgeois society that Kristol constantly finds so difficult to refrain from attacking. By failing to deal adequately with "the full range of man's spiritual nature, which makes more than middling demands on the universe and demands more than middling answers," liberalism has brought on this obsession with equality. It is the lack of a truly religious vision of humanity that "terrifies and haunts" the artist, the worker, and the bureaucrat alike and leads them to "unappeasable indignation."[59] Bell's "reaffirmation" of liberalism calls for the revival of a tragic sense of life and a return to "some conception of religion."[60] This is not to say that a connection between liberalism and religion is impossible, but it does indicate that the new Whiggery's support of liberalism, as they see it, is quite conditional.

All of this effort to create a new Whiggery may only serve to illustrate two ironies. One is that the most strident defenders of liberalism in America are in fact liberals only by virtue of the limited availability of political doctrines in the second half of the twentieth century. The other is that the new Whiggery that emerged from a Whiggery that literally enveloped American society is, to use Bell's earlier critique of Marxism in America, *in* society but not *of* it. Where is there a place for one who longs for a tragic sense of life, devotion to transcendental ends, and awe-inspiring heroism in America today?

NOTES

1. A. J. Ayer, *The Problem of Knowledge* (Baltimore: Penguin Books, 1955).
2. Margaret Macdonald, "The Language of Political Theory" in *Logic and Language*, ser. 1 and 2, Anthony Flew, ed. (Garden City, N.Y.: Doubleday, 1965). p. 184.
3. Ibid., p. 193.
4. Sheldon Wolin, "Paradigms and Political Theories" in *Politics and Experience*, Preston King and B. C. Parekh, eds. (Cambridge: Cambridge University Press, 1968), pp. 125-52.
5. Irving Kristol, *The Democratic Idea in America* (New York: Harper and Row, 1972), p. 28.
6. Clinton Rossiter, *Conservatism in America* (New York: Macmillan, 1955), p. 58.

7. William Graham Sumner, *The Essays of William Graham Sumner*, Albert Galloway Keller and Maurice R. Davie, eds., vol. I (New Haven, Conn.: Yale University Press, 1934), p. 423.

8. Ibid., p. 316.

9. Ibid., II: 42.

10. Ibid., p. 7.

11. Ibid., I: 335.

12. Ibid., I: 95.

13. Ibid., p. 93.

14. Ibid.

15. Ibid., p. 94.

16. Ibid., p. 327. See also p. 104 ff.

17. Ibid., p. 171.

18. Ibid.

19. Ibid., II: 230.

20. Ibid.

21. Ibid., p. 233.

22. Ibid., II: 238.

23. Ibid., II: 239-40.

24. Ibid., p. 240.

25. William Graham Sumner, *The Conquest of Spain and Other Essays*, Murray Polner, ed. (Chicago: Henry Regnery Co., 1965). p. 248.

26. Ibid., p. 54.

27. Ibid.

28. Ibid.

29. Joel C. Edelstein, "Mobilization, Immobilization, and Spontaneous Forms of Fascism" *Politics & Society* (Spring, 1972), 373.

30. Ibid.

31. R. Buckminster Fullet, *Operating Manual for Spaceship Earth* (New York: Pocket Books, 1970), p. 120.

32. J. Peter Euben, "Political Science & Political Silence" in *Power and Community: Dissenting Essays in Political Science*, Philip Green and Sanford Levinson, eds. (New York: Random House, 1969), p. 45.

33. See Lewis A. Coser and Irving Howe, *The New Conservatives: A Critique from the Left* (New York: Quadrangle, 1973).

34. Louis Hartz, *The Liberal Tradition in America* (New York: Harcourt, Brace and World, 1955) p. 89-90.

35. Ibid., p. 108.

36. Ibid., p. 110.

37. Cited in Richard Hofstadter, *The American Political Tradition* (New York: Vintage, 1948), p. 330.

38. It should be noted that of the two, Kristol is the most open opponent of reform. But see his comments in *On the Democratic Idea in America* (New York: Harper & Row, 1972), p. ix.

39. Irving Kristol, "Comment: New Right, New Left" *Public Interest* 4 (Summer, 1966), 7.

40. Irving Kristol, "'When virtue loses all her loveliness'—Some Reflections on Capitalism and The Free Society" *Public Interest* 21 (Fall, 1970), 9.

41. Ibid., pp. 9-11.

42. Ibid., p. 9.

43. Ibid., p. 10-11.

44. Ibid., p. 11.

45. Daniel Bell, *The Cultural Contradictions of Capitalism* (New York: Basic Books, 1976), p. 53.

46. Ibid., 77.

47. Daniel Bell, "Meritocracy & Equality" *Public Interest* 29 (Fall, 1972), 58-59.

48. Kristol, *Democratic Idea in America,* p. 13.

49. Irving Kristol, "Corporate Capitalism in America" *Public Interest* 41 (Fall, 1975), 124.

50. Ibid., p. 125.

51. Ibid., p. 126.

52. Ibid., p. 131. Also see his "Of Populism and Taxes" *Public Interest* 28 (Summer, 1972), 3-11.

53. Irving Kristol "About Equality" *Commentary* 54 (November, 1972), 46.

54. Bell, "Meritocracy and Equality", p. 67. Bell adds the proviso that the opportunity for the best to rise to the top through work and "effort" ought not be diminished. Yet the extent Bell is willing to give priority to the disadvantaged is not inconsiderable. He recommends vigorous enforcement of equal access to public places, liberalization of sex conduct codes, reduction of "invidious distinctions in work," and national medical care and housing programs. These are all matters of simple "security and dignity" (p. 65).

55. Kristol, *Democratic Idea in America,* p. 4.

56. Bell, *Cultural Contradictions of Capitalism,* pp. 281-82.

57. Kristol, "On Corporate Capitalism in America," p. 140.

58. Kristol, *Democratic Idea in America,* p. 29. Earlier he blames the estrangement of the "most gifted painters, poets, novelists and dramatists" from American society on the bourgeois world's own diminution of "disinterested social values or transcendent religious values" (p. 18).

59. Kristol, "About Equality," p. 47. Also see his "Socialism: An Obituary for an Idea" *The Alternative* 10 (October, 1976) p. 8.

60. Bell, *Cultural Contradictions of Capitalism*, chap. 4. Yet Bell does not even attempt to join his discussion of religion with the reaffirmation of liberalism. Without a great deal of effort, the two themes would appear to contradict one another. (See Bell himself on this point at p. 171.)

CHAPTER **6**

From Liberalism to Liberation

If myths constrain men, what myth might free them?
—Henry S. Kariel, *Saving Appearances*

The core beliefs that form the basis of the liberal tradition, the inevitability of human conflict and the plurality of the good, have produced two attitudes toward political and social life that are not totally consistent. From the first comes the liberal's sense of sobriety toward politics and the social order. It is difficult for contemporary political theorists to appreciate the powerful demythologizing role that liberalism has assumed in its few hundred years of existence. Thus it is rare to find a liberal who does not see politics as a potentially dangerous and even mean affair. Historically, the liberal has seen through the claims of those in authority. Prerogative, divine right, noblesse oblige, all were regarded by the liberal as pomposity covering a large share of self-interest. Bentham's attitude toward the "matchless constitution" is typical: "Why must [the Constitution] not be looked into?—Why is it, that under pain of being ipso facto an anarchist convict, we must never presume to look at it otherwise than with shut eyes?" The reason is that it harbors "waste, oppression and corruption in every department in every shape....Those who benefit from it can hardly rally others with such slogans as 'Waste Forever', 'Oppression Forever', and 'Corruption Forever!' But 'the constitution forever,' this a man may cry, and does cry, and makes a merit of it."[1] Later, liberals would resist the enchantment of the *Volksgemeinschaft* as well as the dictatorship of the proletariat. Politics accommodated real and often nasty interests. Locke's civil society was born from "revenge," "passion," "corruption," and "partiality." What sort of offspring could one expect? As such, even Arnold Kaufman, who would fashion a radical liberalism for the 1970s, warns:

> Politics is limited: Those who seek to fulfill apocalyptic visions through political activity are bound to become disillusioned. If Calvin, Hobbes, or Freud are correct in their descriptions of human nature, the salvation sought is beyond our worldly reach. Even if pessimistic accounts of human nature are mistaken, there is a sphere of personal struggle and aspiration that one may never be able to affect through the control of the crude levers of power with which political groups must ultimately be content. The realization that this is so is at once the end of innocence and the beginning of effectiveness in the pursuit of legitimate social goals.[2]

Political authority becomes a mechanism to resolve conflict but not, of course, in any permanent sense. In the words of Richard Friedman, authority "produces a decision to be followed, not a statement to be believed." Since politics does not possess an intrinsic purpose in the determination of the good, the liberal has a difficult time using it as anything other than a remedy, albeit an ongoing one. It is true that Marxism today carries the mantle of the great demythologizer, but it has achieved that role partly because it has promised a vision in which the cold eye of the realist would no longer be necessary. Politics would dissolve into administration, and the poetic would ooze over all social life. Liberalism could never make a promise of this sort.

The other liberal belief, the notion that the universe is a pluralistic one with many combinations of values that could produce the good life, has resulted in an attitude toward the human personality that is peculiar to liberalism. The liberal has insisted that for one to choose, he must be as unfettered as possible from constraints that might hamper his decisions. Liberalism has not been consistently anti-clerical, in fact, two of its greats, Acton and Tocqueville, placed a high value on religiosity and its function in the social order, but it has always preferred an individualized, depoliticized religion. Capitalism was, and is, frequently justified on the basis that it does not authoritatively lay down the nature of one's work or consumption. As heretical as it may sound today, even capitalism was a second choice for the liberal. At least it was an approximation of conditions that might give birth to the flowering of human personalities. Spencer gave his highest accolades to the artist, not the manufacturer. Mill spoke of different persons requiring "different conditions for their spiritual development" and argued for the direct administration of as many social and economic enterprises as possible so that it might produce an "endless diversity of experience." These were less "questions of liberty" than of "development."

This is not to say that liberals have not preferred certain social types. Liberalism still looks fondly upon realistic, active, and industrious persons but its method, especially in its more confident years, was one of example.[3] The rule of thumb was offered by Milton. Better to select virtue over temptation from evil than virtue without contest.

Two problems emerge from these attitudes that are worth exploring in the interest of an examination of post-liberal thought. One is how to combine these two inclinations, sobriety in politics, and a Faustian conception of the individual personality. Sometimes, liberals have emphasized the former almost exclusively. Mechanisms for dealing with human conflict have been devised that, while clearly dispassionate and scientific, have nearly wiped out the other side of liberalism. Bentham's felicific calculus, Smith's market mechanism, Spencer's law of differentiation, Skinner's operant conditioning have produced accounts of political conflict so finely honed that little is left of the men they were designed to measure. On the other hand, others, most notably J. S. Mill, have been accused of confusing society with a debating club. Many more liberals have struggled to stay between both inclinations. The other problem is that the liberal cannot and need not predict precisely what the human personality will do once freed. The freedom that most liberals envisioned was not so deeply buried that it needed to be laid bare on bloodied streets or painfully plucked out on a psychiatrist's couch. It always lay close to the surface. Restraints upon freedom, then, are nearly always external and, once removed, the results nearly automatic. Mill, as always, is the best illustration:

> The only freedom which deserves the name is that of pursuing our own good in our own way, so long as we do not attempt to deprive others of theirs or impede their efforts to obtain it. Each is the proper guardian of

> his own health, whether bodily or mental and spiritual. Mankind are greater gainers by suffering each other to live as seems good to themselves than by compelling each to live as seems good to the rest.[4]

The liberal, then, is placed in the awkward position of fostering a climate that is sympathetic to utopian thinking in the sense that all is possible for the individual while, at the same time, it denies its chance of success in the sense of finding a way to incorporate it firmly in the political order. It is interesting to note, for instance, the ambivalence the liberal tradition expresses when it has confronted the wave of utopian communities that have sporadically swept across liberal societies. The movements of Owenite and Fourierist withdrawal from society to produce heavens on earth are quite consistent with the Lockean injunction to seek one's own freedom in a *vacuous locus.* There is no revolutionary terror to object to; participation is quite voluntary; even evangelism is often absent. We have seen Nozick's fascination with them. Nevertheless, liberals have scorned or worried about the practice of even these mini-utopias. Despite Mill's plea for "experiments in living" free from the restrictions of the majority, it took nearly all his liberal fortitude to insist upon a laissez-faire stance in regard to the Mormons. Lewis Coser's doubts are quite illustrative on this point as well. The Oneida settlement was an example of a "greedy organization" that produced individuals without a private self; "the community had succeeded in sucking up its substance, leaving only a shell."[5] While the liberal vision of the human personality is not so individualistic that it must have Stirnerite independence, it is sufficiently reluctant to be unwilling to posit an ensemble of individuals that do not need some protection against the utopian schemes of each other. The highest flights of the Faustian spirit are always reserved for the individual in his study. These are to be carefully fettered and tamed before they reach the political arena.

A good portion of the American post-liberal tradition is not at all willing to accept this view. This chapter will focus upon works by Henry Kariel, Aristide Zolberg, and Herbert Marcuse, three of the most prominent advocates for a direct connection between the utopian impulse and the political order.

If the efforts of Kariel and those who write from similar perspectives are measured against the critique of liberalism offered by Marxists, one cannot fail to see a certain independence. There are, of course, certain ceremonial gestures of gratitude. Marx "fires the imagination," we are dutifully reminded.[6] But the critique is hardly Marxist at all. What fires Kariel's imagination is Marx's glimpse of human existence "beyond necessity" into the "true empire of freedom."[7] Zolberg insists that Marx was, after all, ambivalent toward the utopian socialists. He "partly shared the sensibility of his enemies."[8] Marcuse speaks of "passing from Marx to Fourier."[9] The stern materialism of the *German Ideology*, the penetrating empirical analysis in the *Civil War*, or the tedious descriptions in *Capital* do not titillate. What does titillate is the "early" Marx; the Marx of the *Manuscripts* supplies a utopian vision more demanding and inclusive than liberalism.

It is important to note that the Marxist critique of liberalism, and not a few variants of socialism as well, contained a bitter Machiavellian realism regarding liberal society as well as a claim that was highly utopian. It is true that the communists believed they had solved the riddle of human history; alienation was not a permanent part of the human condition. Yet, Marx and Engels could be quite clever at emphasizing their own brand of realism and utopianism. Pressed by liberal plans for political freedom, Marx would demand emancipation from "huckstering" and argue for the realization of the species being.[10] Pressed by LaSallians, Marx would puzzle at the "fuss" over distributive justice and also mock the idea of state aid for cooperatives.[11] Pressed by anarchists, Engels would remind his readers of the necessary "despotism" of factory life.[12] The phrase, "abolition of the state," is never made quite clear. But then, any "really human morality" and its consequences become visible not only when class antagonisms are overcome but when they are "forgotten" in practical life.[13]

Despite tactical and logical problems in both positions, Marx is relatively clear about the task of political action and ultimate human liberation. The political struggle against capitalism and the movement of bourgeois society itself eventually integrates the liberal division of society composed of individual, social, economic, and political spheres. The individual in the state of pure communism does have a certain dilettante quality about him. He fishes, reads philosophy, raises cattle, and hunts. However, he is very much a communal creature. In the words of the 1844 *Manuscripts:* "...that which I make of myself, I make of myself for society and with the consciousness of myself as a social being....What is to be avoided above all is the re-establishing of 'Society' as an abstraction vis-a-vis the individual."[14] If Marx's analogy of the orchestra is accepted as an accurate statement of authority in communist society, the extent of close cooperation and discipline he had in mind is clear. Politics may be replaced by administration, but life in communist society, even if it is pluralistic, is anything but anarchical.

Crucial to Marx was his belief that utopia be born of necessity. Politics in a liberal society merely reflected the economic order. If that order was a complex one, its political configuration would be appropriately represented; some elements of course would only be treated as objects of oppression. Thus, in the *Eighteenth Brumaire*, Marx is able to speak of "big landed property with its priests and lackeys," "high finance capital," "large scale capital," "large scale trade," "petty bourgeoisie," "landed property," "lumpen proletariat," proletariat, "peasant troglodytes," "small holding peasants." Such a complex class balance was not desirable from Marx's viewpoint. It blurred the source of oppression:

> The best form of polity is that in which the social contradictions are not blurred, are arbitrarily—that is: artificially, and therefore only seemingly—kept down. The best form of polity is that in which these contradictions reach a state of open struggle in the course of which they are resolved.[15]

Thus political activity had two faces depending upon historical circumstances. In the coming of the Second Empire, it was a "grotesque mediocrity" with a bewildering array of classes, desperately seeking to find a form of order that would promote the interest of each. In the open struggle model, politics does have a liberating effect. The proletariat is moved by a "practical expression of necessity" to a "life-and-death struggle." Needless to say, politics as liberation must contain both elements: class solidarity and revolutionary goals. Without the proper unit and aims, politics would remain encased in the "old democratic litany."[16]

Tedium replaces necessity as the central theme that provides the basis for the critique of liberal society from the liberationist standpoint. From Marcuse to Kariel to Zolberg we are reminded of the intellectual's feeling of ennui when confronted with the liberal order. In Marcuse, the indictment of boredom is offered with dashes of outrage. In Kariel, however, the critique is presented in its purest form:

> From the wealth of case studies of contemporary American politics at all levels of government there emerges a picture whose familiar title—The Decision-Making Process—is altogether fitting. The color of the picture is an almost even grey, its texture smooth, its design agreeable. It would not seem to have been deliberately composed at all, so effortlessly do its soft lines flow through the canvas. While there are some fluttering movements and a few decisive points of color and interest, there is little drama, little confrontation of opposites, little tension and suspense. What motion there is tends to be circular or elliptical.[17]

Kariel yearns for a "pattern heroic," "some dramatic highlight—a point of impact, a dash of interests, a violent thrust, a conclusive decision, a strike and a deadlock."[18] Instead, he is offered only the "precious Whig tradition" with its "Robert's *Rules of Order*, the Sherman Antitrust Act, the System of Checks and Balances, due process of law, the right to privacy, and violence scrupulously aimed only against perverse, uncompromising outsiders."[19] Since no massive change in American politics is in sight, Kariel recommends locating those forces that "devitalize" the political order and subjecting them to the challenge of a "playful" citizen.[20] A polity of people playfully criticizing, playfully mocking, playfully questioning will produce a citizenry "more spectacular, dramatic, winning and attractive—ever seeking to attract others by the scenes they steal or make, roles they create, the alternatives they present."[21] It is true that "millions are hurting" in America. "Politics is not for them, not yet."[22] But then, perhaps in their acts of desperation and self-destruction, they are playing as well "but not knowing it."[23]

Zolberg has even found a thread that connects the series of convulsions that France has undergone since 1848. What connects the overthrow of the July Monarchy, the Paris Commune, the liberation of Paris from the Nazis, and the 1968 May strikes is boredom. The 1848 outbreak was the "first revolution against boredom." Each subsequent liberation benefited from the "collective memories" of past ones. Politics is truly orgasmic:

> Ecstasy or delirium, the thing happened and it was unmistakably political. The recurrence of these moments over one hundred and twenty years, recognizably the same in spite of variations, give the phenomenon a persuasive concreteness each event may not possess individually. The evidence contained in this purposely heterogenous testimony gathered in this essay is remarkably consistent. Whatever the attitudes of the writers at the time of writing, whatever role they played in the events, whatever their mode of writing, they record intense moments of festive joy, when an immense outpouring of speech, sometimes verging on violence, coexists with an extraordinarily peaceful disposition. Minds and bodies are liberated; human beings feel that they are in direct touch with one another as well as with their inner selves.[24]

Zolberg fondly quotes Flaubert's *L'Education Sentimentale* in which Moreau, the young country bourgeois, makes arrangements with a prostitute at the brink of the 1848 outbreak: "The revolution begins as he possesses her...his personal life and history mingle."[25] Like Fourier, the connection between sexuality and politics is of great import. Zolberg even dismisses the subsequent pessimism of those who actually experienced "moments of madness" as a backlash of guilt, a *post coitum omnia animal triste.* Yet revolutionary ebullience is nevertheless worth modeling. Fourier spoke of seas transformed into pink lemonade, the mutations of anti-animals, and a firework profusion of stellar activity. Zolberg is not quite so phantasmagoric, but one can certainly understand Fourier's intentions better by Zolberg's slightly less poetic descriptions: "The streets of the city, its objects, and even the weather take on harmonious qualities. Falsehood, ugliness, and evil give way to beauty, goodness and truth....Dreams become possibilities."[26] The dream becomes a corollary metaphor to the dominant sexual one, and a fitting denouement it is indeed. The libido has the upper hand here; restraint is suspended. Only the nightmare, the model of dysutopians from Kafka to Huxley, is neglected. The commune was a "festival," not a "barbaric and criminal orgy," says Zolberg in quoting Rougerie. The obvious analogy to Dionysian revery in which pleasure and violence rest on the most precarious equilibrium is purposely pushed aside. In a whisper we are informed of the exception of the Bloody Week: "All together fewer than one hundred hostages were massacred."[27]

In Marcuse's works is seen a closer connection between necessity and liberation. The model of Marx is more immediate. Yet Marcuse's agents for revolution, the lumpen proletariat and the lumpen intelligentsia (middle-class youth who refuse to traverse the rite of passage into the bourgeois economic order), are chosen not only for their expendability in relation to the economic system but also for their irrationality and unpredictability in one-dimensional society. Marx heaped scorn on the political base of Louis Napoleon. The Parisian lumpen proletariat, "this scum, offal, refuse of all classes," was the "only class on which he can base himself unconditionally." For Marx, the discipline of factory life was essential to creating the solidarity that would eventually force political liberation. Marcuse tells us, however, that industrial order with its delivery of "efficiency and wealth" has instead produced a happy consciousness.[28] Yet one wonders how much of the alteration of Marx is a tactical one, if the working class still is "objectively" the basis for revolution.

Marcuse is critical of the more sober visions of Marx regarding complete communism. "Marx rejects the idea that work can ever become human play" but it is now possible that the "imagination of such men and women would fashion their reason and tend to make the process of production a process of creation."[29] He is equally disdainful of Marx's reticence in describing utopia. "Such restraint is no longer justified....The growth of the productive forces suggests possibilities of human liberty very different from, and beyond those envisaged at the earlier stage."[30] With Marx's and Engels's admonition against painting "fantastic pictures of future society" pushed aside, Marcuse is able to pick up his own brush. The "new sensibility" has become praxis. The yearning for freedom is derived not from economic necessity but from freedom, especially in sexual form. If the "decline of shame and guilt feelings in the sexual sphere" can be transcended and applied to the political realm, "instinctual revolt turns into political rebellion." The revolutionary slogan becomes *L'Imagination au Pouvoir.*

What precisely does the imagination of the new aesthetic power conjure up? In general terms, Marcuse is able to speak of an image of humanity. Men would develop an instinctual barrier against cruelty, brutality, ugliness; "tender" and "sensuous," they would "no longer be ashamed of themselves." Yet his examples of the new aesthetics reveal the dark side of play. "Systematic linguistic rebellion...smashes the ideological context in which words are employed."[31] Obscenity is clearly a tool of war:

> The methodical use of obscenities in the political language of the radicals is the elemental act of giving a new name to men and things, obliterating the false and hypocritical name which the renamed figures proudly bear in and for the system. And if the renaming invokes the sexual sphere, it falls in line with the great design of the desublimation of culture, which, to the radicals, is a vital aspect of liberation.[32]

The black redefinition of the "soul" transforms it from "the traditional seat of everything that is truly human in man, tender, deep, immortal" to something "violent," "orgastic," "tabooed," "uncanny."[33] Contemporary music is praised for its "erotic belligerency."[34]

The critique of liberal society offered by these theorists outlines a novel approach to society and politics, one that deserves its own appellation. The political philosophy of liberation is derived from accepting one part of the liberal world view while adamantly rejecting the other. The utopian impulse within liberal thought is grasped, measured unfavorably against the public restraint one finds in liberal society, and, then, cast out as the model of political action. The world of free individuals fashioning their own social order is much closer to liberalism than Marxism. Marx was able to see the import of this phenomenon, if only to reject it for reasons extraneous to liberalism. The utopians, by engaging in a "fantastic standing apart from the contest" of class struggle, attempted to move toward the realm of freedom without passing through the caldron of necessity. There are differences, of course, between the utopian socialists and the liberationists. The latter are not patient enough to work out their visions in experimental and small-scale communities. Such an alternative is too cautious. The liberationist has acquired a taste for larger projects. Savor a portion of Henry Kariel's confessional:

> ...I subsequently considered the unfulfilled promise of politics, recognizing how curiously *satisfying* it was to inject private, untamed impulses into the political sphere....[35]

How curious is the phrase "curiously satisfying"! Politics is to be designed to make people happy, not in the sense of providing mere material comfort or even of providing a sense of pride or respect. Politics is to be designed to produce sensual pleasure (Marcuse's term) giving rise to drama and excitement and finally an afterglow of contentment. Nowhere is this more clear than in a series of long rambling passages recently offered by Kariel. Note the appeal to politics as erotica:

> ...it becomes possible to entertain oneself by a vision of people entering a practice field of sorts—an educational arena to which they feel attracted by the way it blends familiar scenes and strange situations—perhaps a theater showing a film that introduces them to America in such a way that they find it easy tomake love to it. The film shows them a land that is marvelously rich—a blessed, generous, spacious country, one they recognize as truly theirs. They comfortably *relate* to what they see: they're home. The mellow color would invite them to caress its familiar regions....The audience is turned on by the eroticized, energetic landscape, by a country with problems, yes, but solvable problems....
>
> As members of the audience allow themselves to be drawn deeper and deeper into the country, they begin to hear and see what goes on beneath America's inviting surface. They slowly reach its secret pain and muck....While shots from the opening part of the film weave in and out to keep reminding them that it's their land, that *this* is what they love, that they love it all the way down.[36]

Why the metaphor? Part of the reason for its selection has been suggested already. If public life in liberal society is factious and dull and private life too constrained by bourgeois niceties, then it becomes understandable for one to select the most obvious image in contradiction. The erotic provides for two related visions. First, it suggests a peak of excitement almost incomparable to other facets of human existence. Susan Sontag, who is hardly Victorian and whose work probably fits into the liberationist model as well, contends that human sexuality "belongs, at least potentially, among the extreme rather than ordinary experiences of humanity."[37] Sexuality remains "one of the demonic forces in human consciousness —pushing us at intervals close to taboo and dangerous desires...." At a physical level, orgasm resembles an "epileptic fit." The appeal of the erotic metaphor for politics explains a great deal more about its use in liberation thought than Marcuse's ostensible justification that the violation of sexual taboos will destroy the image of political authority as a father figure. In Marcuse's analysis particularly, "civil" modes of behavior not only hide serious injustices in liberal societies but internalize aggression. This surplus repression is channeled into socially harmless outlets and must be unleashed. The second function of the erotic metaphor is as an image to indicate the extent of human unity that politics can provide. After all, in the sexual sphere one can lose one's "self" in involvement with another. Erotic politics becomes the ultimate symbol of community, so intense and so encompassing as to even make Marx's vision limited. Zolberg's French revolutionaries find their "minds and bodies liberated" in "direct touch with one another." Kariel's description of American society as "autistic," incapable of real human relationships, is to be replaced with a loss of self at a higher level. Love is what America needs now.

One can raise two closely related questions in assessing liberationist thought. How valid are its premises, and in what political direction are they likely to lead? The obvious answer to both questions within the context of conventional liberal wisdom is to remind the liberationists that life can never be play. Even a continuous string of holidays produces its own boredom. Necessity always creeps back, sometimes in quite unexpected ways. Kariel, the most thoughtful of this group, is not unmindful of this possibility:

> It is best to concede, I think, that this reality may be short-lived. Brute implacable necessity will keep putting an end to it. Forced to retreat to

idealism, people will claim once more that their pain must surely be *good* for something, that they must leave their mark, a monument testifying to their suffering, a true record of some kind of a scar on the landscape.[38]

Yet the liberation mystique deserves a more detailed reply. An answer can be suggested by examining the very basis of its model. Despite all its concern for the hypocrisy and self-interest endemic in American society, the liberationist model is one that seeks to present a moral critique by consciously moving beyond the ordinary demands of morality. In a sense, the works of Marcuse, Zolberg, and Kariel represent an attempt to present an amoral philosophy of life. In this respect, they ultimately owe more to Nietzsche than Marx or even Fourier. The erotic metaphor is instructive in pursuing this line of thought as well. While the analogy to the sexual sphere denotes a longing for community, it also represents a longing that is, at root, a painfully existential one. The union with another offers a relief from the agonies of human existence that is somehow individually structured. If only politics could reflect that same satisfaction. It is no accident then that those who espouse liberation are anxious to avoid the responsibility of accepting any particular role in society. Kariel speaks only of people *playing* at roles, dropping the demands upon him or her that might be assumed if one was a judge or cabinetmaker, and picking up another. One is reminded of Sartre's description of the intricate behavior patterns of a waiter. He bows, he smiles, he delivers food with a flourish, but all these movements are products of the role of the waiter. Nietzsche insisted that what was wrong with morality was the way it imposed itself upon individuals. It prevented us from becoming "a law unto us." "We must free ourselves of morality in order to be able to live morally."[39] Morality, after all, was people's own creation; why must so many be prevented from acting out their creations?

One can more readily understand the disparagement of liberalism at this level. If liberalism promised liberty, why are we so constrained? Yet if one assumes this position, one which is not entirely nonsensical, one is drawn to accept serious consequences. If "true" morality and presumably "true" freedom is to be defined entirely in the service of individual creation, then creation itself becomes the only standard of morality. Sin is conceived in terms of hypocrisy (a form of false creation) or restraint. Nietzsche, who was able to present the most poignant descriptions of the human condition, was also to offer the most ugly accounts of politics as well.

The reason that this must be so is obvious. The liberationist standard is creation. This requires a degree of psychological space, a release from convention. To the extent that such space is to be found privately and individually, the artist can work. Liberal societies, of course, provide ample room for the eccentricities and daring of the artist. The liberationists are not unaware of society's tolerance. However, art as art doesn't seem to be able to push itself into other areas of life: "No matter what sensibility art may wish to develop, no matter what form it may wish to give to things, to life, no matter what vision it may wish to communicate—a radical change of experience is within the technical reaches of powers whose terrible imagination organizes the world in their own image and perpetuates, ever bigger and better, the mutilated experience."[40]

The liberationist cannot live with entirely private expressions of creation. It becomes necessary to "progressively annihilate the dead ends of privacy" and eliminate the "great liberal distinction between self and others, between public and private."[41] It is at this point that the dark underside of liberationism surfaces. Creation itself is an amoral category. The liberationist has already dredged up the Dionysian side of human existence as well as rejected notions of rights or justice or virtue as too constraining. Kariel's fascination with Ad Reinhardt carries over to politics: "They [the individual and body politics] must be treated as if they are nothing, as if they amounted to nothing...."[42] Now, men of goodwill can always dispute how many anchors we need to carry on a decent existence (and liberalism recognizes fewer than others), but who would say that we need none? Thus the liberationist is forced to insist upon fashioning a society of "actors without scripts, films without authors, buildings without architects....nations without founding fathers."[43] And why not? Against the image of "societies whose capacities defy the imagination," who would call for restraint? Kariel, of course, will hesitate. There is a "real danger of getting lost, of failing to communicate." But he shakes his head, casts off the doubt, and quickly pushes on.

What of those who wish to hold on to some anchors—rights for protection, restraint against their selves in bad moments? Nietzsche's answer here was the most direct. If one chooses to live in a "herd" he must pay a horrible price: "If you are too weak to give laws to yourself, then let a tyrant lay his yoke upon you and say: 'Obey, gnash and obey!' and all good and evil will be drowned in obedience to him." Contemporary liberationists are not as blunt as Nietzsche, but the harshness is not far below the surface. Kariel's personal remarks suggest the temptations. He speaks of his "heroic involvements" and "midnight defeats" revealed in "one wild incandescent moment" in academic life in the 1960s:

> It has been possible to express the thought (never more than that) that an academic department...might proceed to pool individual incomes, replace secretaries who would not adjust to such a windfall, discard wives or husbands who would not disarm, and recruit no new chairman who would feel otherwise. We would change offices into lounges, clerks into research associates, teachers into students. We would all become untenured participant-observers whirling beyond schedules, unregistered and out of bounds.[44]

Note the fluctuation in mood in even this short quote. First, there is the elation of a new order of reality. The "wild incandescent moment" focuses upon actual change. But those who will not or cannot "disarm" themselves are to be cast away. This is certainly an unpleasant feature of liberation politics, but one does not dwell upon it. The next sentence shows a recouping of energy, and the "open" nature of the system is pushed before us. Of course, those who have been discarded do not enjoy being "unregistered and out of bounds." Can they be made to enjoy such pleasures?

One can gain a clear notion of what is involved in such a process by briefly summarizing the views of a writer who himself has applied liberation thought to the field of public administration. His work can be especially useful since he does not write from a traditionally revolutionary perspective in which ebullience is understandably apart from the peculiarities of liberationist thought. Orion White poses two models of policy formation.[45] The conventional mode has been a "politics of contract." Here, human relations are seen in terms of "negotiations and bargains" between parties. Public policy is formed "through a structure which balances narrow interests in a deal where all or most parties benefit somewhat." However, the contract model has been challenged by the new generation who demands "limitation of authority in a way that reasserts the autonomy of the individual." In its stead, White proposes the "politics of love" in which parties establish a "deeply personal relationship" and "actualize" themselves. The advance guard for this new administrative politics are the legions of people who eagerly participate in "encounter groups" and "sensitivity training" in their capacity as family, church, or corporation members. White notes that policy differences that might occur in this framework will take on a more "militant" character. Once Madison is rejected in the overt political sphere, Weber will be rejected in the administrative one. This militancy can produce resolution of differences that can more properly be called confrontation rather than conflict. This new mode would demand that all actors in political institutions—but especially administrators—relate to the elements in their environment in a way that stresses that

> interactions continually take place within an explicit framework of principles based on a specification of what man is and what his purposes are. The concepts of decision by compromise, reasonableness, tolerance, or balance of interest would become irrelevant for a much wider range of issues than at present.[46]

For those who disagree over what man is, politics can be nothing less than therapeutic. However, the problem with liberation goes deeper than its open disavowal of tolerance. After all, lovers *can* be extremely tolerant of one another's foibles. The elevation of the notion of love as well as creation to the center of politics transforms emotion in ways that the liberationists are almost totally unaware. Here the sin of hypocrisy, the negative thread that connects the liberation critique of American society as well as the sin of tedium, assumes important proportions. For hypocrisy, the counter emotion, exacts terrible demands when one of the major purposes of political action is to remove it.

Hannah Arendt has presented one of the most penetrating analyses of politics as a war against hypocrisy in order that liberation can govern pure. She notes that the Reign of Terror, unique in history with the French Revolution, arose directly out of a "misplaced emphasis on the heart as the source of political virtue, ou le coeur, une ame droite, un charactere moral." Once the battle against hypocrisy assumed the center stage of political action all human relations are destined to be poisoned:

> The heart...keeps its resources alive through a constant struggle that goes on in its darkness and because of its darkness. When we say that nobody but God can see (and perhaps, can bear to see) the nakedness of a human heart, "nobody" includes one's own self—if only because our sense of unequivocal reality is so bound up with the presence of others that we can never be sure of anything that only we ourselves know and no one else. The consequence of this hiddenness is that our entire psychological life, the process of moods in our souls, is cursed with a suspicion we constantly feel we must raise against ourselves, against our innermost motives. Robespierre's insane lack of trust in others, even in his closest friends, sprang ultimately from his not so insane but quite normal suspicion of himself. Since his very credo forced him to display his virtue, to open his heart as he understood it, at least once a week, how could he be sure that he was not the one thing he probably feared most in his life, a hypocrite? The heart knows many such intimate struggles, and it knows too that what was straight when it was hidden must appear crooked when it is disclosed. It knows how to deal with these problems according to its own "logic," although it has no solution for them, since a solution demands light and it is precisely the light of the world that distorts the life of the heart. The truth of Rousseau's âme déchirée, apart from its function in the formation of the volonté générale, is that the heart begins to beat properly only when it has been broken or being torn in conflict, but this is a truth which cannot prevail outside the life of the soul within the realm of human affairs.[47]

It is this wisdom (although in no way is it a wholesale defense of hypocrisy) that can be derived from the liberal heritage. The marking off of a private from a public sphere is hardly "specifically designed as a defense for the protection of anti-social behavior," a case for a philosophy of "each for himself and the devil take the hindmost."[48] On the contrary, it is designed in part to recognize and protect the complexity of human existence. White's honest relationships and a politics of confrontation and Robespierre's âme déchirée and Reign of Terror are not far apart. Both derive from the attempt to annihilate privacy.

Yet if the politics of liberation can produce citizens so tortured in displaying their motives that they see that others must be hiding doubts, is it possible to construct a model that avoids murder in the name of honesty? Most liberation writers have perceived an alternative. At this point, the image of Robespierre fades and that of Sorel comes to the forefront. Why not conceive a series of leaders who are aware that their motives cannot be completely sorted out? They could stand apart from the agony of liberation while insisting that others undertake the process. One is reminded here of John Humphrey Noyes, the leader of the Oneida community, who held regular encounter sessions to force his subjects to lay bare their sins. Needless to say, he never underwent the same analysis. Marcuse's notorious dictatorship of the intellectuals clearly illustrates this option. Even Kariel has latched on to this Sorelian alternative—"to promote an idea which would eradicate ideas, a truth which would make truth dispensable....If myths constrain men, what myth might free them?"[49] Now the leader is permitted to lie in the service of liberation with the certainty that he will receive absolution because a lie that is believed becomes truth. Dishonesty, the last refuge from an ethics that sees creation as its only duty, is now discarded because a great lie, a really imaginative lie, can produce the most creative act of all—arousing men to become "protean creators continuously identifying and expressing and mastering experiences."[50]

There appear, then, to be few basic directions the liberal model can take. In one, it can stand as an appeal for liberal society to take seriously its own utopian premises. Fourierists can rush about appealing to capitalists to finance phalanxes. Or, solitary malcontents can serve to titillate liberal society. Emerson, the visionary who has no time to liberate slaves when he must liberate the mind; Thoreau, the cranky hermit who occasionally shuffles out into civilization to remind us to act from our "hearts"; Mailer, stumbling up Pentagon steps in order to spend a sober night in jail; all stand for reconstituting the place of the spirit in a hardened technological society. We see them, spend an uncomfortable evening reading their works, and perhaps behave with a bit more sensitivity the next day.

In another direction, it serves as a rationale to applaud any act of violence as a glorification of the self in repudiation of liberal society. But liberationists should be aware that the "laughing of desperate men" produces no pleasure for the victim. It may be true, as Nietzsche said, that the person of superior character harbors no hatred against his victims much as a wolf does not feel any malice toward sheep. However, what Nietzsche did not say (and could not say) is that conventional morality for all its rules and rights and duties would not be necessary if people were not vulnerable to extreme pain and suffering. H. L. A. Hart once remarked that morality would be irrelevant if people were encased in some foolproof armor, immune from injury. Once that truth is recognized, politics in the service of creativity loses its appeal.

NOTES

1. Jeremy Bentham, "The Book of Fallacies" in *A Bentham Reader*, Mary Peter Mack, ed. (New York: Pegasus, 1969), p. 348. The "matchless constitution" was an example of "vague generalities and, for Bentham, was based upon the 'theoretical' supposition," the "wisdom of barbarian ancestors."

2. Arnold Kaufman, *The Radical Liberal* (New York: Simon and Schuster, 1968), p. 11.

3. James Mill made the case with his usual bluntness: "[the opinions of the workers] are formed, and their minds are directed by that intelligent middle rank, who come the most immediately in contact with them, to whom they fly for advice and assistance in all their numerous difficulties....to whom their children look up as models for imitation, whose opinions they hear daily repeated, and account it an honor to adopt." *Essays* (London: Dent, n.d.), p. 12.

4. John Stuart Mill, *On Liberty*, Gertrude Himmelfarb, ed. (Baltimore: Penguin, 1974), p. 72.

5. Lewis Coser, "Greedy Organizations," *European Journal of Sociology* 8 (October 1967), 215.

6. Henry Kariel, *Saving Appearances* (North Scituate, Mass.: Duxbury Press, 1972), p. 80.

7. Ibid.

8. Aristide Zolberg, "Moments of Madness" in *The Politics and Society Reader,* Ira Katznelson, ed. (New York: McKay, 1974), p. 251.

9. Herbert Marcuse, *An Essay on Liberation* (Boston: Beacon Press, 1969), p. 22.

10. Karl Marx, "On the Jewish Question" in *Marx-Engels Reader,* Robert C. Tucker, ed. (New York: W. W. Norton), p. 44.

11. Karl Marx, "Critique of the Gotha Program" in *Marx-Engels Reader,* pp. 387-88.

12. Friedrich Engels, "On Authority" in *Marx-Engels Reader,* p. 663.

13. Friedrich Engels, "On Morality" in *Marx-Engels Reader,* p. 667.

14. Karl Marx, "Economic and Philosophic Manuscripts of 1844" in *Marx-Engels Reader,* p. 72.

15. Cited in Michael Evans, *Karl Marx* (Bloomington: Indiana University Press, 1975), p. 118. See also Karl Marx, "Civil War in France" in *Marx-Engels Reader,* p. 573.

16. Karl Marx, "Critique of the Gotha Program" in *Marx-Engels Reader,* p. 395.

17. Henry Kariel, *The Promise of Politics* (Englewood Cliffs, N.J.: Prentice-Hall, 1966), p. 103.

18. Ibid., p. 101.

19. Henry Kariel, "Making Scenes in a Liberal Society," *Massachusetts Review* 11 (Spring 1970), 226.

20. Henry Kariel, *Saving Appearances,* pp. 8-9.

21. Henry Kariel, "Making Scenes in a Liberal Society," p. 225.

22. Henry Kariel, *Saving Appearances,* p. 8.

23. Ibid.

24. Zolberg, "Moments of Madness," p. 245.

25. Ibid., p. 240.

26. Ibid., p. 245.

27. Ibid., p. 238.

28. It is worth noting that Henry Marcuse's thesis in *One Dimensional Man* itself involved a significant revision of Marxist thought. The notion that modern society was capable of providing for material satisfaction while, or actually because, it neglected spiritual values is, at base, an aristocratic or conservative critique and extends from Carlyle to Babbitt. Marcuse is quite lucid on this point. See, for instance, the following: There is a "kernel of truth in the romantic contrast between the modern traveller and the wandering poet or artisan, between assembly line and handicraft, town and city, factory-produced and the home-made loaf, the sailboat and the outboard motor, etc." Or (on the "democratic domination" of aesthetics): "It is good that almost everyone can now have the fine arts at

his fingertips, by just turning a knob on his set or by just stepping into his drugstore. In this diffusion, however, they become cogs in a culture machine which remakes their content." *One Dimensional Man* (Boston: Beacon, 1964), pp. 72-73, 65.

29. Marcuse, *An Essay on Liberation* (Boston: Beacon, 1969), p. 21.

30. Ibid., p. 5.

31. Ibid., p. 35.

32. Ibid.

33. Ibid., p. 36.

34. Ibid.

35. Kariel, *Saving Appearances,* p. 4.

36. Henry Kariel, "Celebrating Not Celebrating," seminar paper for "The Idea of America," Tanglewood, North Carolina, June 6-12, 1976, p. 17.

37. Susan Sontag, "The Pornographic Imagination" in *Perspective on Pornography,* Douglas A. Hughes, ed. (New York: St. Martin's Press, 1970), p. 153.

38. Kariel, "Celebrating Not Celebrating," pp. 18-19.

39. Cited in Karl Jasper, *Nietzsche: An Introduction to the Understanding of his Philosophical Activity,* Charles F. Walraff and Frederick Schmitz, trans. (Tucson: University of Arizona Press, 1965), p. 147. My argument is indebted to Jasper's penetrating analysis.

40. Marcuse, *Essay on Liberation,* p. 45. Marcuse's doubts about the inspirational impetus of art are more prominent in *Counter-Revolution and Revolt* (Boston: Beacon, 1972), especially chap. 3. While the "internal exigency" of art "drives the artist to the streets," in doing so art becomes "antagonistic" to radical practice (p. 122).

41. Kariel, *Saving Appearances,* p. 5.

42. Ibid., p. 83.

43. Kariel, "Celebrating Not Celebrating," p. 15. In a recent paper Kariel has followed this line to its extreme. If all life is really play "signifying nothing," then the liberationist call for authenticity is itself too narrow: "We would then be content to do nothing more abusive than design and exhibit our own masks....We would then surrender our deadly emblems of authenticity and merely pretend to be authentic, truthful, honest, and truly in touch with ourselves." "Participation Beyond Nihilism," paper delivered at the 1976 American Political Science Association, Chicago, Illinois, September 2-5, 1976, p. 15. Although Kariel is contending that such an attitude surpasses nihilism, one is reminded of the child playfully tearing apart a doll, who when admonished by a parent, replies, "but it's not a *real* person!"

44. Kariel, *Saving Appearances*, p. 10.

45. Orion F. White, "Administrative Adaptation in a Changing Society" in *Toward a New Public Administration*, Frank Marini, ed. (Scranton, Pa.: Chandler, 1971), pp. 59-83.

46. Ibid., p. 79.

47. Hannah Arendt, *On Revolution* (New York: Viking, 1965), pp. 92-93.

48. H. W. Arendt, "The Cult of Privacy," *Australian Quarterly* 21 (September 1949), 69-70.

49. Kariel, "Making Scenes in a Liberal Society," p. 231.

50. Ibid., p. 232.

CHAPTER 7

The "Anarchist" Alternative: The Journeys of Robert Paul Wolff

...there is a temptation here to use the word "dialectical" a lot....As I say, there is a temptation to talk that way. And it sure does sound good. But I must confess that I don't know what those words mean. I cannot now form a concrete conception of a set of social arrangements which would, at one and the same time, respect the nature of each person as a rational moral agent, and also sustain and support each man and woman in a natural human way along the life cycle from birth, through childhood, young adulthood, maturity, old age, to death.
—Robert Paul Wolff, "There's Nobody Here But Us Persons"

The liberationists put forward what amounts to a gnostic heresy within the liberal tradition. They clutch at liberalism's utopian premise as if it were some injured bird. They examine it, stroke it, and ask themselves why it cannot fly on its own. Then they hold their hands to the air and ask it to fly—alone. But within the context of the little understood dialectic of liberalism, the scientific premise can act as a communitarian element. The human penchant for conflict forms the ingredient which forces the liberal to find some means of social cooperation. Let liberal utopia fly off alone and one simply cannot predict what direction it will take.

The efforts of Robert Paul Wolff are an example of other journeys liberal utopia can take. One of the most puzzling aspects of Wolff's *In Defense of Anarchism* was its tone. There was no rage, controlled or uncontained, as one finds in the works of Stirner or Spooner. Nor was there the ebullience of Goodman or the younger Friedman. There was not even that magnificent vision of the anarchist community that is laid before us in Kropotkin or Godwin. All the reader was given was Wolff's "forlorn" description of his journey—"crestfallen and embarrassed," it ended with "chagrin": "I became a philosophical anarchist."[1] It was as if he embraced anarchist political theory in the same manner a dedicated Christian saint would dutifully comfort a dying leper. In place of Godwin's glorious kingdom on earth in which even the universal sentence of human mortality might be licked by rationality is a four-page "glimpse" of a world without states, each proposal tortuously appendixed by notations on the difficulties involved. Critics have seemed to overlook the distinctive nature of this "soft" anarchism. Taken alone, Wolff's essay was more distinguished for its poignancy than for the logic of its arguments.

Now, three years later, Wolff produces a book on Kant and both the nature of his peculiar form of anarchism as well as the reasons for his trepidation can be seen more clearly. If his major works are reviewed, beginning with *The Poverty of Liberalism* and now momentarily resting with *The Autonomy of Reason*, we shall be able to see the road upon which Wolff is traveling perhaps even better than he.

Wolff's 1968 book was his most confident; the bittersweet, confessional style of his latter works is totally absent. In each of the five essays in *The Poverty of Liberalism* Wolff steps firmly and dispassionately on every major shibboleth—tolerance, diffusion of power, privacy, individualism. He even ends the volume on an upbeat with an essay on community, a concept that he is convinced "must serve as the key to a new social philosophy."

Wolff's central premise is that while liberals have absorbed the sociology of conservatives and radicals, they "continue to employ the assumptions and models of an individualist politics."[2] In his essay on tolerance, he sees pluralism as the last grand attempt to provide a merger of these two perspectives. Pluralist democracy, not imperialism, is the "highest stage in the political development of industrial capitalism." However, like the Marxists, Wolff is quite gracious in his assessment of the historical role of now obsolete social systems:

> It transcends the crude "limitations" of early individualistic liberalism and makes a place for the communitarian features of social life, as well as for the interest group politics which emerged as a domesticated version of the class struggle. Pluralism is humane, benevolent, accommodating, and far more responsive to the evils of social injustice than either the egoistic liberalism or the traditionalistic conservatism from which it grew.[3]

Of course, pluralism has lived out its use. It is "blind to the evils which afflict the entire body politic." In fact, as a social theory it prevents consideration of the reforms necessary for a "new philosophy of community."

Like nearly all the "post-liberal" writers in America, Wolff bases his critique of liberalism on its alleged anemic view of human nature. He insists that all liberals are crude hedonists. No mind that this may represent liberalism, or one variety of liberalism, in its most primitive form. Wolff tells us that "it is thus that a philosophy often reveals itself best."[4] Liberals have a "bookkeeping attitude" toward sensation (a "direct reflection of the bourgeois merchant's attitude toward profit and loss"):

> The term "good," says Bentham, means "pleasant," and the term "bad" means painful. In all our actions, we seek the first and avoid the second. Rationality thus reduces to calculating prudence; its highest point is reached when we deliberately shun the present pleasure for fear of the future pain.[5]

Switching analogies, Wolff contends that the political perspective of liberals is equivalent to fashioning a society of balloons (hedonist individuals) with an expanding gas (desire). Justice in the liberal society involves protection of each balloon's interior and the equal apportionment of space to all. Liberals, then, are not only hedonists but egoist hedonists. And not only egoistic hedonists. Since the object of desire is beyond rational resolution, they are, in political theory at least, skeptical egoistic hedonists as well.

Given this assessment, it is not terribly difficult to predict how Wolff can almost lazily bludgeon John Stuart Mill to death. Wolff's attitude is clear. As a "radical," he regards the difficulties liberals have encountered with Mill with "quiet satisfaction." As a philosopher, he is "irresistibly tempted" to try some analysis and clarification much as a doctor might feel his professional interest aroused by a particularly complicated case of cancer in his sworn enemy. These roles do conflict, however, and one wonders in the end if Dr. Wolff has not inflicted a measure of pain himself if only by way of faulty diagnosis.

The critique stems entirely from an interpretation of Mill as a Benthamite utilitarian: "In establishing this point of principles governing society's relation to the inner and outer spheres of individual life, Mill proposes to rely solely upon the so-called Greatest Happiness Principle which he and Jeremy Bentham before him had made the cornerstone of the doctrine of Utilitarianism." Mill tells us that he will "forego any advantage which could be derived...from the idea of abstract right."[6] From here on in, the disposal of Mill is easy. How can the greatest happiness principle possibly establish that society must never interfere with an individual's private life for the purpose of making him happier! Surely we might wish to refrain from forcibly rehabilitating heroin addicts on the grounds of natural rights or dignity of person. "But can [Mill] really show us that it will reduce the sum of human happiness to cure addicts, even against their will?"[7] Obviously, ex-addicts will relieve the rest of society of fear of assault as well as empathetic discomforts. And the cured clearly enter a new world of pleasure unmixed with the grotesque pain of addiction.

Wolff contends that Mill attempts to salvage "so unlikely a claim" indirectly by advancing the theme of liberty of thought and discussion. Again, the battle between the great nineteenth-century liberal and this contemporary "philosophical radical" is necessarily very uneven. That increase in knowledge creates greater happiness is, for the utilitarians, an empirical question; Wolff all too eagerly points out the fatal flaw in the doctrine:

> In order to decide whether we should permit the growth of empirical knowledge, we must settle a question which is itself empirical, and hence a very part of that knowledge whose value we are attempting to estimate. If we allow the question to remain open until it has been decisively settled, then by that very postponement of decision we have come down on the side of the advance of knowledge. On the other hand, if we close off investigation and opt for a static society, we deny ourselves additional data with which to improve our judgment on the issue. In short, so long as we restrict ourselves to the principle of utility, we cannot deal consistently with the question of the relation between knowledge and happiness. Hence, Mill's entire argument rests on an article of faith for which he advances no argument, and for which no utilitarian argument could suffice.[8]

Anyway, says Wolff, offering one last kick, we cannot even say tentatively that there is a plausible relation between freedom of speech and the growth of knowledge. Take the three sorts of knowledge Mill discusses: religious, scientific, and moral. Religious liberty is a "principle for agnostics." "As soon as I see even a glimmer of a case for any religion, I ought on utilitarian grounds to become as intolerant and persecutory as ever the Inquisition was."[9] Similarly, the scientific establishment is "notoriously intolerant of its own history" and can function reasonably well in dictatorial societies. Only in morals and politics does Mill come "into his own." In these matters, Wolff argues that "the freest possible expression of competing views is called for": "Experience [*sic!*] suggests that a vigorous competition of opposed policies, however disruptive of social tranquility, is to be preferred to the enforced quiet of political repression."[10] Here, at least, "Mill is right." But not, of course, for the right reasons.

Wolff's critique of Mill does have flashes of insight. Religious toleration has always been a difficult issue for liberals. Their distrust of the state has been their only convincing argument for it. And Wolff is right; it has been the secularization of Western society that has solved the issue for liberals, although no doubt the liberal mind has had a hand in that development as well. Moreover, the confidence in the "scientific method" as representing some sort of confirmation of a free society has surely been exaggerated. The euphoria of Dewey and Cohen and even the strictures of the stalwart Weldon seem misplaced today. But has Wolff successfully attacked the central thesis of Mill or even offered an alternative to it? I think not. Here is Mill's *complete* statement of the basis for what he tells us will be his argument for freedom of thought and discussion:

> It is proper to state that I forego any advantage which could be derived to my argument from the idea of abstract right as a thing independent of utility. I regard utility as the ultimate appeal on all ethical questions.

Then Mill goes on to add an enormously important qualification:

> *but it must be utility in the largest sense, grounded on the permanent interests of man as a progressive being.* Those interests, I contend, authorize the subjection of individual spontaneity to external control only in respect to those actions of each which concern the interest of other people.[11]

To view Mill as a hedonist requires not only overlooking this principle but Mill's attempt as well to emasculate Benthamism in *Utilitarianism,* to say nothing of his critique in *Bentham* and the anguish ("like Judas, I have denied my master") in the *Autobiography.*[12]

All of this is not to say that Mill's "permanent interests of man as a progressive being" is ultimately the most fruitful way of resolving the problem of free speech and political authority. His rejection of classical utilitarianism required such a mighty effort that a deep and prevailing skepticism pervaded all his subsequent thought. However, crippled as he was by the onslaughts of competing devotions, he still sought to rescue "from oblivion truth which Tories have forgotten, and which the prevailing schools of Liberalism never knew."[13] I have no intention here of defending Mill. He has no surfeit of able advocates. What must be asked is how different is Mill's structure from Wolff's. Wolff insists that Mill must invoke "some notion of man's rights as a free and rational agent, rather than as a receptacle of pleasure and pain."[14] But surely this is not

Mill's position. He knew, as opposed to the utilitarians, that moral injunctions are not a simple catalogue of pain and pleasure, that they also need to be apprehended, "valued" in order to be understood. Heredity creeds, those not subject to debate, were received "passively" until they are given only a "dull and torpid assent" failing to connect at all "with the inner life of the human being." The final result is that the "creed remains as if it were outside the mind, incrusting and petrifying it against all other influences addressed to the higher parts of our nature; manifesting its power by not suffering any fresh and living conviction to get in, but itself doing nothing for the mind or heart except standing sentinel over them to keep them vacant."[15] Now which view, Mill's concern with keeping alive the "higher parts of our nature" or Wolff's analogy of a "string quartet" in which rights are "madness," suffers from moral and philosophic anemia? And can this spirit of free discussion in search of higher natures be kept alive in the political sphere when smaller associations are governed by different rules? This was the problem Mill saw for democracy. The opinions of the masses are "everywhere become or becoming the dominant power." They are "moderate in intellect" and "moderate in inclinations" and since they take their opinions from leaders any eccentricity is a service. Mill's plea for eccentricity is not quite as silly as Wolff makes it sound. He is less concerned here with variety of dress or outlandishness of opinion than with cultivating the capacity to think with "vigor" and "moral courage"—what earlier writers called "virtue." Naturally, Mill's position is only a plea. It was an outside hope at best to be implemented as a long-term plan and some might say that the caution in which he was to advocate it amounted to an abdication. One direction to which it led has been criticized in chapter 2.

It remains to see if Wolff's "new social philosophy" is much different. One can see his essay "Power" as a preface to his attempt. Unfortunately, it is marred, as are all his later works, by an ambivalence in his treatment of ethics and politics. The immediate thrust of this essay is the evaluation of power in American society. Wolff concludes that "America is not ruled by a power elite."[16] But liberals win only a little victory over radicals in this respect since they rejoice in what Wolff regards as the "moral disaster of

American politics." Much of this assessment is based upon an account of the nature of power. There are for Wolff three aspects to the concept of power: an object of decision, the consequence of a decision, and the social importance of that decision. The object of decision (any event or state of affairs which someone or other is in a position actually to choose to bring about) is the crucial concept. Wolff argues that no power elite exists in America because there is no group capable of deciding matters of major social importance and enforcing their decision against widespread opposition (constitutional or violent). Sometimes, the blame for acquiescence to an unjust society is blamed on the "stupidity and viciousness of the American people." In the end, however, Wolff assigns culpability to the liberal intelligentsia. It is they who in their refusal to engage in the kind of "utopian criticism which can map out arenas of social importance accept a condition of social irrationality which is unnecessary and therefore inexcusable."[17]

Thus far, all we have is this Millsian plea, although Mill would have never had the temerity to attribute an existing state of affairs to the intelligentsia. It is only when we examine fully the nature of objects of socially important decisions that we see the confusion in this position. Wolff contends that there is a "law of historical development." Once a matter of social importance becomes an object of decision," it *never* reverts to the status of fact of nature or unintended consequence."[18] He refers to this as "the law of the progress of rationality" and also states, "...to be free is 'to be the author of one's actions, to act rather than to be acted upon'...." A man becomes more rational "just insofar as he brings within the scope of his will some datum of experience which previously confronted him as independent of his will."[19] Not surprisingly, liberals are accused of celebrating the irrational, not because they emphasize the import of the emotive in human existence but because they view ends as given by feeling and hence not open to rational discussion. Rationality is conceived solely as efficiency; liberal social scientists remain at the level of predicting preferences among toothpastes or presidential candidates.

Wolff's concept of power and the law of the progress of rationality can be interpreted in two ways. In one, the groundwork for modern dictatorship is provided. In the other, one is left with the basis of a liberal state (although it may well be a vastly improved one). Take a common example. For centuries the sex of the newborn has been regarded as the result of chance. We now have the ability not only to find out the sex of the fetus but to predict the sex of a child on the basis of the time of its conception. And, of course, both childbirth and abortions have been made far less dangerous than they once were. Assuming that we are in the midst of a serious population explosion, what does the law of the progress of rationality (one that is irreversible) command us to do? Since rationality "requires" us to transform into "objects of decision important matters which are now the consequences of uncoordinated acts," we must recognize that copulation is really a social act just as is playing violin in a string quartet.[20] In Wolff's analogy, the lesson was that the central problem was not one of rights but the coordination of action and the choice of collective goals. Obviously, the population crisis admits a variety of solutions, and reasonable people may differ. But surely the dignity of the individual must play some part in the calculations so that any opposition to the extension of social control is not regarded as irrational. Surely, we would balk at one-way television sets in the bedrooms of America to monitor and prevent sexual intercourse on certain days of the month!

It is clear that in liberal societies the plea to reject the law of the progress of rationality has been tainted with self-interest. The corporate leader who argues for the virtues of a free and random marketplace often has the system carefully coordinated to his advantage. However, the contention that a rational solution to social problems "requires an extension of collective control" to new areas of social life as even a prima facie recommendation is overdrawn.

In what is the most interesting essay in *The Poverty of Liberalism*, Wolff manages to clarify his position. As a result, he momentarily moves away from the charge that he is advocating the chilling optimism of Skinnerism, but he still maneuvers quite close to the edges of the liberal orthodoxy he so dreads. Wolff admits in his final essay that he has not yet reached a new social philosophy. But he does know where to begin. He is convinced that the "key" is the concept of community, and he promises the kind of Kantian deduction of the concept that he was unable to present for authority in *In*

Defense of Anarchism. However, like the *Defense,* what is so intriguing here is not the use of deduction per se but the manner in which it is carried out.

He begins with what appears to be an Aristotelian assumption. "Men are by nature purposive beings." Wolff's deduction, however, does not require examining the ends humans seek. The resulting image is closer to Hobbes:

> In their choice of ends, men are inclined by their attitudes, both positive and negative, toward the objects, acts, experiences, and states of affairs which might possibly serve as their goals. Men desire, yearn, love, want, hope, need, aspire; they hate, shun, deprecate, abhor, reject. Insofar as a man adopts an attitude toward some object or state of affairs which does, or might, motivate him to act for it or against it, we may say that he *takes an interest* in it.[21]

Values are thus defined neutrally. They are "any object of any interest." There are basically two kinds of values, private ones which are "those liberals assume men to be interested in" and social ones among which are the values of community. When social values involve large groups of people they constitute a "reciprocity of awareness" that is called community. These values fall "naturally" in three categories: (1) "affective community" or shared culture, (2) "productive community" (enjoyment in collective work), and (3) "rational community" or political community.[22]

None of these forms of community is in itself novel either in fact or in the imagination. What is important in understanding Wolff's development is how they are justified. For the first two forms of community—affective and productive—"*no valid argument can be constructed.*" "It is morally permissible that men should choose to shun the sharing of a common culture or the fulfillment of socially productive labor."[23] Cultural and economic forms of community are, then, up for grabs; they are a matter of choice. The political ("rational") community can hardly be expected to foster them since they are morally neutral. Men may eschew them if they like, collect beer cans in one's study while the national bicentennial goes by, or skip out from trade union meetings, and there is nothing that we can say by way of moral criticism. There may be private values and social ones (liberals with their stunted social imagination cannot conceive of the latter), but, since all values are interests, how can we deny the pursuit of some rather than others? A rational community, that intrinsic love of discourse for social decision, must preside over this sea of interests, some private, some social. Do we have here anything more than American pluralism with a slightly expanded sphere of what Dahl called political professionals who devote themselves to public service at least in part for the fun of it? There had been some very brave talk in Wolff's essay on power about the need for radical utopian criticism as opposed to the practical reformism of liberal societies. But is it any wonder that those who preside over such variety of equally "morally permissible" "interests" should resemble Levi-Strauss's bricoleours more than talkative and confident social engineers? Wolff cannot even give a justification of the value of a rational community although, at this point, he does believe that an a priori demonstration can eventually be given.

In the end, *The Poverty of Liberalism* restates liberal hopes under another name and with a post-liberal vocabulary.

In Defense of Anarchism created something of a storm upon its publication. There are a score of articles and at least one full-length book denouncing it.[24] It became for political philosophers what a British friend referred to as that "terrible little book." But the *Defense* is much more important for what it leaves out.

The book's entire argument rests upon the delineation of two concepts, authority and autonomy. Wolff manages to define each through the other. It is only when we force them apart that we are able to see that the book's conclusion that "philosophical anarchism would seem to be the only reasonable political belief for an enlightened man" is based upon the acceptance of Wolff's apparent intentions and the reader's inclusion of traditional anarchist criteria into the concepts. Of course, reliance upon either is not logically compelling.

Wolff does give the skeptical reader a cue, however, in his preface: "I have been forced to assume a number of very important propositions about the nature, sources, and limits of moral obligation. To put it bluntly, I have simply taken for granted an entire ethical theory."[25] He promises a full-scale work in the "reasonably near future." But how can Wolff possibly manage to construct a defense of anarchism, one of the most bold steps a modern political theorist can undertake, with anything less? Nearly all anarchists have been the most demanding moralists and the most well-read sociologists. The vehicle for such a shortcut is the Kantian deduction. Deductions of empirical concepts consist simply in pointing out instances of objects that refer to the concept. But nonempirical concepts are different, and deductions must proceed in a different manner. "All normative concepts are non-empirical, for they refer to what ought to be rather than to what is."[26] Political philosophy must, then, demonstrate by an "a priori argument that there are forms of human community in which some men have a moral right to rule."[27]

There are several significant problems left unexamined in this approach. First, the rigid distinction between concepts amenable to empirical validation and those that are not is a positivist assumption and a unreconstructed positivism as well. As early as 1956, Waisman pointed out the open textures of concepts, even the most commonsense ones. Certainly the deduction of the concept of *horse* consists in more than exhibiting a horse. On what basis did we arrive at the concept of *horse* and how is that related to our entire classificatory scheme of animal life? How do we distinguish a "real" horse from a statue or a mechanized one or a donkey? While this is not the place to settle the extraordinarily difficult problems of fact and value, a stern separation raises as many problems as it solves. Yet, the normative deduction of authority is achieved by precisely this kind of sleight of hand.

Second, why must the concept of normative authority involve the proof that some men have a *moral* right to rule? There are innumerable normative concepts that are not moral ones. Of course, it could be said that no human community can survive without some sense of morality and, therefore, a deduction of the concept of the state must necessarily involve a moral dimension. This is a persuasive argument but it is, broadly speaking, at least an empirical one. It requires an examination of various societies or at least the concept of different social arrangements. Or, Wolff could have said that the concept of authority is legitimate provided that it rests upon the acceptance of moral truths independently arrived at, truths discovered, to use Mill's words, inside and not outside the mind. However, such a position involves constructing a political and social system that not only discourages torpid assent but also relies upon the belief that there is, in fact, a single valid set of moral truths capable of discovery. Wolff comes close to adopting the second view when he offers the utopian community as an example of the authority problem resolved: "A community of persons inspired by some all-absorbing religious or secular ideal might find itself so completely in agreement on the goals of the community and the means for achieving them that decisions could be taken on all major questions by a method of consensus."[28] Of course, here Wolff remains skeptical on empirical grounds. Eventually, factions will appear. What is important, however, is his belief that any set of moral beliefs will do, so long as they are mutually agreed upon. One begins to wonder if it is not the concept of autonomy per se that prevents the deduction of authority, but Wolff's belief, now suppressed, is that the results of autonomous individuals will produce a radical dissension of belief, leaving authority to be represented only in terms of a command structure.

A look at the concept of autonomy as presented by Wolff will show little to disconfirm such a suspicion. The autonomous individual takes responsibility for his actions which, in a strong interpretation of that phrase, entails attempting to determine what one ought to do. There is, quite rightly, no assumption of infallibility in this formulation but one is not very clear about other restrictions. Wolff contends that the responsible man is not "capricious or anarchic." Wolff does acknowledge being bound by moral constraints. However, even without specifying any direct substantive criteria, he leaves his autonomous man perilously close to capriciousness. He notes that he may listen to advice. But is the individual who constantly makes judgments "off the top of his head" in regard to the great issues of the day as well as crucial personal ones truly autonomous? Either he is recklessly irresponsible, deciding the fates of others on whim, or, more likely, moved by unexamined prejudices accumulated over time like barnacles.

By failing to ask how moral principles are learned, what are the possibilities for acting responsibly in the modern world, how one is able to distinguish self-interest from morality, Wolff has gone far to continue autonomy's bad reputation. With as many unanswered questions as these it is no small wonder that few "rational men" would wish to risk life in an association that guaranteed moral autonomy. The reason for such reluctance is that Wolff, the post-positivist philosopher, has used a positivist account of morality to reduce authority to sheer command. At this point, Wolff has accepted neither a Hobbesian nor a Marxian account of morality. Neither false consciousness nor insatiable appetite prevents the immediate attainment of anarchist society. What does thwart it, although Wolff does not say so here, is the belief in a gray void that is in the center of all moral systems. At their base, they all rest upon unjustifiable premises, beyond rationality, beyond goodwill, beyond what Nietzsche called "good and evil." In the face of such an image, determination steps in to fill the void and the sole function of morality is, ironically, its social use.

The Autonomy of Reason is probably Wolff's best book. It is a labored exegesis of Kant's *Ground of the Metaphysic of Morals.* Sometimes Wolff marvels at the intricate arguments of Kant, sometimes he is puzzled, and occasionally he is critical. But he is always respectful and, frequently, illuminating. A discussion of the accuracy of Wolff's interpretation of Kant is not necessary here. His basic judgment appears to be the conventional one. Wolff is of more interest than Kant. Those that looked for the presupposed moral theory promised in the *Defense* are told that meeting that commitment is still forthcoming. Wolff says he has much further to go. Actually, there is less left of the remaining journey than Wolff imagines.

The book's conclusion tells what is right with Kant and what is wrong. Kant's "great achievement" is "his analysis of the nature of rational agency." The "will," the stumbling block of even Kant's sympathizers, is simply a description of causality, the conception of the connection between a self-defined end and the behavior consistent with that end. Shades of "liberal" social science? Wait, there is even more to come. Kant also acutely articulated the conflict between natural and rational interpretations of human behavior. Behavior, the same behavior, can be explained psychologically and predicted statistically as well as issuing from the autonomous action of practical reason. Aside from this, Wolff finds comfort in Kant's Kingdom of Ends. Once its membership is conceived in terms of rational agents rather than in the nature of reason, "some of the elements of a theory of rational community and, thereby, of the origins of moral and political obligation" emerge.[29]

Even with these hymns to Kant are found subtle indications of Wolff's direction. The will is not a mental faculty—"indeed, is not the name of anything at all"—the free will-determinism distinction is not resolved by Kant adequately, and the concept of reason in the Kingdom of Ends needs to be reduced to rational agents. How much of Kant is left? Was Wolff's preoccupation with this great philosopher a gamble that he lost? Was his wager that discovery could only come from philosophical reconstruction a successful one? Again, as with all Wolff's works, one wonders. One wonders if Wolff is headed in the direction he thinks he is.

The section "What is Wrong in the Groundwork?" is truly astonishing. The most acerbic critic of Kant could not have arrived at more damning conclusions. Kant failed to establish substantive moral principles from the Categorical Imperative. This much is conventional. Many writers have appraised this grand effort and found the Categorical Imperative to be simply too weak for the burden assigned to it. But Wolff states: "The truth of the matter, I think, is that Kant fails to find a plausible argument for the validity of substantive moral principles because there simply are no such principles!"[30] No modern positivist, not A. J. Ayer, not T. D. Weldon, not Felix Oppenheim, not Herbert Simon, none could have said it more clearly! And there is still more. The second tenet of Kant's moral philosophy that must be rejected is his account of the relationship between the rational and affective elements in man:

> The drama of conscience must be construed, as, in fact, later psychologists and sociologists have construed it as a causally determined psychocultural phenomenon....It ought to be possible to predict the socioeconomic and historical circumstances in which persons of strong conscience will appear, to predict the forms that their internal struggles will take, and even, if science were sufficiently successful, to predict the outcomes of particular conflicts between conscience and temptation.[31]

Wolff has gone beyond liberal social science now; he is in the camp of Bentham and the Skinnerites, smartly throwing daggers into soft-headed liberal concepts of freedom and dignity. It is "sentimental" of us to deny that all behavior, "anti-social" and "social," is rooted in the circumstances of heredity and childhood environment.

Just as in *The Poverty of Liberalism* and in *The Defense,* Wolff offers only a few tantalizing passages on his next embarkation. He still is a "long way" from a "full-scale theory" of morality and politics, but the digestion of Kant has now allowed him to see the direction in which "enlightenment" can be found. Needless to say, this involves "some significant revision" of his commitment to anarchism.

In the *Defense,* Wolff argued that political philosophy was a branch of moral philosophy. He now insists that that statement is still true, but his new perspective allows us to speak of branches only in the broadest metaphorical sense. He now says: "There is, at base, no difference between moral and political obligation. All obligations are founded in the collective commitments of a society of rational agents."[32] The distinction, let alone the autonomy of morals and politics, has disappeared in the evanescence of a positivist sky. The political implications are far-reaching and Wolff is able to see many of them. A separation of ethics and politics, even if it is only an analytic one, enables us to judge the purposes of each and ultimately, perhaps, use each to assess the other. Most contractarians want to submit all of morality to reciprocity and the demands of politics. The sphere of moral autonomy may be large or small but it becomes the core of the resulting political system. Both Locke and Rousseau refused to justify a slavery by contract.

Wolff's positivism, however, leads him into wholesale contractarianism. So long as there is no inner core of morality, however small and fragile, apart from the consensus of a community there can be no substantive limitations on political arrangements.

> There is absolutely no substantive limitation to the character of the ends to which a society of rational agents may choose collectively to commit itself. They may choose a system of thoroughgoing, alienating mutual hostility, such as laissez-faire capitalism, or a system of reciprocal coop-

> eration and communal intimacy or, indeed, a system of regulated reciprocal murder, such as the institution of dueling essentially was. So long as the agreement is explicit, consistent, unanimous, and confined only to those who actually participate in the choice of the system, there is no rational, which is to say, no moral ground for selecting one system rather than another.[33]

Wolff still has "moral sympathies." His descriptions of capitalism and Marxism clearly reveal that. However, as a moral and political philosopher he tucks them away out of professional sight where all affairs of the heart ought to be. How strange where "utopian criticism" can take us! Wolff has become one of those skepticist liberals, alternately smug and anguished.

It is always difficult to predict the intellectual development of an active and incisive mind. Wolff's apparent intellectual volatility would seem to make the task doubly difficult. However, the meandering journeys of Wolff do show a pattern, and it seems likely that he will not stay long in the same house occupied by men who exhibit such a different temperament. Liberal skepticism requires either a crusading but negative spirit or a timid one. Wolff possesses neither. After a brief respite, Wolff will be faced with selecting one of two paths. While it is impossible to predict which he will eventually choose, it is possible to describe the alternatives available to him. But, alas, neither will allow him to escape the barrenness and "poverty" of liberalism.

Note that Wolff has slid back and forth in embracing two contradictory accounts of morality. One prefers to reduce moral utterances to psychological dispositions. In his *Poverty of Liberalism,* Wolff insisted upon portraying liberalism as hopelessly committed to moral psychologism in the form of utilitarianism. By necessity, Wolff was a bit skittish in his treatment of Marx. He had engaged in basically the same kind of reduction as Bentham. But Marx had a dialectic built into his system that enabled him to see beyond the immediate pleasure-pain nexus of existing society so that, without pushing things too far, Wolff could avoid a potential dilemma. In the *Defense,* Wolff could embrace another account of morality, one that insists on describing moral statements in terms autonomous to psychology, in this case using Kant's rational agency. From Wolff's viewpoint, this adoption permitted him, by his definition, to go beyond liberalism. He then found himself in an intellectually uncomfortable cul-de-sac. He had not accepted a rationalist morality as anything more than a working hypothesis—a marriage of convenience in his bout with liberalism—and the relationship could not bear the strain placed upon it by political anarchism. In *The Autonomy of Reason,* he discovered that Kant could not get him out, and he slid into a psychological account of morality but insisted upon retaining a now unrestrained contractarianism.

Unfortunately, the moral language of the contract does not mix well with the view of man as a network of motor responses. In the former, one views action in terms of individual calculation, reflection, and choice. In the latter, the only autonomy comes from the moment of discovery on the part of the onlooker. That is why Wolff must certainly push on. But now, after three major books, there is very little room left to maneuver. Wolff rests with the assertion that human beings can be viewed both as psychological and rational actors. But of what use is there in seeing them as the latter? If human actions can be both understood and predicted scientifically and if there is no substantive morality to be found, we are left to conceive of the rational agency solely in terms of our ability to engage in social engineering. Here is where rationality comes in; it can handle the language of the contract by creating the conditions under which people will "freely" choose certain collective agreements. Wolff can become a Skinnerite; his law of progressive rationality leads him in that direction as well. He then would have not refuted Bentham but outdone him! After all, Marx was partially right when he said that Bentham, that "leather-tongued fool," was too bourgeois to see the implications of his own arguments.

Or Wolff can move in one other direction. In its path stands a specter that has haunted the liberal mind long before Marx described its form in the opening line of the *Manifesto.* That, of course, is the genius of Hobbes. Hobbes took the principles of psychological determinism and rational calculation and produced an unbridled contractarianism with a logic unparalleled in Western political thought. He was able to achieve such a feat by using a "key," the principle of introspection which laid bare the nature of human will and permitted its holder to see life as an insatiable quest for power ceasing only in death. Such passion would drive men to voluntarily give up their right to pursuit and would form the mighty leviathan. It is the "Passions that incline men to Peace," and it is "Reason [that] suggests convenient Articles of Peace." "Partly in the Passions, partly in his Reason," man forms a machine equivalent to the Creation.[34] And all is conceived as contract, the product of will and reason, not only the leviathan, but mother-child, husband-wife, slave-master, and servant-lord relationships as well.

Wolff has not found such a key, but he is poking around quite close to the area in which it is likely to be discovered. He is searching for a "purely a priori rational proof" to claim that one has an obligation to broaden the scope of his commitments "with other persons into elements of rational community grounded in collective commitments."[35] No Hobbesian man could choose life in the State of Nature, and, with the key, no Wolffian man will either.

Wolff's journey has been a long and tortured one sparked by moments of vision and nobility of purpose. However, it appears to have ended quite close to a completed circle. Such a journey could no doubt be described by some wag with a greater capacity for vengeance than I with a remark about the poverty of philosophy in the post-liberal era.

NOTES

1. Robert Paul Wolff, *In Defense of Anarchism* (New York: Harper Torchbooks, 1970), p. viii.
2. Robert Paul Wolff, *The Poverty of Liberalism* (Boston: Beacon Press, 1968), p. 50.
3. Ibid., p. 160. See also p. 123.
4. Ibid., p. 140-41. Does Marxism "reveal itself best" in Stalin?
5. Ibid.
6. Ibid., p. 5.
7. Ibid., p. 8.
8. Ibid., p. 10.
9. Ibid., p. 15.

10. Ibid., p. 17.

11. John Stuart Mill, *On Liberty*, ed. Currin V. Shields (Indianapolis: Library of Liberal Arts, 1956), p. 14. Emphasis mine.

12. Could the man who spoke of Bentham as a "one-eyed" visionary possibly be interpreted as a crony of the utilitarians? For a more accurate view, see Isaiah Berlin, *Four Essays on Liberty* (New York: Oxford University Press, 1969), pp. 172-206. Even the left has appraised Mill more sympathetically. See: J. E. Parsons, Jr., "J. S. Mill's Conditional Liberalism in Perspective" *Polity* V (1972), p. 147-168; Herbert Marcuse, "Repressive Toleration" in Robert Paul Wolff et al., *Essays on Toleration* (Boston: Beacon Press, 1963) pp. 48-81. Also see Gertude Himmelfarb, *On Liberty and Liberalism* (New York: Knopf, 1974).

13. J. S. Mill, *Collected Works*, vol. 10 (Toronto: University of Toronto Press, 1969), p. 163.

14. Wolff, *Poverty of Liberalism*, p. 9.

15. Mill, *On Liberty*, p. 49.

16. Wolff, *Poverty of Liberalism*, p. 118.

17. Ibid., p. 119.

18. Ibid., p. 90.

19. Ibid.

20. Ibid., p. 91.

21. Ibid., p. 168.

22. Ibid., p. 170.

23. Ibid., p. 194. Emphasis mine.

24. Some of the most prominent are: Harry G. Frankfurt, "The Anarchism of Robert Paul Wolff," *Political Theory* I (November, 1973), 405-14; Benjamin R. Barber, *Superman and Common Men* (New York: Praeger, 1971), pp. 34-36, 93-97; Jeffrey H. Reiman, *In Defense of Political Philosophy* (New York: Harper Torchbooks, 1972); Kurt Baier, "The Justification of Government Authority," *Journal of Philosophy* 69 (November 9, 1972), 700-16.

25. Robert Paul Wolff, *In Defense of Anarchism* (New York: Harper Torchbooks, 1970), p. ix.

26. Ibid., p. 8.

27. Ibid.

28. Robert Paul Wolff, *The Autonomy of Reason* (New York: Harper Torchbooks, 1973), p. 218.

29. Ibid.

30. Ibid., p. 219.

31. Ibid., p. 221. Compare B. F. Skinner: "Krutch has argued that whereas the traditional view of man supports Hamlet's exclamation 'How

like a god!' Pavlov, the behavioral scientist, emphasized 'How like a dog!' But that was a step forward. A god is the archetypical pattern of an explanatory fiction, of a miracle-working mind, of the metaphysical. Man is much more than a dog, but like a dog he is within range of a scientific analysis." *Beyond Freedom and Dignity* (New York: Bantam Vintage, 1972), p. 192. One would have thought that Wolff might have pondered the implications of such social engineering, especially given his description of Gene Mason's "1984 Revisited" as "chilling." Mason writes that "the reliance on science and technology to solve problems of human behavior have fundamentally altered the pursuit of the ideal and freedom." He recounts Arnold Hutschnecker's proposal to place children who fail a psychology test for criminal potential to "rehabilitation centers" in a "romantic setting with trees out West." *1984 Revisited: Prospects for American Politics* ed. Robert Paul Wolff, (New York: Knopf, 1973), p. 41-74.

32. Wolff, *Autonomy of Reason*, p. 224.

33. Ibid., p. 219.

34. Thomas Hobbes, *Leviathan*, ed. C. B. Macpherson (Baltimore: Penguin, 1968), pt. I, chap. 14, p. 188.

35. Wolff, *Autonomy of Reason*, p. 226. Even Wolff's essay "On Violence," written at the height of his anarchist conversion, contains surpressed Hobbesian elements. The distinction between violence and nonviolence rests upon two elements: a subjective one based upon the accepted uses of force and an objective one based upon those interests that are central or periferal to the individual. Violence then is reduced to a Hobbesian framework of regularity and interest aggregation. The diversity of views on violence in America is the result of the existence of different social groups with "different central interests." "In the complex class struggle for wealth and power in America, each of us must decide for himself which group he will identify with." What do we do once we abandon anarchism as a fruitful exit from this American state of nature? See also "There's Nobody Here But Us Persons," *Philosophical Quarterly* 5 (1973-1974), 125-41 in which he reflects for a moment on the whirlpool he has constructed about him. After noting that we must forge "a new society in which the reintegration of the public and the private into the human whole is accommodated through freedom rather than through necessity," he wonders: "As I say there is a temptation to talk that way. And it sure does sound good. But I confess that I don't know what these words mean." (p. 140).

CHAPTER **8**

The Tyranny of Fraternity in McWilliams's America

The dream of the revolutionary and the bastion of the reactionary, it is a word to conjure with at all times and by all fires.
—Wilson Carey McWilliams, *The Idea of Fraternity in America*

If liberalism's use of its utopian premise has angered many writers who had hoped for more, it has frightened others who hoped for less. Thus it is not a novel observation to note that liberalism has nurtured not only a radical opposition but also a conservative reaction. It is in this context that Carey McWilliams's *The Idea of Fraternity in America* will be examined. This is a superb book. In fact, it is something of a *sui generis* in post-liberal political thought. Lacking the moral geometry of Rawls, Nozick, or Wolff as well as the frenetic energy of Kariel, McWilliams apologizes for the occasional introduction of "rigorous structure" and opts for presenting his case as a "rich fabric" of discourse. *The Idea of Fraternity in America* sits on one's bookshelf like an old friend who is to be consulted rather than studied or refuted.

However, McWilliams can dazzle the reader as well. Confronted with what is probably the best writing style to be found in political philosophy since Rousseau, the reader is so fascinated with the aesthetics of the meandering path of fraternity in political thought that he becomes more absorbed in following McWilliams's trials than asking himself about the justification for the trip itself. *The Idea of Fraternity in America* is a reactionary work, one which attempts to reintroduce the "old words" of political thought: "obligation, honor, authority." Once McWilliams's argument is unraveled, it exhibits all the liabilities of that tradition of political thought. Since McWilliams has chosen to work with a concept that has been the *crie de coeur* of modernity and, more recently, approriated by America's radical academe, it is not so apparent that there is an attempted resurrection here as well. However, what is proposed in *The Idea of Fraternity in America* is a conception of politics that is not only hopelessly inapplicable to modernity (except in a critical sense), but is subject to severe internal faults. None of what follows is meant to detract from the tribute to McWilliams. From a historical perspective, it is fitting and perhaps necessary that one of the masterpieces of political thought in the post-liberal era should be profoundly conservative. But *The Idea of Fraternity in America* represents a curious kind of conservatism. Babbit, More, and Santayana attempted to rediscover a pre-liberal world through an examination of the classics. McWilliams has his Athens, too, of course, but, more importantly, he offers Calvin's Geneva and Winthrop's New England as his alternatives. It is true that both the latter represent determined efforts to find a common public space to establish, in McWilliams's words, "the best city, short of which no failure is adequate or excusable."[1] But who can deny the bourgeois core of the larger vision? Even if we simply acknowledge the place of property and commerce in the City on the Hill, can we ignore that alongside grace stood sin, alongside election stood fallibility? Then there is the question of the use to which McWilliams puts the concept of fraternity itself. Can the concept overcome liberal truths or merely disguise them?

McWilliams has not been propped up to make the critic's kill seem heroic. What follows is fraternal criticism, affectionate and, I hope, demanding.

McWilliams finds a considerable significance in the fact that the idea of fraternity is "a cry that survives the ages."

> The dream of the revolutionary and the bastion of the reactionary, it is a word to conjure with at all times and by all fires. It may in fact be a proof of human kinship that all men find a need to claim the word as a talisman.[2]

Certainly, historical preoccupation with an idea can indicate a basic human longing. But it can also indicate a more prosaic and less pleasant desire as well. As Hobbes noted, deception and confusion are universal constants made possible and perpetuated by language. Fraternity, for all its complexities, is one of what J. L. Austin described as substantive-hungry words. Austin, always reaching for the understatement, once noted the apparent similarity and the hidden difference between the sets of words "These diamonds are real/These are real diamonds" and "These diamonds are pink/These are pink diamonds" and concluded:

> But whereas we can *just* say of something "This is pink," we can't *just* say of something "This is real," and it is not very difficult to see why. We can perfectly well say of something that it is pink without knowing, without any reference to, what is is. But not so with "real." For one and the same object may be both a real *x* and not a real *y*; an object walking like a duck may be a real decoy duck (not just a toy) but not a real duck. When it isn't a real duck but a hallucination, it may still be a real hallucination—as opposed, for instance, to a passing quirk of vivid imagination. That is, we must have an answer to the question "A real *what?*," if the question "Real or not?" is to have a definite sense, to get any foothold.[3]

Now, fraternity is not at base a substantive-hungry word in the way Austin's "real" is. If it were, its use in political discourse would be much more limited. We can understand what one means by fraternity. But fraternity suddenly becomes a substantive-hungry word when we recommend it. When we say "fraternity is good!" we have recommended fraternity without assuming the burden of giving it a substance. The correct response here, as is the case with "real," is to ask what is good, a fraternity of plunderers or a fraternity of saints? It is precisely because fraternity is a substantive-hungry word and substantive-hungry at the level of recommendation that it is especially suited as a concept of political discourse. This certainly explains a good deal about why Martin Luther King and the Dragon of the Klan—two of McWilliams's examples—can speak of "fraternity as high, if not highest, among the relations of men."

The moral neutrality expressed in the idea of fraternity is not total, but the ethical element, while expressing a fundamental idea, is too weak to permit it to stand alone as an evaluation of conduct. The idea of equality works much the same way. Perhaps it can help as an illustration. Political philosophers are fond of pointing out that regard for another as equal to oneself before God or in rational discourse is an essential element of morality. Yet respect for another person does not resolve problems of income distribution, punishment, or conscription without associated moral concepts. Similarly, few would deny that bonds of "intense interpersonal affection" are not desirable elements of any conception of morality or even that morality has little purpose without their encouragement and existence. Yet the fraternity of Leopold and Loeb and the sorority of the Manson girls show us the perversity of "intense interpersonal affection" when it exists in a moral vacuum.

Even more troublesome, because it is not so obvious, is the basic antagonism between the idea of fraternity and the idea of politics. There are several levels at which this antagonism is manifested and the best course is to take each in turn. One is closely related to the substantive-hungry dimension of fraternity just discussed. Imagine a society of satanists practicing their creed in one instance in a fraternitarian polity such as Massachusetts Bay under John Winthrop and in the other instance in a modern liberal society. Even if the satanists avoided such practices as human sacrifice they are likely to have trouble in both communities. Despite satanist pleas of fraternity in the Puritan polity it is certain that the elect would be suspicious of their existence. Measures certainly would be taken to insure their elimination. No doubt the Puritans would not deny their claims to fraternity. In point of fact, their image of "intense interpersonal affection" is likely to be much more graphic and grandiose than the rather pathetic sociology of devil worship would indicate. They would not deny the power or the glory of a fraternity of satanists. The Puritan case would rest on the contention that the powers of darkness must be challenged else they envelop the fraternity of the holy. That they should refuse to share any quarter with evil is entirely consistent with the idea of fraternity and the fraternitarian idea in politics.

The fate of the satanist in a liberal society, at least one not totally given over to the secular fascination with the demonic, is likely to be the same. Certainly, the methods of the liberal society might be less straightforward and less jarring than setting funeral pyres. Income tax audits and zoning restrictions are more appropriate liberal solutions. But the liberal conception of politics, procedural and cautiously limited, still requires a certain personality set to sustain it. The satanist's call for submission to the powers of evil with his attendant beliefs of despising the good and rational make him an unlikely choice for a neighbor or city councilman. Liberals like to think that their conception of politics affords fair treatment for a greater spectrum of personalities than other conceptions allow. The fact of the matter is that liberal politics has its limits of toleration as well. And the point of this example is that whether one's view of politics emphasizes substance or procedure it must of necessity question the nature of a fraternal relationship. When it does, the purpose of political discourse and action involves reaching an assessment, and a frankly authoritative one, about the desirability of the group in question. The issues rarely revolve around the legitimacy of holding "intense interpersonal affections" but around the purposes to which those affections are put and the social ramifications that may follow. If one of the functions of politics is to assess and discourage or encourage certain fraternal relationships, political action goes beyond the idea of fraternal relationship in an important way.

There are other instances in which conflicts between the two ideas become apparent. One can appreciate these by looking at some of the basic characteristics of fraternity. Generally, "intense interpersonal affection" does not develop quickly. One has to share a range of experiences with another over time in order to enter into the joys of fraternity. This in itself places severe restrictions upon the number of fraternal relationships one can enjoy in a lifetime. It also involves considerable (though not unjustifiable) sacrifices in the choices of partners one selects with which to spend a life. Chance encounters with others must be limited to mere acquaintances in favor of nourishing and sustaining existing relationships. New fraternities require the demise of others. Even the most gregarious Hollywood star must limit himself to six or seven marriages before one begins to question the quality of his relationships.

Moreover, the very depth of the fraternal relationships leads us to assume more exacting duties toward our participants than toward the rest of the world. We may feel obligations to help a brother or a friend get out of debt, how ever foolishly he might have managed his affairs. Others may very well regard stern refusals on our part as cruel and unfeeling. Yet this is not to say that there are not limits to help friends and relations. There certainly are. Fraternal duties cannot be allowed to override general obligations to humanity. One does not protect a friend who cold-bloodedly kills a stranger out of a duty emanating from "intense interpersonal affections."

There are then severe moral tensions in the duties one owes to one's comrades and in those one owes to humanity at large. A moral philosophy that does not recognize these misses much of the import of the human condition. They comprise the stuff of which great tragedies are made; the inability of moral philosophy to provide guidance in extreme situations shows not a deficiency but a healthy respect for the complexities of existence. Nevertheless, there are tendencies inherent in the morality of fraternity that are dangerous and need to be recognized. It is no accident that fraternal relationships rest and feed upon a hatred or disdain for those not within their circle. One finds this simply by observing the activities at an elementary school playground for a few minutes. The bond which creates a "special" relationship between members of a group makes outsiders less than "special." Rituals and secrets are part of the apparatus of fraternity. They serve to initiate new members into a new world of intimacy and cement the ties of old ones. As such, the outsider is viewed with polite condescension or disdain. This, in turn, further integrates the fraternal group. Such antagonism becomes more pronounced when it is easy to identify the outsider by his speech, color, dress, or mannerisms. Any fraternitarian theorist must take into account this underside of fraternity. Lifted unfettered into the political sphere where the personal confrontation with the outsider is diminished and a generalized image takes its place, the vision of the right due to humanity at large shrinks grotesquely. The results can be horrific. To the extent to which the function of politics involves an intergenerational resolution of conflicts at a generalized level, the idea of fraternity may function best only as a goad to take into consideration needs that are more deep but also more temporary and smaller in scope.

There are, however, ways in which the idea of fraternity can be cast into the framework of political order. One does so by telescoping the gestation period for fraternal relationships. A mark of human relationships in times of relative social and economic calm is the extreme routinization of lives. Enormous portions of one's day are spent in performing mundane tasks. The time spent grocery shopping, servicing cars, raking lawns, and paying bills leaves precious few hours to engage in the idle talk and companionship necessary for fraternity. Certainly, part of the rancor of youth which is directed at parents results from the small portion of a day spent by those over thirty cultivating meaningful relationships. The young lead less cluttered lives and are ebullient at the untested grandeur of fraternity. Only the power of nature and the polity can alter the plodding path to fraternity. Place individuals in positions of extreme stress, even in survival-testing situations, and the ingredients for the production of instant fraternity appear. Natural disaster, war, and revolution require the complete attention of participants. There is no concern over bills to pay when one is building dikes or charging an enemy. Cooperation is demanded; knowledge of others' abilities is essential for survival; the participant's vicarious sharing of the flush of victory (or the certainty of defeat) is personal, immediate, and uniform. In days individuals know one another better than they might in years of contact in ordinary times. No wonder that old army buddies feel the bonds of fraternity through a lifetime.

Yet the acceleration caused by disaster, war, and revolution is short-lived. Barricade and trench fraternity can sustain a generation perhaps because its memories are so vivid. However, societies slip back to more routine tasks, and one's mind begins to focus upon seeding the lawn. Political systems can sustain this fraternity by initiating new and long wars and finding more internal enemies. When those on the front lines perceive the orchestration involved, however, sadness and fatigue set in. The citizen soldiers have been had. Only the professional, one who fights for glory as its own end, can find succor in this situation. But we all know the kind of situation that emerges when the polity becomes the soldier writ large. And even battlefield fraternity in a war fought for just reasons has its liabilities. Not all men can survive the intensity of its life, and the glories of victory have a different effect on those that lie maimed and scarred from the battle.

Rather than intensify personal relationships, some have chosen to expand the scope of fraternity itself. If fraternity is limited by time and space, the political order can expand both. Men love their friends and families. The polity can teach them to love all humanity as they do their intimates. The "brotherhood of mankind" is politicization of the idea of fraternity as demanding and, ultimately, as futile as soldierly comradeship. Fraternity, like its more general formulation—love—is a transitive word. To love is to love someone. To love everyone and to love everyone equally is impossible. The consequence is to love no one.[4] Yet, to the extent to which fraternity is given a political dimension, even in the smallest of communities, there exists a universalist impulse. The injunction to treat those whom you do not love with civility and decency is a function of politics that for the fraternitarian is hopelessly restrictive.

What appear to be the major objections to the idea of fraternity as a basis for a philosophy of politics have been set down briefly. McWilliams's account is acutely sensitive to these problems, more so than any other writer of this sort. On every point he tries courageously to answer them.

McWilliams denies that fraternity is a "substantive-hungry" word. His denial involves acceptance of a set of assumptions that are so essential that some effort needs to be expended in spelling them out. Somewhat unwillingly, he lays out his definition of, and his case for fraternity in outline form and in the same package. Fraternity is:

1. a bond based on "intense interpersonal affection"
2. limited in the number of persons and in the social space to which it can be extended;
3. it also involves shared values or goals considered more important than "mere life" and
4. is closely related to the development of "ego identity," since it

5. includes a recognition of shortcomings and failure in the attainment of ultimate values, but
6. provides the emotional courage and sense of worth ("assurance of identity") which make it possible to endure such tensions without betraying one's own values, and finally,
7. implies a necessary tension with loyalty to society at large.[5]

None of these seven points allows us to distinguish between the fraternity of saints and the fraternity of plunderers. For that, McWilliams reaches deep, very deep, into the history of political thought:

> In more than one sense, my assumptions are "reactionary," for the definition of fraternity that I seek is an essentialistic one. That is, I presume that there is a nature of man, and consequently a nature of fraternity.[6]

It is clear that McWilliams has more in mind than nature as a biological construct. Nature ought not to be restricted to "biology and the mechanics of inheritance." Even modern philosophy has mistaken its import. Both analytic and existentialist philosophy "seek man's conquest of nature, his emancipation from, and lordship over the world of physical things, and deny his status as a part of nature." Placing quotation marks around "nature" is a tool of attack. Nature is treated as a "foe, an enemy separable from man." McWilliams wishes to assume, "as the classics did, that man is a part of nature and that human nature is a fact which affects the life of men." He asks: "May it not then be possible to consider a nature of the relations of men, a nature of fraternity, even a natural law?"[7]

Now, the idea of nature involves the introduction of a concept whose purpose is to restrict the notion of fraternity by giving it substance. Not all bonds based upon "intense interpersonal affection" are fraternal. Only those consistent with the nature of man deserve that name. The reader must know, then, what nature is and precisely how it functions in order to appreciate the idea of fraternity. Without this knowledge McWilliams's entire argument remains incomprehensible. Here are three possible "translations" of McWilliams's use of nature:

First, by offering the idea of fraternity based upon the nature of man, McWilliams is showing that the distinction between those relationships which are not fraternal and those that are is based upon some intuitive perception of an intrinsic value. McWilliams seems to suggest as much when he says that "those who believed [fraternity] to have a nature" felt it "as an immediate thing." "When we have examined fraternity from that perspective, that perspective in turn may be examined in terms of our own observations."[8] Nature is used here in much the same way that G. E. Moore used the word "good." While particular "goods" can be justified in terms of things which are good in themselves, the concept of the good is indefinable. We can attempt to discover to what degree things possess the property of goodness and determine causal relationships between goods. But Moore contended that the subject matter of ethics is that "there is a simple, indefinable, unanalyzable object of thought by reference to which it must be defined."

> By what name we call this unique object is a matter of indifference, so long as we clearly recognize what it is and that it does differ from other objects. The words which are commonly taken as signs of ethical judgments all do refer to it; and they are expressions of ethical judgments solely because they do so refer.[9]

If nature is the unanalyzable source of all expressions of fraternity then one can begin to appreciate how McWilliams feels entitled to deny that juvenile gangs are not examples of fraternal relationships because their chivalry is "dignidad without the Christian ideal." Yet there are several problems with this interpretation of McWilliams's use of nature. First, McWilliams is not content to restrict himself in the way that Moore did when he was asked how we recognize the good in itself when we see it. Moore replied by saying that "wise men know." McWilliams, on the other hand, does lay down a "path of argument," and he quotes approvingly from Hobbes's method. There is more than "feeling" the idea of fraternity based upon nature. Presumably, those feelings can be analyzed in some manner capable of replication. The basis for such analysis rests on the peculiarity of fraternity. "Gases may be free; they cannot be fraternal." McWilliams insists that "an analysis of the relations between human beings must take into account the primary fact of human, if not of organic, life: the consciousness itself."[10] But surely a recognition of consciousness does little to establish the idea of nature. For McWilliams, consciousness entails volition and purpose. He contends that the true (natural) idea of fraternity contains both purposive and expressive behavior. The absence of either makes us unhappy. No doubt this is true. When a husband comes home excited about a raise he has received, it is very disappointing to be greeted only by an unexpectedly empty house. However, is there something in the concept of purpose that selects some actions as natural and some as unnatural? Purpose and expression again are procedural concepts and to the extent to which McWilliams wishes to rely upon them alone to feed substantive-hungry fraternity, they are food without nourishment. Remember McWilliams has offered an "essentialistic" definition. He wants to make a stronger argument than one which denotes bad fraternal relationships and good ones. Bad ones, since they are inconsistent with nature, are not fraternal relationships at all, at least not to the discerning eye. Had McWilliams stuck to the proposition that nature is unanalyzable but nevertheless knowable and uniform he would have made an internally consistent case. But as it stands, the idea of nature sits between two fences in a yard without a name.

Second, at other points McWilliams seems to suggest that since fraternity represents universal human longing, it is natural to try to secure it.[11] Here is a meaning as close to the commonsense usage of natural as a commonly observed disposition as when we say "It's natural for you to miss your friends," or "Of course, it's natural for you to be jealous." Those dispositions which appear in human society relatively uniformly over time may well deserve to be called natural although one must be especially cautious in designating them as such since many may derive solely from uniform social structures. Yet some natural things we look on with approval; others horrify us. It may be natural for us to wish others ill will and even to want to murder. These dispositions we attempt to restrain. Some of us are more successful than others. However, if we gauged culpability by our thoughts, precious few resist the natural. When McWilliams says fraternity is a cry that survives the ages we can be sympathetic. But, then, any fraternal relation is consistent with nature as disposition. There have been as many fraternities of gangsters in history as there have been fraternities of saints. Both have satisfied deep-seated longings.

Finally, the most likely interpretation of nature is that it does not directly denote either an unanalyzable property of the human condition nor a disposition but that it is a part of a euphemism and, to put it bluntly, a confusing one for expressing a moral point of view. This is certainly what such writers as Aristotle, Aquinas, and even Locke had in mind when they spoke of natural law. Rules derived from nature were moral rules. Locke's state of nature was a state of freedom but not of licentiousness; there were moral laws which governed men. When McWilliams complains that modern political theorists define "relations" by genes and kinship in purely physical terms rather than in terms of "right relations," he is using the old terminology, one which distinguished positive from natural law and practical from right reason.

One of the great difficulties with McWilliams's work is that the philosophy of nature upon which he rests his conception of fraternity is never detailed. It is true that McWilliams speaks fondly of the "ancients." But there is no analysis of classical thought in the way in which Strauss and Arendt use them to approach political problems. What stands in place of such analysis is McWilliams's discussion of traditional societies. The model for nature and the nature of fraternity is to be found among the Humangia, Tipokia, Omaha, Trukese, and ancient Israeli with the help of interpretation by Freud, Hegel, Lorenz, Firth, Crawley, Simmel, and Tonnies! A few pages are devoted to Plato and Aristotle in order to illustrate their appreciation of the traditional society. McWilliams's nature is clearly a sociological construct. He derives "lessons" from the analysis of fraternity in "kinship societies" and the ancient city.

Nature, then, is not a shorthand expression for a philosophical system or even a way of philosophizing. McWilliams's search for an "essentialistic" definition of fraternity resting upon a "nature of man" and "even a natural law" is not to be found in a set of absolute moral principles that somehow represent the order of things. Nature is a word that stands for a way of life. The way in which we must judge fraternity is to judge the way of life of which fraternity is a part. The elements of fraternity are, of course, procedural. What is substantive is the way of life that McWilliams is recommending. When we see what appears to be a fraternal relationship and we are told by McWilliams that it in fact is not one, we are told that although this relationship is characterized by a bond of affection it is not part of the way of life McWilliams is describing.

If McWilliams has been translated accurately up to this point the most that can be criticized is that the idea of fraternity is presented in a confusing manner. But we have sorted all that out. The task remains, however, to judge the way of life that surrounds the idea of fraternity. If McWilliams's way of life is regarded as undesirable or somehow lacking, fraternity again stands alone, substantive-hungry, and not especially particular about from whom it gets its next meal.

McWilliams's critique of modern society is Rousseauan. There are no social groups "with the ability to win loyalty and deep commitment."[12] There is nothing in an individual's life to justify sacrifice. A bloodless rationality prevents appreciation of intrinsic value in social institutions. The corporation does not aim at "a way of life internal to itself...but at the production of a commodity for sale by criteria determined elsewhere."[13] Life is privatized, competitive, and careerist. The result is that despite all the fitful motion no one has mastery over himself. All labor is alienated and intellectual activity is given over to sophistry. In contrast, the traditional society (by definition, societies which take the idea of kinship as a basis for social order) provides an alliance between emotion and vision, recognizes man's needs as a social animal, and unites the "private" with the "shared" soul. The result is contentment. Fraternal encouragement replaces modernity's prudence, and the individual can "run risks he would otherwise shun." Fraternal reproof replaces modernity's hubris; everyone is reminded of the corrosive nature of pride and his "imperfection in relation to the idea."[14]

There are two models from which McWilliams draws support for his idea of fraternity: "kinship societies" and ancient cities. From the kinship society we learn about the movement from "blood" to "covenant" kinship. This allows us to appreciate the primordial character of the idea of fraternity as a means of dealing with the human condition as well as learn about the genesis of fraternal politics. From the ancient city we learn about fraternal politics full-blown. However, there is a serious conflict between the "lessons" that these prototypes offer, and they may well damage the plausibility of the way of life McWilliams offers.

The traditional society is, for all McWilliams's distaste for the term, a post-liberal surrogate for a state of nature. The extent to which the logic of departing from it is faulty indicates a problem in the idea of fraternal politics itself. McWilliams denies that his conception of traditional society is romantic. "Human beings in traditional orders have desires for power and dominance and are often manipulative in their relationships."[15] Yet the conception is not factual. The communality of traditional societies is not "nature" but the result of "massive peril and insecurity." "They are only more conscious of their dependence on other men; predatory man must hunt in groups...." Traditional societies "surround man with iron-clad custom out of individual anxiety, not communal love."[16] Thus blood kinship "is, in fact, a beneficient myth...."[17] Covenant fraternity rests upon myths as well. And secrets can leak. "A hundred conditions conspire to deprive ritual of its impact...."[18] Yet all these "false promises" work toward a way of life that is worthy of emulation: "In the companionship of his initiate brothers, the individual finds an 'unambiguous moment' in which purpose and affection are one, and private and external souls, though not united, are at least fulfilled."[19]

For all this fulfillment, there are, to use Locke's words, certain "inconveniences" to be found in traditional societies. Clan alliances are no substitute for citizenship. Covenant fraternity only works to create a political order. Only the polity truly grasps the idea of politics. While men in kinship societies can be seen to be living the tensions and ambiguities of fraternity, these doubts are imputed by the outside observer. To the man in kinship society, the social order is a constant, so encompassing that the idea of doubt is impossible. It is this feature of kinship authority that led Engels to note that "the mightiest prince and the greatest statesman or general of civilization may look with envy on the spontaneous and undisputed esteem that was the privilege of the least gentile Sachem."[20] The reason for this is that "the one stands in the middle of society, the other is forced to assume a position outside and above it."[21]

For McWilliams the city-state is the remedy. Political society recognizes the shortcomings of traditional norms and requires a belief that there is a law and authority common to all:

> The idea of the polis is based on a law of higher standing than bloodright, one which logically involves a conception of unity in nature behind the multiplicity of appearance and experience. The separation of the "male principle" from blood descent becomes elevated to an explicit status in the construction of the state.[22]

For McWilliams, the idea of politics and the idea of the good life rest upon an appreciation of the genesis of private fraternity which one never entirely rejects along with the search for a "true, natural law imperfectly grasped." The distinction now becomes one of "mere life" in kinship society to the "good life" of the ancient city. The political order is "made to support and aid the search for the true and the good."[23] The citizen is bound in beatitudes of fraternity. Respect for custom and the "new duties" owed one another in the search for the creation of a life beyond it form networks of ties that give off pleasant and, need we say it, even orgiastic feelings.

McWilliams's model now does seem to allow for certain exclusions. Man totally free from custom is a slave of the emotions. Kinship supplies a crucial leavening for political fraternity. Moreover, political fraternity requires the existence of certain conditions: (1) an absence of continuous war and crisis, (2) a small state, and (3) a nonmaterialistic standard of value. The trouble with this formulation is that its conception of politics does not look carefully enough into the nature of the transition from kinship societies. The idea of authority it claims to offer is different from the inclusive and paternalistic one represented by the kinship society and the impersonal and atomistic one represented by modern society.

The place of McWilliams's conception of authority can best be illustrated by a recent essay by Richard Friedman.[24] Friedman draws a distinction between being "an authority" and being "in authority." The former assumes a sharing of a basic inequality between "an authority" and his follower. The relationship is hierarchical. In modern societies, "an authority relationship" may well be limited to certain definable roles (doctors, engineers, professors). They do not seem to converge to society-wide roles, ones which would be called political. This is not so in traditional societies:

> Authority involves the absence of justification (at the level of the particular action or belief in question). But the point is that justification may be absent not because the subject desists from demanding one, but because it does not occur to him that he is capable of evaluating the demands authority makes on him. That is, he may not conceive the possibility that he could stand back from the established ways of society and make up his own mind whether or not those ways are deserving of his allegiance. The grip that the established authority structure has over a person's mind may be so complete that it does not occur to him that that structure could be judged in the light of any standards external to it....[25]

Friedman's concept of "in authority" is neo-Hobbesian. It assumes a recognition of dissension of belief and a recognition that all opinions are "equally 'private.'" Men then set up a procedure by which a designated person has authority to make decisions for society.

The first conception of authority (an authority) is clearly an inadequate one for the good life. Rousseau's primitive man represents a pristine existence. Looked at from the viewpoint of modernity, he is nostalgically virginal. But there is always something subhuman about such primitivism. One's sympathies go out to the modern man, anguished and tormented, pathetic in his attempts to free himself. The docile and ignorant sheepherder holds little more than a superficial attractiveness. On the other hand, the Hobbesian view of authority is equally nonpolitical. Persuasian is rejected; crucial decisions are left to the impartiality of procedure. Politics is reduced to the lowest common denominator; moral judgments, reflective and uninformed, are equally crushed into an arbitrary constitutional machine. The result for Plato was a city of pigs. For McWilliams, the ancient city stands suspended between both specters. Its size permits face-to-face persuasion. Close proximity to the household guarantees an appreciation of the demands of fraternity. The sharing of social roles supervised personally emphasizes human rather than material standards of value. Yet for all its splendor this model of the ancient city represents a real refusal to come to grips with the excruciating problems of justifying political authority. In McWilliams's polity there are no rulers and no ruled. Even power in its feeblest form, persuasion, is severely limited since brothers are want to use any method of control too forcefully. Brothers never push an advantage to a conclusion which totally exposes the other.

However, does the absence of authority in the ancient city rest upon supporting structures? What conception of authority (and fraternity) did the female of the household and its servants hold? It is clear that the ancient city employed a conception of authority that was traditional in the extreme for the majority of society. How were "outward Christians" tied to the Puritan polity? How many individuals moved (or were permitted to move) beyond blood right? How many were to learn virtue, in Aristotle's words, solely by imitation of the master? McWilliams is correct in noting that secrets must be kept. This is the essence of the message of the *Republic.* What McWilliams neglects to consider is that the period of nonage is extended indefinitely for major portions of the fraternal polity. For some, secrets are never revealed, fraternal covenants never contracted, and the "true natural law" never exposed to the scrutiny of convention.

McWilliams's claim that the ancients were right in seeing fraternity as a means to freedom and equality may be correct in a limited sense. But it is a grave error for those who share at least some sympathy with modernity. Here, numbers are important to political truths. If the road is well traveled but only traversed by the same few, precious little is gained by an attempt to reverse the modern ordering.

All of this goes far in explaining why the politics of ancient cities never appear "to do anything." The flurry of modern political activity, liberal or Marxist, may well be frantic, like a shivering man who throws books on a fire. This is because modern states have a broader polity, and they seek to use politics to meet very prosaic needs like human misery. The liberal did not invent the stationary state.[26] Every major proposal of a Plato or Calvin is designed to resist change so that political activity remains pure and nonauthoritative, a search for beauty and truth among brothers. Lesser goals are to be managed by elaborate supporting institutions so that politics will not become contaminated by the needs of lesser men. Thus when McWilliams insists that political fraternity needs to be limited to small communities, his polity is much smaller even than he thinks. When McWilliams notes that the Calvinists were "wiser than liberals" in recognizing that because of "the ignorance and carnality of men, error tends to prevail in the marketplace of ideas," he goes far toward picturing the dilemma of the fraternal polity. A broad conception of tolerance reintroduces the problem of political authority, as ugly and unfraternal as the concept is. Ideas must be confronted in all their ghastly variety. Some must be acted upon, and others consciously rejected. Decisions that previously could be relegated to the natural workings of the silent but powerful traditional community must be publicly and willfully made. Political leaders must stand naked, enforcing conduct not just "entertaining each other in brotherly affection" to "delight each other" in "cohabitation and consortship." No doubt Winthrop saw the specter of political authority being perceived by the whole polity when he opposed the movement to enact a "Body of Liberties." Its promotors held it to be their "dutie and safetie...to collect and expresse all such freedomes as for present we foresee may concern us, and our posteritie after us...."[27] Roger Williams, who receives very critical treatment by McWilliams, appeared to be tormented by doubts over the fraternal polity. He recognized that "conscience is found in all mankind, more or less: in Jews, Turks, Papists, Protestants and pagans..." and wondered that in "fighting against several sorts of consciences; is it beyond all possibility and hazard that...I have not persecuted Jesus in some of them?" Williams's eventual conception of authority was to the Puritan orthodoxy much too clear. The polity was like a ship at sea. "Papists, Protestants, Jews and Turks may be embarked in one ship." No one ought to be compelled to come to the ship's worship but the captain ought to "command the ship's course, yea and also command that justice, peace and sobriety, be kept and practiced, both among seamen and all the passengers." If some refuse to perform their services or pay their freight or refuse to obey the common laws and orders of the ship, "the commander or commanders may judge, resist, compel and punish such transgressors, according to their deserts and merits."[28]

Oddly enough, McWilliams's recommendations for fraternity in the modern polity may well offer good advice. Here, his analysis rests just on the edge of resignation. Political fraternity is "impossible in the great industrial states, and even more limited brotherhood is difficult."[29] Modern attempts to found the fraternal city have resulted in "totalitarian nightmares." The "worst errors" have been committed by those who "yearn for fraternity." Desperation produces reveries of "romantic dream of self" and "violence and romanticism are twins." The liberal state is still the best and the only alternative that modernity can offer. "In the modern state, the best, or rather the safest, approximation of justice is procedural rather than substantive, limited to external conduct, and leaves the development of man's justly fearful spirit to other than the state."[30]

The place that McWilliams assigns fraternity in modern society is very limited. He speaks of three moral imperatives. One should recognize fraternity when it occurs, broaden the chance for others, and feel compassion for those denied the opportunity of fraternity. The most important message of these imperatives is to "keep the idea of fraternity alive and its language accessible to humankind."[31] The irony of this advice is that all of it would be acceptable to the most determined liberal. Although McWilliams has separated fraternity from the way of life he advances and has thus made it substantive-hungry again, his caution allows us to see and to search for fraternity in its most valuable form.[32] Precious, extremely fragile, not to be manipulated or enforced, fraternity is like love. Its existence is less an act of will than good fortune. When one has found it, it is to be treasured. But it is far too delicate a thing to be made the basis of political order. Certainly Twain and Hawthorne accepted this as did Jefferson and King. It would be unwarranted to say that the liberal idea that fraternity will follow liberty and equality is correct. However, to say that the voice of fraternity in the liberal society speaks with the softest "whisper" is less a criticism than a reassurance. Should its voice be heard louder, more likely than not it will be heard as a cry of terror or hate. In the end, the dreams of the fraternal and the liberal polity may both become tyrannies. One must choose which nightmare with which to share his slumber. I suspect that, after all is bravely said and done in the assurance of the light of day, McWilliams has decided, like many others, to bed down with the latter.

NOTES

1. Wilson Carey McWilliams, *The Idea of Fraternity in America* (Berkeley: University of California Press, 1973), p. 149.

2. Ibid., p. 1.

3. J. L. Austin, *Sense and Sensibilia* (New York: Oxford University Press, 1966), p. 21.

4. See Aristotle's characterization of Plato's communism as a "watery sort of fraternity." *The Politics of Aristotle*, Ernest Barker, ed. and trans., (New York: Oxford University Press, 1962).

5. McWilliams, *The Idea of Fraternity in America*, pp. 7-8.

6. Ibid., p. 5.

7. Ibid., p. 6.

8. Ibid., p. 7.

9. G. E. Moore, *Principia Ethica* (Cambridge: Cambridge University Press, 1966), p. 21.

10. Ibid., p. 6.

11. Ibid., pp. 2, 94, 624.

12. Ibid., p. 70.

13. Ibid.

14. Ibid., p. 24.

15. Ibid., p. 10.

16. Ibid., p. 16.

17. Ibid., p. 31.

18. Ibid.

19. Ibid.

20. Frederick Engles, *The Origin of the Family, Private Property and The State* (New York: International Publishers, 1972), p. 230.

21. Ibid.

22. McWilliams, *The Idea of Fraternity in America*, p. 25.

23. Ibid.

24. Richard B. Friedman, "On the Concept of Authority in Political Philosophy, in *Concepts in Social and Political Philosophy*, Richard E. Flathman, ed. (New York: Macmillan, 1973), pp. 121-45; what follows is not to suggest that Friedman's distinction satisfactorily resolves the problem of political authority.

25. Ibid., p. 136.

26. This is not to say that both do not attempt to find their own versions of the stationary state. The liberal tendencies were noted in chap. 2. Alvin Gouldner has outlined the current attraction of functionalism in current Communist thought. *The Coming Crisis of Western Sociology* (New York: Avon, 1970), pp. 255-477.

27. *Puritan Political Ideas*, Edmund S. Morgan, ed. (Indianapolis: Bobbs-Merrill, 1965), p. 179.

28. Ibid., p. 223. Also see Perry Miller, *Roger Williams* (New York: Atheneum, 1962).

29. McWilliams, *The Idea of Fraternity in America*, p. 65.

30. Ibid., p. 74.

31. Ibid., p. 81.

32. An attempt is made in chapter 10 to dislodge the concept of friendship from fraternity.

CHAPTER 9

John Schaar and the Commonwealth Alternative

We must reject the gods of efficiency and display.
—John H. Schaar, "The Case for Patriotism"

The recent history of the concept of citizenship provides a convenient and instructive focus for the development of post-liberal thought. The post-liberal's concern for a resuscitated political order has led him to reevaluate the role of the citizen in modern society. Two broad images of the citizen have provided the basis for criticism. One of these models may be called autonomous citizenship and the other, communitarian. The first allegedly stems from Locke. The second includes two variants, one conservative and Burkean or Aristotelian, and the other radical and Rousseauan. Nearly every current political philosopher has declared himself sympathetic to one or the other. In the post-war period dichotomies were arranged to flatter the autonomous model. Sabine spoke of two democratic traditions, one liberal and one radical. Talmon arranged two types of democracy, one liberal and one totalitarian.[1] The latter was driven by the implications of "the assumption of a sole and exclusive truth in politics" and took on a "messianic" state of mind. Dante Germino developed a trilogy of "humanisms" that collapsed into a contest between those accounts of politics that called for a "change of heart" and those that envisaged a qualitative transformation (metastasis) of existence.[2] Isaiah Berlin framed his view in terms of negative and positive liberty and concluded that the latter could become a "monstrous impersonation."[3] According to these judgments, the ideal citizen in one polity was reasonable and tolerant, not given over to strong emotions, save perhaps in his devotion to the system which supported such sentiments. On occasion, some issues could engender severe disputes, but the fact that a plurality of values was institutionalized in society prevented recurrent animosity between the same parties. Individuals might rarely act in their capacity as citizens. Robert Dahl formulated this view well when he said that in "liberal societies politics is the sideshow in the circus of life."[4] However, individuals were always free to enter and citizenship held at least residual status in the lives of the population. That such political activity was really only "pseudo-politics" since it was directed in support of the claims of a group and not the entire polity, was countered with the charge that concerted action in the pursuit of a single goal was not politics either. It was fanaticism, action devoid of both realization of the tactical value of compromise and concern with the possible value of other viewpoints. Autonomous citizenship, then, seemed an appropriate model for those that (1) could not make up their mind about what sort of life was best, (2) enjoyed the clash of opinion and accepted a moral marketplace as an intrinsically desirable existence, (3) preferred to be left alone to pursue the kind of life they wished, and (4) feared the consequences of an expanded connection between morality and politics. A political system that held out its arms to all but the most extreme zealot seemed to be an accomplishment of the highest order.

Throughout this period there stood a rearguard movement within the confines of liberal democratic thought that challenged this model. Leo Strauss warned against the "retail sanity and wholesale madness" of social scientists.[5] American political science had indeed given itself over to the morass of relativism, and Strauss could skillfully trace its consequences. Yet, despite his devotion to a classical conception of politics, he was never willing to carry his critique to the American political order. Bloom's eulogy is informative on this point:

> His attachment of the American regime was deep. He studied its history and was charmed by its particular genius. Practically, he was grateful for the refuge it gave him, and he was aware that the liberal democracies are the surest friends of his people. From both experience and study, he knew that liberal democracy is the only decent and just alternative to modern man.[6]

One of his students aptly conveyed the nature of the commitment to the current model of citizenship as follows:

> The Madisonian system (in either its original or its present form) is not exciting. Its politics of moderation, its endless piecemeal compromises among interests and viewpoints do not inspire the mind with noble visions of the political good. But it does operate to prevent many evils. Representative and constitutional democracy may not be the best regime that the mind of man can envision, but it embodies many good things—things most difficult to replace when one has lost them. And this regime provides means by which it can be improved without being destroyed. But it will be neither improved nor preserved if we cannot teach the youth how to reflect responsibly upon many-sided political realities, and how to live with dignity in a necessarily imperfect world.[7]

Other writers in this interlude between World War II and the Vietnam War critically examined the autonomous model as well. In a book that is still compelling, Robert Nisbet described the specter that haunts the modern mind:

> Surely the outstanding characteristic of contemporary thought on man and society is the preoccupation with personal alienation and cultural disintegration. The fears of the nineteenth-century conservatives in western Europe, expressed against a background of increasing individualism, secularism, and social dislocation, have become, to an extraordinary degree, the insights and hypotheses of present-day students of man in society. The widening concern with insecurity and disintegration is accompanied by a profound regard for the value of status, membership, and community.[8]

Nisbet's solution to the problems of modernity can be found in the pairing of terms he offers. To the words "disorganization, disintegration, decline, insecurity, breakdown, instability" would be placed "integration, status, membership, hierarchy, symbol, norm, identification, group"—the vocaculary of community. The belief in equality through participation in power only aggravated the dilemma. It required the full force of the state to create individuals who would regard the status of citizenship as the basis of their existence and hence be "free":

> Only through the elevation of political power to the point where it supersedes all other power and constraints, to the point where it becomes the sole power in men's lives, is it possible to create that scene of rational impersonality demanded by the needs of individual liberation.[9]

Yet once the political community became so exalted, the citizen had no bearing from which to make judgments. Liberated from church, family, and union, from where could one find sentiments upon which community could be built? Nisbet has faith in neither a species-being nor felicific calculus. Masses are not citizens at all but the most discreet and lonely souls. Contrary to current writers, however, Nisbet refuses to regard liberalism with total disdain. "It would be calamitous," he writes, "if the creative, liberal purposes of individualism were to be lost...."[10] Privacy and privileges of personal choice are essential to any good society. Nisbet's account, as well as Strauss's, are not invulnerable to criticism. One wonders how much "inequality" is necessary to produce this nation of citizenship, if the hierarchies are so great as to produce such different kinds of citizenship that some might rightfully be called fraudulent. One also wonders if there are enough traditions left to rebuild the pluralist community.

The current theories of communitarian citizenship are, however, far removed from this view. They encompass an enormous number of academics today, perhaps enough to produce a new orthodoxy on the notion of citizenship in America. Yet there is variety here as well, and perhaps the best way to sketch this position is to begin with the new dichotomies designed to illustrate the differences between the two models of citizenship. As early as 1960, Sheldon Wolin was to present the same categories as Sabine, democratic radicalism and liberalism, but this time the flattery was with the former. In 1968, Robert J. Pranger spoke of two kinds of politics, one of power and one of participation, and the citizenship roles attached to each. The former produced no citizen at all but a "curiously childlike but hardly exemplary creature."[11] Pranger used contemporary political scientists as the focus for his critique and while one had the feeling that behind the attacks against Almond and Verba stood the ghost of J. S. Mill, the thrust of the *Eclipse of Citizenship* was cautious. Parochialism and stupidity among social scientists seemed to be the source of our discontent. Much the same could be said for Bachrach's *The Theory of Democratic Elitism* which posed similar dichotomies, a year earlier. But there were more strident voices.

Christian Bay has been quite courageous in this regard. There were two kinds of politics, one genuine and one fraudulent. Unless politics promised a conception of the public good it was not politics at all.[12] Current conceptions of the citizen ("cheerful, loyal, pliable, law-abiding and basically privatist") prevented the rise of ideal democracy.[13] In later work Bay outlines his conception of citizenship as designed to meet certain needs, the frustration of which create pathological behavior. These needs liberalism either fails to recognize or is incapable of bringing to fruition through politics.

There appear to be a number of elements that distinguish this model of citizenship from the prevailing model of the 1940s and 1950s as well as from its conservative variant.

The universally accepted cure for the malaise of the human spirit brought about by liberalism is an increase in the level and quality of citizen participation. Through political action one transforms oneself from a petty, privatistic individual to a self-conscious citizen:

> The real alternative to bureaucratic welfarism is to be found budding in the experience of men who form communities—whether a freedom school, a community union, a teach-in, or a wildcat strike—to struggle as equals for their own self-determination. Such communities come and go, existing at their best during intense periods of solidarity. But even where they fail to achieve institutional reality, these communities become a permanent part of this generation's consciousness of the possible.[14]

Community, then, is not conceived as participation in a social tradition as such but in the struggle to reject tradition through the united efforts of a group. This, as Hayden noted, is especially effective when confronted with the scent of the hunt (presumably as either pursuer or quarry). In Alan Wolfe's words: "The type of community worth having is highly political."[15] Nor is the devotion to the participatory community designed to retrieve lost or stolen rights. It is designed to be a permanent attribute of life which produces, in the words of the early Students for a Democratic Society, power "rooted in love, reflectiveness, reason, and creativity." As such, the participatory community knows no bounds or restraints. All aspects of social life can profitably be subjected to new organization.

Yet lurking behind the hatred of liberalism and the devotion to politics, which appears to be the driving force of this approach toward citizenship, stands a conception of self. As has already been noted, it obviously is not the self with which liberals are preoccupied, capable of improvement yet marred by both the most persistent egoism and lethargy. It is a self that does not know a purpose save its own liberation.

Kariel writes: "Ideally we would all write in disappearing ink. We would let the sounds fade out, even while resoundingly affirming that for us the members of a community we have no greater treasure, no finer plaything than our words and our sounds."[16] The self's connection with politics is vague but somehow important. The relationship between "self, society and the state" are "deeply interwoven" and the "two great streams of self-consciousness and social consciousness" are "coming together again":

> Our society is filled with people who are ardently yearning and consciously striving for authenticity: moral philosophers who are exploring the idea of "self-realization"; psychiatrists are those who are working to develop and strengthen "ego-identity"; artists and writers who gave the word "authenticity" the cultural force it has today—some consciously influenced by existentialism, others ignorant of it, but all bent on creating works and living lives in which their deepest, truest selves will somehow be expressed; young people, hip or straight, "seeking to get themselves together," determined above all to "do their own thing"; countless anonymous men and women all over who are fighting to preserve, to feel, to be themselves. All these seekers after authenticity are just beginning to learn a fact of life which our first seekers always knew; that whoever you are, or want to be, you may not be interested in politics, but politics is interested in you.[17]

By contrast, liberal human nature and the sort of citizenship it conceives seems a paltry thing. But again, one wonders. Egoism takes many forms and need not be relegated to material consumption. One wonders what this new community and the citizens in it will consume.

Of course, not all academics have succumbed to the fascination of the new communitarian model. A. James Gregor darkly points to a "fascist persuasion" in modern politics that embraces the generation of the American New Left and the Italian Futurists.[18] J. G. A. Pocock has expressed his doubts.[19] Richard Friedman has carefully considered the assumptions of both models.[20] Daniel Boorstin has bravely suggested that America has communities after all. They are just different from the ones our historical sense leads us to seek. America possesses the consumption and statistical communities, transitory and individualistic. Comradeship is based upon the millions of *Lucky Strike* smokers and insurance policy holders.[21] But attempts at a synthesis have been rare. Rawls manfully struggles with liberal and communitarian conceptions. McWilliams's *The Idea of Fraternity in America* attempts to merge the older paternal conception of community with the newer one but the linchpin of an "essence" of fraternity is philosophically too weak to hold such strain. John Schaar is another writer who has undertaken the study of citizenship. His work is ideal for examination. Schaar's writing shows great sensitivity and commitment. He generally avoids the impulse to truculence so common among our colleagues. That he enjoys the respect and gratitude of his fellow scholars and the emulation of prospective ones is so obvious that it is a bit commonplace to even mention. Moreover, his recent work comes so close to the desperately needed reconciliation between models of citizenship that it deserves the most careful attention.

Schaar's most recent essays are all explorative. They include an examination of the consequences of various conceptions of political authority, the failure of contemporary radicalism, the agonizing choices contained in acts of political participation, and interpretations of Watergate.[22] Central to these themes is Schaar's attempt to reevaluate the concept of patriotism. Patriotism is more than one of the battery of "essentially contested" concepts of political thought. Its appeal is less protean since it represents a concept in a way of life that is difficult for other views to appropriate without a good deal of wrenching. That it is no more than an anomaly for contemporary liberal thought shall be discussed. Its roots are too deep in historical development for the patient dissection of ordinary language analysis. Marxists rightly loathe it, and phenomenologists (given the experience of one of their major disciples) wisely ignore it.

Schaar's devotion to its rejuvenation pushes him away from the new communitarianism: "Decent relationships among human beings are problematic. They do not flow from the spontaneous well-being of our essential humanity, our species being."[23] They cannot be conjured up by "moral exhortation." Nor, as liberals would have us believe, do they individually bloom as wild flowers: "The establishment of a decent common history and just relationships of power among human beings is a work of art, specifically of the political art."[24] Schaar refrains from demanding that the identity of the self be co-terminous with the political. He asks only that public concerns come first in our priorities, realizing that while the state evolves from the most noble sentiments it rarely fails to employ the most evil ones as well. Moreover, although by sleight of hand he blames the glorification of an expansionist self on the liberals, Schaar bemoans the fact that the left "lost all coherence" and transmuted social justice into "the baser coin of personal liberation."[25]

But this is no bemused conservative analysis. The renewal of the concept of patriotism in America is designed to create a "revitalized radical politics." The refusal of the left to seriously consider the import of the patriotic idea led to an unrestrained hubris that prevented tapping into the wisdom of the American political tradition. By implication, it left the idea of patriotism dormant, ready to be dredged up by the forces of reaction and united with its "bloody brother," nationalism. The recent American left, disillusioned by the promise of a liberal society, reached for Marxism, liberalism's stepbrother, instead of looking even further back in history.

Schaar speaks of varieties of patriotism. "Natural" patriotism focuses upon the land, "the love of one's homeplace." We become devoted to "the people, places and ways that nurture us and what is familiar and nurturing seem also naturally right."[26] For love for our surroundings, we learn the idea of reverence," which defines life by its debts." The wisdom accrued here is preserved for us only in American letters. Only Faulkner, Frost, and Wilson wrote in the language of natural patriotism.

Instinctive patriotism, the love of one's city, while it once consumed the attention of classical political philosophers, is but a memory. The closest modern equivalent is devotion to sports teams. Even the shrunken analogy is largely inapplicable. Local gods never moved at the behest of corporate management. What remains is not patriotism, love of one's country, but nationalism. Somewhere along the road, the latter fought and defeated the patriotic idea. Nationalism rests on its ruins and grotesquely nurtures from it. Schaar is very sensitive to the belief that patriotism and nationalism are allied concepts. That the two are "warp and woof" is a belief that is composed of "genuine objections" and held by "many thoughtful people." Schaar, however, believes differently. Each owes its intelligibility to different vocabularies, indeed, to different world views. Nationalism is based upon an inhuman "instrumental rationality." Its god is power to be used to systematically convert the world into economic and political resources. Patriotism reflects other "modes of knowledge" that are "rich in memory or history and is solid and sensuous in its texture." The patriot speaks in terms that are "concrete and conservative":

> Its emotional tone is made up of reverence mixed with nostalgia. Such knowledge has little of the abstract about it and is not easily packaged for export.[27]

Schaar's model here is Burke. The anguish, however, is more like Rousseau's who complained that "we have physicists, geometers, astronomers, poets, musicians, painters; we no longer have citizens...." and worried that once national hatred died out so would love of country.[28]

The blame for the rise of nationalism is placed upon liberalism and capitalism. An ethic of competition and mastery in the economic sphere prepared the ground for individualism, the "deadliest enemy of civic virtue." But skepticism regarding all notions of disinterested, public-regarding behavior was not always the basis of American political thought. It is here that Schaar introduces the concept of the covenant community, the lodestar of his conception of American political thought. The Puritan "city on the hill" forms the "center of American nationality."

> Individuals became members of the community only upon acceptance of certain articles of religious faith and morals. That acceptance had to be proved in practice, and to the satisfaction of the guardians of the covenant. Social institutions were designed to encourage performance of

> the covenant. The Puritans discouraged the formation of isolated, private farmsteads and tried to keep all persons in the towns, in sight of each other, and with life centered in the meetinghouse. In sum, membership was not a right of birth. It had to be earned, and was the reward of choice and effort. Institutions were designed to encourage the choice and supervise the effort.[29]

Of course, the "city on the hill" failed. But the "idea of earned membership," albeit now a cheap replica of its original, still remains. And Schaar finds this idea fascinating; "at once universal and generous and parochial and narrow." More and more the profession of republican principles was turned over to propaganda and the loyalty test:

> An American became one who would *not* do certain things: from belief in anarchism, to the practice of polygamy, to joining the Communist Party, and on to disavowing the use of revolutionary force and violence. A nation of strangers, ignorant of the most important things about the man next door, we attempted to assure predictable behavior by requiring ritual disavowals of feared beliefs and practices. The quest for consensus in national politics followed almost naturally—as through patriots were persons who did not disagree, as though patriotism were a matter of professing certain doctrines and supporting the party policies of the day, rather than a steadfast devotion to the founding principles and a disinterested search for the good of the whole.[30]

Covenant patriotism degenerated into a Rousseauan civil religion, a veneration of the nation itself. But Schaar believes that it need not have been so. His model for a distinct and truly republican patriotism is Lincoln. It was Lincoln who captured the spirit of the covenant. Generations of men must remain committed to the principles of the Declaration of Independence. Without such dedication the citizenry will fall prey to the ambitions of a demagogue and lose the nobility of sacrifice to the pursuit of self-interest. For Schaar, Lincoln teaches that patriotism is a "burden and a promise." "It sets a mission and provides a standard of judgment." By setting a principle "it tells us when we are acting justly and it does not confuse martial fervor with dedication to country."[31] It gives America a "teaching mission" in the world rather than a superiority or hostility.

For the resurrection of Lincolnesque patriotism in America, Schaar recommends decentralization ("All power to the Fragments ought to be the catchword") and austerity (reduce luxury and suppress "by moral and education means all consumption of display"). By rejecting the "gods of efficiency and comfort" and the "squalid promiscuity that says anything goes and all desires are equal," we create the conditions for a memory of resistance and tie the broken thread of the American ideal.[32]

No one can pretend to be unimpressed with this analysis. It is sensitive to objections while at the same time attempting to forge a new perspective. Yet there are points of severe stress in Schaar's vision that will not hold. These can be seen clearly if a closer look is taken at two concepts central to the defense of the image of a patriotic, as opposed to a self-interested, traditional, or liberated, citizen. One is the notion of the cultural and political debt that the patriot so willingly acknowledges, and the other is the function of leadership for the patriotic citizen. Since the latter is bound up so closely with Schaar's commitment to the "republican perspective" as he understands it, it will be necessary to briefly review America's flirtation with that experience in the early period of our republic.

In an earlier essay, Schaar insisted that there must be a notion of authority different from both Sorel and McNamara. Schaar, however, appears to have missed in his attempt to find one.

Schaar argues that the patriot lives in a world of reverence which defines life by its debts:

> ...one is what one owes, what one acknowledges as a rightful debt or obligation. The patriot moves within that mentality. The gift of land, people, language, gods, memories, and customs, which is the patrimony of the patriot, defines what he or she is.[33]

This is a far different world from that of Hobbes. He defined gratitude as a "free gift" and insisted that it created obligations only because the giver must have expected something in return. For the sake of peace the recipient must not cause him to regret his actions.[34] The reason for Hobbes's position becomes clear when his presuppositions are examined. Hobbesian men do not form friendships; they have no bonds of affection. Even the relationship of the parent and child (which was to bring a tear to the cold eye of Herbert Spencer) is one of fear. A child ought to covenant with the object of his fear. Since a mother can dash a child against a rock, he owes allegiance to her. Contemporary liberal revisionists write in the same spirit. John Kenneth Galbraith would have us see the purpose of the family as an efficient consumption machine. Parental affection is simply a "convenient social virtue" designed to advance the well-being of those destined to perform unpleasant tasks. Freeing the household by placing it in the hands of professionals can produce a "very great economic bargain" by increasing the productivity of labor and destroying the consumer management function of the family.[35] Similarly, the family becomes an undiscussed appendage in Rawls's effort to further rationalize liberalism.[36]

Here, of course, Schaar is correct. Friendship and love are the stuff from which gratitude is made. That such alchemy can occur only at the personal level is as far as liberalism has wished to revise Hobbes. E. M. Forster, whom Schaar nervously dismisses, saw obligations of gratitude to larger entities as monstrous. Secrets between brothers, chatter with children, confidences between husband and wife must be kept. One's duties rest with those who stand in a "special relationship" to one's self. Neighbors who spy on one another, children who retell the stories of parents to authorities do not exhibit a higher loyalty at all. Without the customary debts to one's friends, there can be no obligation anywhere. Forster hoped he had the courage to "betray" his country in the service to a friend.

The current counterargument, and one which Schaar employs, is that the solidarity of family and friends simply can not exist as an island in a sea of self-interest. Corrosion sets in. Friends become acquaintances; children are packed off to nursery schools, and spouses bring home their anxieties from life in the marketplace and act out a thousand daily private tragedies with each other as antagonists. Hobbes smiles knowingly from his grave as Galbraith and Rawls tinker with socialist equality. But the new wisdom tells us that there need be no conflict between man and citizen in the good polity. Reverence and gratitude carefully nurtured can produce complementary loyalties.

Perhaps the most perceptive proponent of this viewpoint, and one whom Schaar can rely upon, is Gabriel Marcel. His analysis is so thoughtful and humane that it allows us to see clearly the complexities of such an effort. Marcel recounts his horror at hearing a friend's experience with an American officer in a town in Burgundy that had been totally destroyed: The soldier had said: "You should be grateful to us for bombing all this old stuff. Now you can have a clean new town." For Marcel, this attitude is a symptom of a disease grown to epidemic proportions: "There is a growing number of people who no longer recognize their heritage or, rather, who refuse it like a legacy to which burdensome obligations are attached."[37] An awareness of a heritage "can only survive in a certain climate of diffuse gratitude."[38] This conception of gratitude has none of the structure that we are able to see in its common language base. The giver does not know to whom he is giving, and the receiver does not know to whom he owes gratitude. The feeling is much like the one of a viewer of a painting. The sense of gratitude emanates less as a sense of a gift from the individual artist who painted it than from the tradition that gave forth such a creation. Only in this sense does Marcel's conception have a link with ordinary discourse. The ingrate is one who refuses or is unable to recognize the depths of his surroundings.

But what sense of "diffuse gratitude" are we to employ when we contemplate things political? Equivocation is necessary here on several points. To focus gratitude on specific political objects or leaders is to miss the point of a spiritual heritage. Our appreciation might not be directed toward Lincoln or Roosevelt but to the tradition that enabled them to speak to us. The concreteness of the language of patriotism seems to fade into an evanescence. This is not to deny that like its natural counterpart such a sensation is not a precious one or that one who experienced either would feel a real loss without it. But is gratitude made of the stuff that moves men to accept the rigor of "disciplined austerity"? How closely can politics be made to imitate art?

And in what way does the concept of diffuse gratitude apply to those who choose to select Thomas or Bellamy as the focus of their appreciation? On this model, which seems central to an account of patriotism, the dissidents and the disinherited for whom they speak can only be appreciated in terms of the larger spiritual heritage, a heritage formed and controlled by the oppressors. This is the context from which they are able to speak and which makes their actions intelligible. Is the Russian to acknowledge a debt of diffuse gratitude to Stalinism for permitting him to appreciate Solzhenitsyn's *Cancer Ward?* Or is the American to owe gratitude to the slave experience for permitting him to appreciate Ellison's *Invisible Man?* Does Schaar's "language of patriotism," debt-conscious and memory-bound, demand it? In order to be grateful for acts of resistance, are we not also to be grateful for the context in which they occur? If Thoreau's night in jail (Schaar's example) titillates the political imagination, might we not also promiscuously extend our gratitude to slavery and imperialism as well? It is no wonder that some patriots, logic aside, wished instead to wipe the slate clean.

Marcel's answer here is instructive: "My first duty is to reject the lie that after all the disinherited are also heirs." The appreciation of a spiritual heritage requires living "in such material conditions that the human being is not crushed under the weight of care, and that his consciousness is able to develop an awareness of both self and other—and also of a reality which transcends the opposition between the two." These conditions relate to "the satisfaction of basic needs—food, housing and the rest...."[39] The disinherited are then in a Hobbesian state of nature with no heritage at all and it is the task of those more fortunate to bring them home to the safety and warmth of the patriotic idea.

It is here that even Marcel's analysis eases into the world of the paradox. There is "an immense problem of which it is indeed hard to find the positive solution": "How shall the heirs so transform the world of the disinherited that they in turn may share in the spiritual heritage?" Indeed, we might ask if the heritage is part of a system that presupposes that world of the disinherited? And here we reach the dead end of paradox. Marcel asserts that while it is true that religion may be used to veil the realities of exploitation, it is "radically illegitimate" to suppose that conclusions can thus be reached about the essence of religion. "The Christian has simply to declare that by reason of human weakness it is always possible to pervert that essence but, with real injury to the context of faith." The "volition" lies in an even *stronger* commitment to the heritage. Marcel quotes approvingly from Cardinal Newman:

> The stronger and more living an idea, that is, the more powerful hold it exercises on the minds of men, the more able is it to dispense with safeguards and trust itself against the danger of corruption.[40]

The answer to a challenge of the validity of an idea by the disinherited can be dealt with by those sympathetic to the allegation by holding even more strongly to the idea itself! Radicalism ought to be treated by an ever more strong commitment to the way of life which allowed inequities to pile up. No one is more aware than Schaar that "certain peoples were excluded from the covenant, some from the beginning, some later on." How is the idea of covenant patriotism and the burden that is associated with it able to confront such a betrayal? If the standard of radicalism lies in "persuading our fellow Americans that we genuinely care for and share a country with them," are we led to the unpleasant truth that Tom Watson was a better patriotic radical than Thoreau or DeLeon? Certainly Watson captured the ambience of diffuse gratitude and the nature of the "spiritual heritage" of America more concretely than most other dissidents.[41] That Watson peaked his career with the most ugly appeals to racial hatred forces us to ask if the idea of covenant itself as it works its way through American history depends upon disinheritance for its intelligibility. Many have reached that conclusion, of course. More than a century ago, Frederick Douglass concluded that "your celebration is a sham; your boasted liberty, an unholy licence; your national greatness, swelling vanity...your prayers and hymns, your sermons and thanksgivings...mere bombast, fraud, deception, impiety, and hypocrisy—a thin veil to cover up crimes which would disgrace a nation of savages."[42] The point is not that Douglass or Watson was correct but whether the patriotic idea in America can function in the manner Schaar intends. Even Schaar admits that the moral thrust of patriotism is "inherently ambivalent" but reasserts his faith that it is compatible with the most "generous humanism." Between

Watson and Douglass there may be not an intellectual vacuum but an emotional one. This space perhaps may be filled, in Marcel's analysis, by a belief in the divinity of the tradition for which one has committed oneself. But precisely how can it be maintained in a system offered by Schaar that openly speaks in terms of myths and defines those that are "best" as those that are "strongest"?[43]

Perhaps the most unfortunate aspect of Schaar's argument is that he regards his position as decidedly nonliberal and that, in fact, it was "liberalism" that corrupted the covenant. Indeed, if we must look for rogues at all we might be able to point our finger at liberalism in the commercial age, a Hobbesism with a Darwinist mask. Even here we might be mixing cause with effect. There are other forms of the liberal idea in history, and it is a major failure of post-liberal thought to refuse to measure its own political perspective against all forms of the liberal experiment.

In Schaar's favor, however, the appropriateness of selecting that band of American revolutionaries as his model of civic life must be recognized. Here were men committed to a notion of citizenship quite different from the prevailing models.

The conventional wisdom regarding revolutionary thought in America is that it was heavily Lockean (or to translate into post-liberal vocabulary, hopelessly Lockean). However, like all conventional wisdom this belief is only partly correct. Locke was only one of a series of writers whose works were studied by American revolutionaries. That his name was mentioned so frequently may be partially explained by the fact that he was something of an anomaly in what had become a discredited tradition in England. Some writers have even suggested that the prominence of Locke in the writings of American revolutionaries may well have been the result of simple prudence.[44] The tradition Americans borrowed from has often been referred to as that of the Commonwealthmen.[45] However, the tradition extends beyond supporters of republican government and the Cromwellian revolution.

Who were the Commonwealthmen? Recent scholarship has done much to give a picture of their political thought.[46] Clearly they were republicans. But this tells us little about the crucial outlines of their thought. These descriptions might help: devout parliamentarians, opponents of monarchy, defenders of peoples' rights, opponents of commercialism. But what distinguishes them most of all is their belief in a historical oddity called "republican virtue." It is extremely difficult to convey the meaning of this concept, so riveted is the modern mind to both contemporary liberalism and Marxism. Roughly put, it meant love of the people for the polity. It was interpreted, however, as having substantive content as well. Holders of republican virtue were courageous, self-sacrificing, austere, honest.

The importance attached to virtue is best captured by an account of two revolutionaries cited in a recent history of the colonial period.[47] Monarchies are able to maintain stability by two things: the splendor surrounding the prince and the "multitude of criminal laws, with severe penalties." But republicans did not maintain obedience from the "passion of fear." The Commonwealth did not have a complicated system of titles; elected rulers were only "servants of the people" known to all "to be but men." Regime support must come from below. In Adams's words: "Love and not fear will become the spring of their obedience." The question of the day became how liberty could be separated from licentiousness. Tories believed the idea of republican virtue was not an account of how authority could be maintained at all and that it was "clearly and literally against authority." Until the revolutionaries "could give some assurance that...ambition, pride, avarice and all that dark train of passions which usually attend them were absent in America," they would doubt the truth of their assertions.

Two factors combined to give the Americans a wisdom rarely found in the history of revolutions. The first was the belief that America was rapidly following the path set by European societies.[48] Class privileges were beginning to appear; American society was soon to be given over to luxury. Commerce was diminishing the spirit, "both of patriotism and military defence....The more men have to lose, the less willing are they to venture."[49] Those who manufacture depend upon "the casualties and caprices of their customers" and come to live as "mobs of great cities." "Let our workshops remain in Europe."[50] America was in its youth, and "youth is the seed time of good habits, as well in nations as in individuals." Soon, very soon, Boston or Philadelphia would be like London, "submitting" to "continued insults with the patience of a coward." And who can "give to prostitution its former innocence"?[51]

Second, American revolutionaries focused upon the ancients as a source of inspiration. But as Bailyn has noted, the attention paid to antiquity was selective. It rested almost exclusively with the chroniclers of the breakdown of the Roman republic. The works of Cicero, Sallus, Tacitus, Plutarch, the literature of "critical lamentation and republic nostalgia," were the inspiration of the revolution.[52] The warnings were carefully documented and the parallel was never beyond the vision of the revolutionaries. There probably has never been a more sober revolution. The more confident might flirt with the notion that America could easily travel a different road than the one that led to the ruins of Rome and Greece. Charles Lee told Patrick Henry that he "used to regret not being thrown into the world in the glorious third or fourth century of the Romans" but now his hopes "at length bid fair for being realized."[53] On the eve of independence, Paine would object to "yielding the palm of the United States to any Grecians or Romans that were ever born."[54] But the predominant expression was one of "hopes and fears"; Samuel Adams was "infinitely more apprehensive of the Contagion of Vice than the Power of all other Enemies."[55]

Faced with Tories and skeptics on this side of the Atlantic ("We must have Trade. It is prudent not to put Virtue to too serious a Test"), the new Whig trimmers on the other, and haunted by the nightmare of antiquity as well, the American revolutionary asked himself if virtue could be soundly created and maintained.[56]

The conclusions of the American revolutionaries and their consequences can be especially instructive to Schaar's case for virtue, and although any broader study could indicate numerous variations within these themes, our limited purpose can be achieved by merely sketching them.

The martial spirit. Very much overlooked in the Commonwealth tradition is the belief that war-making constituted an efficient and desirable method of sustaining public virtue. Self-sacrifice slackens in peacetime; the preparation for battle provides a focus for the inculcation of courage and frugality. Algernon Sidney, the martyred hero of the real Whigs in England, whose *Discourses* have been described as a bible for American revolutionaries, was painfully blunt on this point: All governments "deserve blame or praise as they are well or ill constituted for making war." Sydney's major argument for the superiority of republics rested upon this premise: the "mortal error" of the Venetian people was their "too great inclination of peace."[57] This theme is expressed in Harrington as well. Its point was not lost upon Paine. The friendship formed in misfortune was the "most lasting and unalterable." A war for independence could fix "a memorable area for posterity to glory in."[58]

The model of Sparta was not an idle choice for Americans. Adams was convinced that a republican polity must have "all great, manly, and war-like virtues."[59] Lee spoke of "honor, property and military glories." Benjamin Rush envisioned a Lycourgan citizen: "Every man in a republic is public property. His time and talents—his youth—his manhood—his old age—any more, life, all belong to his country." Rush, in fact, was concerned that the war be of too short a duration. "A peace at this time would be the greatest curse that could befall us...Liberty without virtue would be no blessing to us."[60]

Habitual virtue. Despite the intrinsic value that a war for independence might have for the fortification of virtue, few Americans saw America as a republic that maintained itself by foraging for virtue in perpetual conquest. There were more settled ways to sustain republican fervor. In this motif, the answer involves a commitment to nothing short of a civil religion. By "recalling the lost images of virtue; contemplating them, and using them as motives for action, till they overcome those of vice again and again until after repeated struggles, and many foils they at length acquire the habitual superiority."[61] The saving grace of this political education, however, was that it was regarded by many as providing a means whereby the people could discern the ambitions of the rulers. Jefferson's tree of liberty which grew from the "blood of patriots and tyrants" was the outcome of a people trained in virtue. Education would make the people "safe...guardians of their own liberty" and teach them "to know ambition under every disguise it may assume."[62]

Republican leadership. The treatment of political leadership by the American Commonwealthmen did much to destroy the inculcation of a republican virtue that looked upon the state with suspicion. That the covenant did degenerate into a civil religion that venerated the state was as much a fault of the original model than any intruding capitalist rationality. Again, classical antiquity provided a source of ambivalence. Was leadership itself a corrupting phenomenon or was it only leadership in nonrepublican government that was at fault? Lycourgos was admired and Nero despised. Could the same be applied to George II and Washington?[63] The function of leadership in Machiavelli remains essentially the same in *The Prince* and *The Discourses.* The only difference is that in the latter it is tempered by a virtuous people. Perhaps, after all, the corruption of power rested in artificial avenues of mobility in society. In a polity that permitted a "natural aristocracy" to flourish, the leader would be a giant replica of the people, without the blemishes of any corruption and with the virtues magnified. In a system of education in which "the best genius will be raked from the rubbish annually," fear of the leader could be replaced with veneration and respect.[64]

Both propositions regarding political leadership flow from America's Commonwealth heritage and can hardly be traced only to the Madisonian model. It is this that makes Schaar's idolization of Lincoln so puzzling. Perhaps a recapitulation of Paine's argument here would be helpful. Paine warned that if independence was not fought for now, when the people had some hold on virtue, independence would no doubt occur later with a different scenario. "It may not always happen that our soldiers are citizens, and the multitude a body of reasonable men; virtue...is not hereditary, neither is it perpetual." If independence is not attempted now independence will come later through the actions of a mob. There will be a temptation for "some desperate adventurer to try his fortune." Without a plan for independence and an attempt to form a government, the "property of no man is secure." "The mind of the multitude is left at random, and seeing no fixed object before them, they pursue such as fancy or opinion pleases." Tories ought to help plan for "a wise and well-established form of government and become Whigs, if not out of virtue, certainly out of prudence."[65]

It should not surprise us that fear of the mob, a fear as old as political thought, should be so much of a concern among these radicals. The mob thinks itself at liberty to do as it pleases. It is to

Commonwealth thought what indolence is to the advocate of aristocracy. Lincoln's comments on this point are central to the problem. Schaar is quite correct in selecting the Lyceum speech as a basis for Lincoln's thought. Despite the fact that it appears to be Lincoln's first major address, it serves as the basis for his later efforts in regard to slavery and reconstruction. Lincoln speaks in 1838 amidst outbreaks of rioting and lynching. He declares the subject of his remarks to be "the perpetuation of our political institutions." While America is at peace internationally and under a government "conducing more essentially to the ends of civil and religious liberty than any of which the history of former times tells us," dangers are "spring[ing] up amongst us" precisely because of our success. This generation found itself the legal inheritors of these blessings: "We toiled not in the acquirement or establishment of them; they are a legacy bequeathed us by a once hardy, brave and patriotic, but now lamented and departed, race of ancestors."[66] Thus far, however, the "powerful influence" of "interesting scenes of the Revolution" upon our passions forced the "basest principles of our nature" to lie dormant. But this feeling "must fade, is fading, had faded":

> At the close of that struggle, nearly every adult male had been a participator in some of its scenes. The consequence was that of those scenes, in the form of a husband, a father, a son, or a brother, a living history bearing the indubitable testimonies of its own authenticity, in the limbs mangled, in the scars of wounds received, in the midst of the very scenes related—a history, too; that could be read and understood alike by all, the wise and the ignorant, the learned and the unlearned. But those histories are gone. They were a fortress of strength; but what invading foreman could never do, the silent artillery of time has done—the leveling of its walls. They are gone.[67]

What makes matters even worse is that while the memory of the revolution still lived and the American experiment was still an idea, the ambitious man was a benefit to the republic; "all that sought celebrity and fame and distinction expected to find them in the success of that experiment." But now "the experiment is successful"; "the game is caught"; the "field of glory is harvested."[68] But what of the "new reapers"? Lincoln was convinced that men and ambition and talents will continue to spring up among us. The question is: can the gratification of their ruling passion be found in supporting and maintaining an edifice that has been erected by others? For Lincoln, the answer was clearly negative. Some may have ambition that aspires to nothing more than a seat in Congress or a presidential chair. But what of those who belong to "the family of the lion, or the tribe of the eagle"?

> What! Think you these places would satisfy an Alexander, a Caesar, or a Napoleon? Never! Towering genius disdains a beaten path. It seeks regions hitherto unexplored. It sees no distinction in adding story to story upon the monuments of fame erected to the memory of others. It scorns to tread in the footsteps of any predecessor, however illustrious. It thirsts and burns for distinction; and if possible, it will have it, whether at the expense of emancipating slaves or enslaving free men. Is it unreasonable, then, to expect that some man possessed of the loftiest genius, coupled with ambition sufficient to push it to its utmost stretch, will at some time spring among us?[69]

Lincoln's answer to this challenge, the rise of nonrepublican leadership in a republic, was "reason—cold, calculating, unimpassioned reason." Passion can help us no more. And cold reason tells us to formulate a civil religion:

> Let every American, every lover of liberty, well-wisher to his posterity swear by the blood of the Revolution never to violate in the least particular the laws of the country, and never to tolerate their violation by others....Let reverence for the laws be breathed by every American mother to the lisping babe that prattles on her lap; let it be taught in the schools, in the seminaries and in colleges; let it be written in primers, spelling books and in almanacs; let it be preached from the pulpit, proclaimed in legislative halls and enforced in the course of justice. And, in short, let it become the political religion of the nation; and let the old and the young, the rich and the poor, the grave and the gay of all sexes and tongues and colors and conditions, sacrifice unceasingly upon its altars.[70]

There is no room for the right of resistance here. Bad laws, until changed, should be "religiously observed."

From the memory of resistance and the language of patriotism comes cold reason and civil religion. The logic is joined at another level. Ambition is checked by venerating the state, the temple of leadership. Gone forever is Jefferson's charge that "God forbid we should ever be twenty years without rebellion." If Lincoln is in Schaar's words the "supreme authority on patriotism" and if it is indeed a "calamity that his idea of patriotism has been so corrupted and subverted among us," then Lincoln is himself the enemy and patriotism harbors within it the seed of nationalism.

The connection between the acceptance of leadership—in Schaar's words, strong men who not only have views but "are their views"—and the notion of citizenship Schaar advances goes even beyond the implications of the devotion to Lincoln. In accepting the notion that politics is an art, Schaar has more in mind than reveling in or refinishing a product of history accidentally created. Like Machiavelli, his admiration extends to the artist in pure form, acting when everything is up for grabs and order can be created from chaos. The ideas of great actors (Gandhi, Lenin, Lincoln, and Malcolm X are Schaar's examples) may be simple, but they "worked very hard for them" and they are able to think in "mythic terms."[71] For us to pare and qualify these views necessitates assuming the role of the spectator and is an act of condescension. Note that the adjective *great* is reserved for the supreme activist regardless of his substantive views. This is not only because a "mythic mentality" is necessary for action but also because political authority is conceived solely in terms of "humanly meaningful leadership" (clearly a euphemism for the myth creator). It carries "its own principle of legitimacy."[72]

Schaar, however, is a sensitive man. He is unwilling to espouse a Machiavellian or Sorelian realism that permits power to be construed as authority whenever it captures the aspiration of a people whether they happen to be virtuous or corrupt. Mythic authority without the limits of tradition and philosophical reason can be as "pathological and dangerous, and as illegitimate, as the processes of power-without-authority characteristic of modern states."[73] As a result, a sense of despair often pervades Schaar's work. Citizens do not need to hear his arguments and noncitizens cannot hear them.[74] Modernity has destroyed the "established processes and formal statutes" necessary for the growth of genuine authority. Only false prophets will multiply in contemporary societies. Here we have Schaar as a modern Tacitus lamenting the pathetic copies of true republican leadership. Yet, in a sense, Schaar has produced a pessimism of his own making. We need to ask why it is somehow unworthy to question the simplicities of "great" actors. Is it because by qualifying and questioning the simplicity of a myth we rob it of its effectiveness to move men? Surely not. For then we arrive at the notion that political truths are only determined by their function. Is it because when we question we will implicitly refuse to participate as citizens? Of course not; it all depends on how we question. If we read at the breakfast table that Malcolm X says that all whites are devils and we mutter to ourselves how that is obviously absurd and then proceed to open up our rent checks from slum dwellings, Schaar may be right. But if we try to show that all whites are not devils by working in appropriate political action groups or by speaking out against attempts to form disastrous coalitions, then Schaar is certainly wrong. To belabor the point, we ought to be able to say that the early Malcolm X and the late Tom Watson were great men only in the most technical sense of greatness. There must be, we want to say, a way to distinguish them.

Natural virtue. In all fairness to the American Commonwealthmen, republican virtue was conceived less as a result of warmaking, or leadership, or quaint social engineering than as a consequence of simple good fortune. Paine told his readers that however our eyes may be dazzled with show, republics were the most natural form of government and Americans were republicans by nature. This more than any other principle was to give some measure of confidence to American revolutionaries. "Character is much easier kept than recovered" and in fact America may have even escaped original sin: "Rome, once the proud mistress of the universe was originally a band of ruffians. Plunder and rapine made her rich and her oppression of millions made her great. But America needs never be ashamed to tell her birth, nor relate the stages by which she rose to empire."[75] However, the connection the revolutionaries had made between republican government and natural virtue was the same made by the Commonwealth tradition in England.[76] Ownership of land was what made republicanism natural. What made America so fortunate was that ugly class conflict was absent: "the people of America are a people of property, almost every man was a freeholder."[77] Jefferson writes, in parody of

Locke, that "those who labor in the earth are the chosen people of God, if ever he had a chosen people, whose beasts he has made his peculiar deposit for substantial and genuine virtue...."[78] What made this belief so natural was that it was in no small part true. Despite slavery and bondage, America was still very much a nation of the middle class without aristocracy and serfdom. The idea of a political order maintained through a balance of social forces, a notion that formed the core of the Whig tradition, was unavailable to the American. Paine had attacked this "wisdom" forthrightly. A balanced constitution contained two ancient tyrannies, monarchy and aristocracy, "compounded with some new republican materials." Britain was in some measure a free polity despite its constitution. The "plain truth" was that England was not like Turkey because of the virtues of its people. Belief in a balance of social orders was not a question of reason but of "prejudice" and "national pride."[79] Others, however, were not so convinced. Adams was disturbed with the absence of "any attempt at any equilibrium or counter poise" in Paine's plan of government. Jefferson's draft for a Virginian constitution included a senate to which he admitted he would submit, if necessary, a proposal for life tenures.

Although the radicals accepted the position that republican virtue was natural in America, it did not require cataclysmic events for them to succumb to a proposition that effectively destroyed the experiment with republican virtue almost before it had begun. It involved the belief that there was, after all, a strong connection between virtue and self-interest. If virtue came naturally with property ownership and if the perpetuation of virtue could be managed through the pursuit and protection of property, government could assume a placid Lockean dimension. After bouts with inflation and rebellion in the 1780s, the state would lose its comfortable Lockean character and assume the proportions of an embattled dictatorship of the propertied class. The unvirtuous now become the majority, those without property. While Madison's "latent causes" of faction are still to be found "sown in the nature of man," the emphasis is upon the most "common and durable source of factions"—the "various and unequal distribution of property." The problem of republican government is "domestic convulsion" at the hands of majority faction. Gone is the ogre of monarchy, the ministry's secret wishes, and the siren of luxury. The threat now comes from an "unjust" majority, with its "schemes of oppression." Neither moral nor religious motives can be relied on as an adequate control when "impulse and opportunity" coincide for a majority. Nor can virtuous leaders be relied upon for support: "Enlightened statesmen will not always be at the helm."[80] But the effects of faction could be controlled, in part, naturally. America was a large republic, and with a national government at its head it could quarantine the flames of faction until they burnt out. Commercialism, in fact, could be encouraged since it might increase the number of factions and make coalitions less likely. That the purpose of government was announced as providing "for the security, advance of property, [and] support of the reputation of the Commonwealth" in one place and promoting "our safety, tranquility, our dignity, our reputation" in another could be glossed over as only an apparent contradiction.[81] It was not only safe for America to open the doors to self-interest and to let a thousand factions bloom, but it was prudent and necessary as well.

It really is a bit off the mark to regard the Federalists as counter-revolutionaries who sabotaged the American experiment or even to regard them as consistent bearers of the revolutionary tradition. They carried the idea of republican virtue to one conclusion. The anti-Federalists were powerless against it because they were never quite willing to take republican virtue anywhere else. Unwilling to create a Sparta bustling for war or to inculcate virtue firmly in the populace or to rely on a Homeric leader, how could they say their vision should not be filled in the manner offered by the Federalists?[82] As it turned out, it was the anti-Federalists who received the label of pessimists, "men of little faith," who could not see a large bustling commercial republic as a lasting possibility. Although they would have been the last to admit it, it is they who would consent to the Rousseauan lawgivers of the Constitutional Convention despite the fact that their best efforts were directed against it.

If the preceding analysis is correct, and, hopefully, there is some measure of truth in it, it is the Commonwealth idea now advanced by Schaar that gave birth to the interest-dominated liberalism he despises. While it is possible that the liberalism of Paine and Lincoln and the liberalism of Madison and Dahl work reciprocally, it is unlikely that the history of liberalism in American can be retraced, and the spirit of the patriot recaptured. Once seduced by the siren of luxury, innocence can always remain a noble idea but hardly much more than that. As Schaar himself has said in an essay analyzing a recent attempt to revise contemporary liberalism:

> For a very long time now, men in liberal states have been conditioned to want *more* and to regard more as their right.[83]

Whether there is an alternative between letting the patriot rest peacefully in his grave and mindlessly digging our own, still remains the central question of our age.

NOTES

1. George Sabine, "The Two Democratic Traditions," *Philosophical Review* 61 (1952), 451-74; J. L. Talmon, *The Rise of Totalitarian Democracy* (Boston: Beacon Press, 1952).

2. In his more recent book Dante Germino softens his position: "...it now seems to me that many of the proponents of messianic humanism were and are also sensible of these dangers, and as determined as I to combat them." *Modern Western Political Thought* (Chicago: Rand McNally, 1972), pp. 15-19.

3. Isaiah Berlin, *Two Concepts of Liberty* (London: Oxford University Press, 1958), p. 18.

4. Robert Dahl, *Who Governs?* (New Haven, Conn.: Yale University Press, 1961), p. 305.

5. Strauss's critique of American political science in *Natural Right and History* (Chicago: University of Chicago, 1953), is something of a contemporary classic, left unexplored by the new post-behavioral radicals.

6. Allan Bloom, "Leo Strauss: September 20, 1899—October 18, 1973," *Political Theory* 2 (November 1974), 374. See also Strauss's "Liberal Education and Responsibility" in *Liberalism Ancient and Modern* (New York: Basic Books, 1968), esp. pp. 24-25.

7. Harry M. Clor, "American Democracy and Radical Democracy" in *How Democratic Is America?*, Robert A. Goldwin, ed. (Chicago: Rand McNally, 1969), p. 108.

8. Robert Nisbet, *The Quest for Community* (New York: Oxford University Press, 1953), p. 3.

9. Ibid., p. 181.

10. Ibid., p. 150.

11. Robert J. Pranger, *The Eclipse of Citizenship* (New York: Holt, Rinehart and Winston, 1968), p. 102.

12. Christian Bay, "Politics and Pseudo Politics: A Critical Evaluation of Some Behavioral Literature," *American Political Science Review* 59 (March 1965), 39-51.

13. Christian Bay, "Civil Disobedience: Prerequisite for Democracy in Mass Society" in *Political Theory and Social Change*, David Spitz, ed. (New York: Atherton Press, 1967) pp. 163-84. Bay, "Needs, Wants and Political Legitimacy," *Canadian Journal of Political Science* 1 (September 1968), 240-59.

14. Tom Hayden, "Welfare Liberalism and Social Change," *Dissent* (January-February 1966), 75-87.

15. Alan Wolfe, "Conditions of Community: The Case of Old Westbury College" in *Power and Community*, Philip Green and Sanford Levinson, eds. (New York: Vintage Books, 1970), p. 218.

16. Henry Kariel, *Open Systems: Arenas for Political Action* (Itasca, Ill.: F. E. Peacock Publishers, 1969), p. 142.

17. Marshall Berman, *The Politics of Authenticity: Radical Individualism and the Emergence of Modern Society* (New York: Atheneum, 1972), p. 325.

18. A. James Gregor, *The Fascist Persuasion in Radical Politics* (Princeton, N. J.: Princeton University Press, 1974).

19. J. G. A. Pocock, *Politics, Language and Time* (New York: Atheneum, 1973), pp. 273-91.

20. Richard Friedman, "On the Concept of Authority in Political Philosophy" in *Concepts in Social and Political Philosophy*, Richard E. Flathman, ed. (New York: Macmillan, 1973), pp. 121-45.

21. Daniel Boorstin, *The Americans: The Democratic Experience* (New York: Random House, 1974).

22. John H. Schaar, "Legitimacy in the Modern State" *New American Review* (January 1970). Citations that follow are from the reprint in *Power and Community*, pp. 276-327: "The Case for Patriotism," *New American Review* 17 (May 1973), 59-94; "Power and Purity," *New American Review* 19 (January 1974) 152-79; Francis M. Carney, coauthor, "The Circles of Watergate Hell," *New American Review* 21 (October 1974), 1-41.

23. Schaar, "Power and Purity," p. 121.

24. Ibid.

25. Schaar, "Circles of Watergate Hell," p. 38.

26. Schaar, "The Case for Patriotism," pp. 62-63.

27. Ibid., p. 63.

28. Jean Jacques Rousseau, *The First and Second Discourses,* Roger D. Masters, ed. (New York: St. Martin's Press, 1969), p. 38.

29. Schaar, "The Case for Patriotism," p. 24.

30. Ibid., p. 76.

31. Ibid., p. 72.

32. Ibid., pp. 97-98.

33. Ibid., p. 63.

34. Thomas Hobbes, *Leviathan,* C. B. MacPherson, ed., vol. I (Baltimore: Penguin, 1968), chap. 14: 193.

35. John Kenneth Galbraith, *Economics and the Public Purpose* (New York: Houghton Mifflin, 1973), p. 236.

36. For reviews on this point from opposite perspectives see Robert Nisbet, "The Pursuit of Equality," *Public Interest* 35 (Spring 1974), 119-20; William L. McBride, "Social Theory Sub Specie Aeternitatis: A New Perspective," *Yale Law Review* 81 (1972), 1001.

37. Gabriel Marcel, *The Decline of Wisdom* (London: Harvill, 1959), p. 22.

38. Ibid., p. 24.

39. Ibid., p. 54.

40. Ibid., p. 35.

41. For a penetrating examination of Watson and the dilemma faced by American radicals see C. Van Woodward, *Tom Watson: Agrarian Rebel* (New York: MacMillan, 1938).

42. Douglass accused his audience of "inhuman mockery by asking him to speak on Independence Day." *The Life and Writings of Frederick Douglass,* Philip Foner, ed., vol. I (New York: International Publishers, 1950), pp. 188-89.

43. Schaar, "Legitimacy in the Modern State," p. 324-25.

44. John Dunn, "The Politics of Locke in England and America in the Eighteenth Century," in *John Locke: Problems and Perspectives,* pp. 45-80. John W. Yolton, ed. (Cambridge: Cambridge University Press, 1969); Caroline Robbins, "Algernon Sidney's Discourses," *William and Mary Quarterly* (July 1947), 3d ser., pp. 267-92; Clinton Rossiter, *The Seed Time of the Republic* (New York: Harcourt, Brace, 1953).

45. While it was historically a description of both approbation and contempt, the description "Commonwealthmen" has been used by modern

scholars. Especially influential here is Caroline Robbins, *The Eighteenth Century Commonwealthman* (Cambridge, Mass.: Harvard University Press, 1959).

46. Robbins, *The Eighteenth Century Commonwealthman: Pocock, Politics, Time and Language,* chap. 3; Z. S. Fink, *The Classical Republicans* (Evanston, Ill.: Northwestern University Press, 1962). For the influence of the Commonwealthmen in American political thought see Gordon S. Wood, *The Creation of the American Republic, 1776-1787* (Chapel Hill: University of North Carolina Press, 1969); Clinton Rossiter, *Seed Time of the Republic;* H. Trevor Colburn, *The Lamp of Experience: Whig History and the Intellectual Origins of the American Revolution* (Chapel Hill: University of North Carolina Press, 1965); Bernard Bailyn, *Political Pamphlets of the American Revolution* (Cambridge, Mass.: Harvard University Press, 1965); Bailyn, *The Ideological Origins of the American Revolution* (Cambridge, Mass.: Harvard University Press, 1967); Bailyn, *The Origins of American Politics* (New York: Knopf, 1968).

47. Wood, *Creation of the American Republic,* p. 66.

48. See Wood, ibid., chaps. 3-4. Bailyn has been especially impressed with the American fear that British policies were a "deliberate conspiracy" to destroy their society. *Ideological Origins of the American Revolution,* chaps. 3 and 4 and especially pp. 144-59.

49. Thomas Paine, "Common Sense," *The Essential Thomas Paine,* Sidney Hook, ed. (New York: New American Library, 1969), p. 55.

50. Thomas Jefferson, *Notes on the State of Virginia,* William Peden, ed. (Chapel Hill: University of North Carolina Press, 1965), p. 164-65.

51. Paine, "Common Sense," p. 55-56.

52. Bailyn, *Ideological Origins of the American Revolution,* p. 25. See also *Intellectual Origins of American National Thought,* William Ober Clough, ed. (New York: Corinth, 1961); Richard M. Grummere, *The American Colonial Mind and the Classical Tradition* (Cambridge, Mass.: Harvard University Press, 1963).

53. Cited in Wood, *Creation of the American Republic.*

54. Paine, "The Crisis," p. 164.

55. *The Writings of Samuel Adams,* H. A. Cushing, ed., vol. 3 (New York: Putnam's Sons, 1907), p. 402.

56. John Zubly, cited in Wood, *Creation of the American Republic,* p. 121.

57. Algernon Sidney, *Discourses Concerning Government* (New York: Eaton, 1805), 22, 23. On this point see Fink, *Classical Republicans,* chap. 6; Robbins, "Sidney's Discourses," pp. 267-96.

58. Paine, *Common Sense,* p. 56.

59. John Adams, *Works of John Adams,* Charles Francis Adams, ed.,vol. 4 (New York: Little, Brown, 1851), p. 199.

60. *Letters of Benjamin Rush,* Kyman H. Butterfield, ed., vol. 1 (Princeton, N. J.: Princeton University Press, 1951), p. 52.

61. Samuel Stanhope Smith in *The Writings of James Madison,* Gaillard Hunt, ed., vol. 1 (Chicago: University of Chicago Press, 1962) p. 208.

62. Jefferson, *Notes on the State of Virginia,* p. 198.

63. Washington adored Addison's *Cato* and even wanted to be cast in a rendition. Juba spoke of Cato as an example of "what a godlike height the Roman virtues lift up mortal man." Clough, *Intellectual Origins of American National Thought,* pp. 219-22. On Washington as the epitome of a republican hero see Marcus Cunliffe, *George Washington: Man and Monument* (New York: Macmillan, 1958).

64. Jefferson, *Notes on the State of Virginia,* p. 196.

65. Paine, *Common Sense,* pp. 49, 59, 66.

66. *The Life and Writings of Abraham Lincoln,* Philip Van Doren Stern, ed. (New York: Random House, 1940), p. 232.

67. Ibid., p. 240.

68. Ibid., p. 238. For some evidence of the truth of Lincoln's assertions on this point see Stanley Elkins and Eric McKitrick, "The Founding Fathers: Young Men of the Revolution," *Political Science Quarterly* 76 (June 1961), 181-216.

69. Ibid., p. 239.

70. Ibid., pp. 236-37.

71. Schaar, "Power and Purity," p. 168.

72. Schaar, "Legitimacy in the Modern State," p. 317.

73. Ibid.

74. Schaar, "The Case for Patriotism," p. 61.

75. Paine, *Common Sense,* p. 26; *Crisis,* p. 114.

76. Pocock, *Politics, Time and Language,* chap. 3.

77. Wood, *Creation of the American Republic,* p. 100.

78. Jefferson, *Notes on Virginia,* pp. 164-65.

79. Paine, *Common Sense,* p. 28.

80. *Federalist Papers,* Clinton Rossiter, ed. (New York: New American Library, 1961), pp. 79-80, 83.

81. Ibid., pp. 119, 107. Hamilton saw the former as the means to the latter.

82. See Bailyn, *Ideological Origins of the American Revolution,* p. 318.

83. John H. Schaar, "A Critique of John Rawls's A Theory of Justice or, Does Kant Succeed in Banishing Cephalus?" paper presented at the American Political Science Convention, New Orleans, 1973, p. 31.

CHAPTER 10

Conclusion: Friendship and the Liberal Society

> ...there have ever been...two types of excellence...in the world. There have ever been stern, upright, self-controlled and courageous men, actuated by a pure sense of duty, capable of high efforts of self-sacrifice, somewhat intolerant of the frailties of others, somewhat hard and unsympathetizing in the ordinary intercourse of society, but rising to heroic grandeur as the storm lowered on their path, and more ready to relinquish life than the course they believed to be true. There have also been men of easy tempers and of amiable disposition, gentle, benevolent, and pliant, cordial friends and forgiving enemies, selfish at heart yet ever ready, when it is possible, to unite their gratifications with those of others, averse to all enthusiasm, mysticism, utopias, and superstition, with little depth of character or capacity for self-sacrifice, but admirably fitted to impart to receive enjoyment, and to render the course of life easy and harmonious.
>
> —W. E. H. Lecky, The History of European Models

This book has advanced two claims, each closely related to the other. One involves those who have expressed a disenchantment with liberalism and attempted to move beyond it. The other involves the nature of liberalism as a social and political theory. It has been stated that liberalism's dilemmas are not the ones offered by the post-liberals; that is, liberalism's problems run deeper than appetitive individualism and, in fact, this individualism is but one consequence of (or one solution to) certain beliefs about the nature of society and political order. This claim has then been applied to the efforts of the post-liberals. In fact, numerous theories derived from liberalism's beliefs have actually been found. None of them—scientific liberalism, welfare liberalism, pluralism and Whiggery in their several forms, and utopian liberalism—were unconcerned about appetitive individualism and the disorders associated with it. The diagnosis of liberalism offered by post-liberals has been wrong. It should not surprise us then that their own political theories are in error.

The post-liberal has consciously cut himself off from his own historical roots. For an American, the rejection of liberalism involves a break of enormous proportions. The post-liberal has murdered his father or at least banished him. Some surrogate is hurriedly sought as a replacement. Plato, Rousseau, Marx, Nietzsche, and Fourier are hastily placed upon the empty pedestal. It is no accident that these writers theorize on founding new societies. It is also no accident that the crisis of liberal America for the post-liberal is a crisis of the spirit. There is a great deal of talk in post-liberalism about equality, either the lack of it or its excess. But equality is judged as a remedy for or, in the case of Bell, Kristol, and Nozick, as a consequence of this sickness of the liberal heart. What the post-liberals want more than anything is a rebirth of the emotive in society. It is from this perspective that one must ask if liberalism, even as properly appreciated, can meet such a challenge.

It will be helpful to briefly review the post-liberal efforts of reconstruction. Virtually every post-liberal surveyed in these pages has devised an account of community based upon emotive closeness. Rawls has his "union of social unions"; Nozick, his intentional communities; Dahl, his neighborhood councils; Lowi, his reformist groups; Bell, his public household; Kariel, his networks of playful citizens; Wolff, his rational community; Marcuse, his hippie barricades; McWilliams, his collage of fraternities. Four basic lessons have emerged from these efforts.

First, the efforts of Rawls, Nozick, and Wolff, as disparate as they appear, are based on a singularly liberal conception of conflict and hence suffer from all the dilemmas their accounts attempt to avoid. All these writers posit irreconcilable differences among human beings that can only be resolved reasonably by the acceptance of uniform procedures of settlement. As Wolff has so poignantly illustrated, there is no real substantive limit to the procedures which free and rational individuals might adopt. He would permit societies based upon dueling; Nozick would appear to allow "voluntary" slavery. Rawls must place envy on the far side of his veil of ignorance to avoid similar conclusions. As Hobbes so brilliantly suggested, a conflict-prone conception of the individual may require the most heavy-handed governance. Thus, there is really little place for sentiment in this view. The family, for instance, which historically has been the liberal's safe cul de sac for the affairs of the heart, becomes a useless appendage in Hobbes as well as in Rawls, Nozick, and Wolff, not because it thwarts revolutionary momentum but because it is insufficiently rational.

Second, the efforts of Dahl and Lowi to unleash and explore the ties of the group in the context of a liberal pluralist society are in some ways the most promising development of post-liberal thought. Yet neither they nor their forerunners, Madison and Tocqueville, have been able to suggest how a political order based upon enlightened self-interest can sustain these platoons of sentiment.

Third, the efforts of the liberationists represent less an independent repudiation of liberalism (as Bell suggests) than the attempt to institutionalize a heresy which has long attacked liberalism. Like any successful heresy, liberationism holds to a certain common ground with its parent. The self is merely celebrated *in extremis;* the vision of the liberationist proclaims the same neutrality liberals have touted. It will welcome any citizen, how ever he has sinned, provided he is committed not to the open society of competing claims but to the open society of the liberated self. As such, the liberationist can never hope to establish the community of which he joyfully speaks. What he hopes for is the impossible. He seeks the ecstasy of participation in the whole without the ability or the inclination to fashion the whole itself. The liberationist wants communion without community. Unfortunately, the believer cannot enjoy the joy and peace of holy supper without the church and its bishops and priests who support it. Thus, the liberationist can only offer us the great leaders to forge existential explosions of energy into a new order.

Finally, the efforts of fraternitarians fall into two distinct groups. One longs for the hierarchically ordered society, extending from the little platoons of which Burke spoke to the various leadership rings of society. However, the post-liberals are not anxious to pursue this image any further than troubled liberals have offered. McWilliams is just as eager to cage man's "fearful spirit" as Tocqueville or Weber. Bell and Kristol, unable to fully accept the fraternitarian order, alternately defend liberalism against what they regard as grotesque alternatives and bemoan the passing of a nobler society. Schaar faces the idea of a more Rousseauan order squarely but is ultimately unable to examine the consequences of his own model. Macpherson's fascination with the notion of class solidarity carries him to the verge of Leninism.

It would be unfair to the post-liberal to simply relate the faults of their heavy reliance upon the need for a return to the emotive in politics and society to their own estrangement from America as a liberal society. The alienation is the result of the failure of liberalism to seriously come to terms with such needs. No matter how romantically the communal life is portrayed, there are elements in that longing that beg to be recognized. It may be that liberalism has been living off the capital of premodern institutions and that only now has it come to realize that it has failed to reinvest in a heritage that quietly supported it. There is, however, another vantage point which must be pointed out again. The communal order can represent a stultifying narrow existence. Rousseau was not unaware of the price to be paid for such a choice. Few post-liberals share his wisdom. It is interesting to note as an example the invigorating impact of reading Heinlein novels. Heinlein's heroes are independent, profit-oriented individuals, precisely the kind of men so despised by the post-liberals. Yet these petty enterprisers look positively heroic when contrasted against the systematic corruption of a static order. They think for themselves, carve out a sensible existence in a brutally organized world, and are willing to let others do the same. In this regard one cannot avoid the inescapable comparison to the pleas of the dissident Soviet intellectuals. Their writings are not always clear and free of confusion and, needless to say, they do not posit any Heinlein ideal. However, central to their efforts is a plea for some intellectual space in order to speak or write and freedom from arbitrary edict. One simply does not find that concern in Rousseau or Marx. One does find it, however, in Milton, Locke, and Mill.

Isaiah Berlin once wondered aloud: "It may be that the ideal of freedom to live as one wishes—and the pluralism of values connected with it—is only the late fruit of our declining capitalist civilization: an ideal which remote ages and primitive societies have not known, and one which posterity regards with curiosity, even sympathy, but little comprehension."[1] Is it true that liberalism represents a world view appealing only when it is struggling in opposition? That once its beliefs assume hegemony over society its vision of a plural world will shrink in an effort to reach a conflict-resolving moral settlement. Do its values inevitably become debased by those willing to use them for immediate purposes? Does privacy become a cloak for manipulation and freedom of speech an arena for huckstering? Does its use of rationality breed a yearning for ecstatic impulse? I think not, notwithstanding the point made repeatedly throughout this book that a genuine liberal order in whatever several forms it might appear is an exquisitely fragile form of social existence.

The liberal's search for stability has led in several directions that the post-liberals have mistakenly assumed represent the liberal vision itself. The most common one, of course, is the liberal's desire to fashion a stable political and social order upon some neutral and reliable foundation whether it be enlightened self-interest, an armor of rights or the moral settlement of the contract. Liberals have always believed that the real growth of society could arise independently around these structures. Spencer, for instance, was very fond of asserting the desirability of the natural and spontaneous growth of society. Gentile, a liberal who embraced fascism, derided the notion that a free society could be treated like a plant to be pruned and even transplanted if necessary. Yet most liberals have been troubled by the awareness that those hard, rational principles,which were to govern politics and protect a measure of plurality,would seep into the social order and poison the very practices they were designed to sustain. C. W. Mills once complained that liberals did not possess the political and social theories to match their moral vision. His comment is perhaps more to the point than most of the post-liberals' efforts.

When other writers have been treated with almost unremitting criticism, there is almost a moral imperative to offer some alternative. Criticism, especially political criticism, is a form of close guerrilla combat. Without some open display of vulnerability it can become an intellectual cannibalism. One gorges on the mistakes of others.

Let us begin by suggesting that there is an alternative between the appetitive individualism that is alleged to be endemic in liberal societies and the various alternatives offered by each of the post-liberals. An alternative can perhaps be derived from a brief summary of the reasons for the failure of John Schaar's position. All of his faults stem from a single source. The "republican perspective" of Schaar is too resolute. It is determined to reject bureaucratic efficiency as a criterion for political life and insists upon cultivating a sense of love for tradition. When that tradition proves to be morally ambiguous—as all traditions are—one is led to pick and choose from it on bases other than traditional ones. It calls for an active solidified citizenry but requires "myths" that are "strong," myths that can only be conceived by great actors. Political fraternity is achieved by accepting definitions of the situation forged by others. Even great leaders need be hemmed in by traditions. Yet these traditions recognize devotion and reverence in order to survive, an attitude Schaar is not quite willing to embrace. Thus, we move more and more frantically in interlocking circles escaping one paradox only to slide into another.

Schaar wants us to acknowledge our debts. But, in a peculiar way, his effort fails for lack of a more stern look at America's past. He sees both greed and somnolent self-indulgence all about him and finds their rejection in America's Commonwealth heritage. What he ought to have asked is how are small islands of presently desirable behavior—the efforts of the young, if you insist—related to the political tradition America has offered. His answers would probably have been different.

A brief summary of the reactions of a British liberal and liberal critic, E. M. Forster will serve as an illustration. Lionel Trilling has captured Forster's position well when he said that although all of his work is in the "liberal direction," he is not quite playing their game. "They [liberals] feel he is challenging *them* as well as what they dislike."[2] Forster described himself as belonging to the "fag-end of Victorian liberalism."[3] That age "practiced benevolence and philanthrophy, was humane and intellectually curious, upheld speech, had little colour-prejudice, believed that individuals are and should be different, and entertained a sincere faith in the progress of society."[4] What the liberals failed to realize was that their beliefs rested upon money. "In came the nice fat dividends, up rose the lofty thoughts, and we did not realize that all the time we were exploiting the poor of our own country and the backward races abroad, and getting bigger profits than we should."[5]

Yet despite his awareness that a post-liberal era had arrived, Forster was unwilling to simply declare that liberal profits automatically disgraced individualism. He could accept the necessity of socialist economics but worries about its consequences for the world of the spirit. Economic planners laughed at fears of a new materialist tyranny, and Forster wondered if there was some deep connection between sneering and planning psychologists should explore. He was heartbroken at the government's destruction of a village for the creation of a satellite town for suburbanites. Yet he could still whimsically experience the corrosive effects of private ownership. When he bought a woods with royalties from *A Passage to India,* he tells the reader of his initial reaction to a sound in "his" forest:

> The other day I heard a twig snap in it. I was annoyed at first, for I thought that someone was blackberrying, and depreciating the value of the undergrowth. On coming nearer, I saw it was not a man who had trodden the twig and snapped it, but a bird, and I felt pleased. My bird.[6]

Would he, too, a man of intellect become "enormously stout, endlessly avaricious, pseudo-creative, intensely selfish" and walk in his wood "until those nasty Bolshies come and take it off again and thrust me aside into the outer darkness?"[7]

If Forster had his doubts about private property and socialist materialism, he was certain that the retreat to a vitalistic political order was a mistake as well. In his "Anti-Nazi Broadcasts" he warned against making fun of fascists. What they say sounds at first sensitive and even noble:

> For instance, they say that instinct is superior to reason, and character better than booklearning. I agree. Baldur von Schirach, who was until lately one of their youth leaders: "The Nazi revolution is and always has been a revolution of the soul. It reveals that power which the intellectual will deny, since it is inconceivable to him as is the god who gave it: the power and soul and sentiments.[8]

But Forster asks why does "the soul always require a machine gun"? Why is "character" "an opportunity for brutality"? Why does the "instinct instinctively persecute"? Part of the answer lies in Forster's belief that Germany rejected its tradition, its "national culture," in favor of a "governmental" one. In a speech Hitler asks, "What is it to be German?" and he replies, "The best answer to this question does not define: it lays down a law." The result is "gangsterdom forever." Force comes to the forefront and Germany "shouts and bullies her neighbors" as it does its own citizens.

If we "drop tradition and culture we lose our chance of connecting work and play and creating a life which is all of a piece." The Fascist style produces "madness and cruelty"; the socialist, a realm that is "earnest," "cheerful," and "consistent" but that blinds the vagrant sensibilities and is "not wholly alive"; the liberal, the world of the "black market and the capitalist jungle."[9] The solution for Forster—or at least what passes for a solution—does not involve the selection of a tradition to reinvigorate the body politic. There may not be any surviving remnants intact enough. And in any case, tradition has never represented the complete argument. What needs reconsidering is the purpose for which traditions are followed. For Forster, this implies a return to personal relationships. Note that he does not call for a return to the self either as a bundle of interests or as an imaginative possibility. Nor does he move straight to the glories of community. Eventually, he will give but "two cheers" for democracy and leave aside the devotion to the "Beloved Republic." He gains a "little order" by asserting that "one must be fond of people and trust them if one is not to make a mess out of life." But personal relationships require a measure of reliability. This cannot be managed by the liberal contract—"the heart signs no documents"—nor by republican virtue. "As soon as people have power they go crooked and sometimes dotty as well, because the possession of power lifts them into a region where normal honesty never pays...the more highly public life is organized the lower does its morality sink."[10]

Forster's description of the ideal citizen will certainly appear inordinately privatistic to many. He does not live in a "Beloved Republic" but simply in a society that "starts from the assumption that the individual is important and that all types are needed to make a civilization":

> It does not divide its citizens into the bossers and the bossed—as an efficiency-regime tends to do. The people I admire most are those who are sensitive and want to create something or discover something, and do not see life in terms of power, and such people get more of a chance under a democracy than elsewhere. They found religions, great or small, or they produce literature and art, or they do disinterested scientific research, or they may be what is called (ordinary people), who are creative in their private lives, bring up their children decently, for instance, or help their neighbors.[11]

However, there is none of the harshness of American pluralism here. Forster's citizens are "sensitive, considerate, and plucky." And a few can survive in the most nightmarish political regimes. "Its members are to be found in all nations and classes, and all through the ages...they represent the true human condition, the one permanent victory of our queer race over cruelty and chaos."[12]

Now, in the standard liberal pattern, Forster refused to carry his analysis toward a complete view of the political order. It was a "tragedy" that "no device has been found by which these private decencies can be transmitted to public affairs."[13] That omission is not completely incurable. What Forster managed to do (and no suggestion is being made that he was the only one to do it), is to offer a distinction between the notions of friendship and fraternity. Clearly fraternity is the stronger concept, one more congenial to nourishment and enforcement by the political order. This is one of the reasons that Schaar latches on to it as well as other post-liberals; it seems to provide a clear alternative to the liberal idea of politics. But, because fraternity is more resolute, it has the capability of producing grisly variations. It is based on the notion that personal intimacy and affection is secured by mutual devotion to one or two beliefs. Such beliefs must be firmly accepted else fraternity disintegrates. It begins to lose its bond and adherents feverishly work to re-cement it. Moreover, since affection is based upon common belief, there is a tendency to feel that more and more members can be encompassed by it. The affection becomes less personal than ideological and intimacy shifts and rests with the movement of party or cause. Friendship on the other hand is more diffuse. Friends become so because they share numerous beliefs in common or perhaps because they share few at all. They enjoy the laughter of another or their cooking or their ability to listen. Another's faults are often recognized, sometimes accepted, and often ignored. Soldiers can become instant comrades. Only years later, after innumerable dinners and football games and movies do they become friends.

A good illustration of this distinction can be found in a short story by Flannery O'Connor. A father and son have nothing in common until they discover that they both hate blacks. Race hatred had produced fraternity. But one would be hesitant to say that it produced friendship. This is not to say that friendship excludes all furies. Bands of friends can do horrible things to others and even to one another. There may be no way to create a social model that produces relationships that are automatically good and beneficient. One can imagine two aging Mafioso chatting over dinner recalling how they first met and patted each other's children's heads. The point is this: force is eminently compatible with fraternity since it consolidates its aims and provides food for nourishing the relationship. Friendship is a more delicate, perhaps even a more sloppy concept. It seems to be placed under the most stress by force and is most often destroyed by it. This is why Forster was anxious to keep it in the background or at the least to revel in it in intervals when it has not managed to come in the front. It is possible, at least, to imagine a liberal and a Marxist becoming friends, but never fraternal brothers.

There is one more distinction worth mentioning. Republican virtue, comradeship, community devotion, liberated selves all hold out the possibility—and understatement is used here—of substituting paternity for fraternity. If belief is the nature of the bond, it must be enforced. People must be reminded that they are equal, or free, or publicly conscious, and this requires direction and compliance. The great fraternal polities were all paternal if one examines the entire base of the political system. It is possible to conceive of friendship within paternal structures—mothers and daughters, fathers and sons, protégés and stars, masters and servants—but they are difficult and tenuous relationships (as indeed they ought to be) in which the structure can dissipate to pure friendship or pure paternity.

The importance of the incompatibility between friendship and fraternity can be illustrated from still another source, one to which liberals are not likely to look and one which others are likely to gloss over. Leszek Kolakowski, the Polish Marxist, posing the question of what separates a "pseudo" from a "genuine" Marxism, separates Marxism as an institutional phenomenon in the form of Stalinism and Marxism as an intellectual enterprise. In the former sense, one was a Marxist to the extent that he was "always ready to accept as its content each recommendation of the Office."[14] Marxism here was not a "doctrine with a specific content" but a "doctrine defined purely formally," its context being in every case supplied by "the decrees of the Infallible Institution which during a certain phase, was the Greatest Philologist, the Greatest Economist, the Greatest Philosopher, and the Greatest Historian in the World."[15] But it is Kolakowski's concept of Marxism as an intellectual movement that can illustrate this point. For all of Marx's cantankerousness toward rival versions of socialism it is impossible to imagine him decreeing the linguistic theories of Marr a "vulgarization" of Marxism as if by kingly fiat. When one does take Marxism seriously as an *intellectual stance,* Kolakowski tells us that "a forteriori historical materialism does not determine whether ...Pascal's philosophy is to be taken as an expression of bourgeois thought, or something else again."[16] While it would be difficult to develop a Marxist angelogy, "the fact is that within the boundaries of science, where various styles of thinking and various types of methodology can very well co-exist and compete, the borderline between Marxism and non-Marxism is extremely fluid."[17] This plea for a pluralist view of Marxist social science is made because:

> In sociological investigations, and even more so in philosophical ones, there is hardly a single perfectly unambiguous term. Vacillations in meaning are inherited by the most fundamental theses of a doctrine; none can be regarded as precise. If terms such as "matter," "social consciousness," "cognition," "superstructure," "causal determination," "relations of production," and so on are not clear, it follows that no methodological rules and no assertions of the theory in which they are involved have a precisely defined meaning.[18]

Kolakowski concludes "the same, or nearly the same, stock of factual knowledge lends itself to a great number of *well-founded* and rationally justified—though radically different interpretations."[19]

As a consequence, the principle of historical materialism must be formulated in "general terms." "It is...extremely harmful to interpret this principle as holding that fundamental class structure [in Marx's sense] determines *unequivocally* all other divisions in the social institutionalist intellectual life of society throughout the entire history of mankind."[20]

Now, of course, it is not at all clear that the Marxism of the "Office" was the result of its capture by forces who insisted upon fashioning Marxism into a "political or religious phenomenon rather than as a science" just as it is not clear that John Stuart Mill's claim that the prevailing image of Benthamite utilitarianism was the result of "misconceptions" concerning the greatest happiness principle. Marx and Bentham possessed one view of society, and Kolakowski and Mill begin to appreciate another. There are journeymen who continue to accept the authority of their pontiff's vision, and there are those who do not.

What model of citizenship does Kolakowski draw from his reformulated Marxism? Once the Marxist model of class solidarity enforced by the "Office" is even partially challenged, a new kind of citizen emerges. Kolakowski's foil is not the privatistic citizen of the American post-liberal but the "consistent" one. A consistent citizen "will always be proud to cooperate with the secret police, knowing it to be necessary to the existence of the state, to its glory and growth. To prove this is so is the easiest thing in the world and every citizen who hesitates to write systematically to the secret police informing on his neighbors is surely inconsistent."[21] However, the citizen moved by consistency in the name of fraternity does not produce comradeship since he can hardly "object to imposing our idea by means of war, aggression, provocation, blackmail, assassination, intimidation, terror, murder or torture."[22] The result is not fraternity but the worst form of atomization, individual quiescence based upon fear with a dose of spite.

Compare Kolakowski's description of the ideal citizen to that of Forster's:

> The race of those who vacillate and are soft, the inconsistent people, precisely those who happily eat steak at dinner and are totally incapable of slaughtering a chicken; those who do not wish to contravene the laws of the land yet do not denounce others to the secret police; those who go to war but in a hopeless situation surrender as prisoners rather than die in a last-ditch fight; those who prize frankness but cannot bring themselves to tell a famous painter that his work is terrible, nervously uttering words of praise which they do not mean—continues to be one of the greatest sources of hope that possibly the human species will somehow survive.[23]

No heroes here—not even those stamped with republican virtue or existential ebullience. Yet, when Kolakowski tells the reader that "total consistency is tantamount in practice to fanaticism, while inconsistency is the source of tolerance" we become aware that he has a citizen in mind more morally conscious than the privatistic model of the autonomous citizen. Of course, where Forster was to leave the relationship between friendship and the political order hanging in some problematical union, we should not be surprised to find Kolakowski less vexed. There are "elementary situations" in which the limits of inconsistency are reached. The praise of inconsistency must also be inconsistent and Kolakowski wraps up his ode to the reluctant believer in such a neat dialectic that one wonders whether the consistent citizen is not to be recalled after all:

> For let us carefully bear in mind that to be consistent in inconsistency means to contradict by an act (the application of a certain consistency) something the affirmation of which (the affirmation of inconsistency) is the substance of that....To this extent, therefore, we mold our praise of inconsistency to a perfect form, protesting against the practice of inconsistency in its perfect form.[24]

No doubt some will find Forster's formulation preferable to Kolakowski's, and vice versa. However, the point is that the broad outlines of both, citizens modeled after the concept of friendship, is a different perspective and one that needs exploration. Naturally there will be those who will speculate if widespread friendship is possible in liberal societies. My own inclination is that if it is not, then it is not possible anywhere.

Does friendship provide the missing part that completes the dialectic of liberal theory? Does it successfully connect liberalism's scientific and utopian elements? I think, with important reservations, the answer may be yes. Little is known about the sociology of friendship, but some additional analytic features beyond these comments can be suggested.

One of the most central features of friendship is its noninstrumental character. Consider the likely response to the question "why did you do that?" from one who has just done some task for a friend. Perhaps the action performed was a simple everyday favor such as babysitting, perhaps it was some act of consolation, perhaps it was even some action bordering on the truly supererogatory. In any case, if a friend were asked to explore his motivation, he or she might answer: "...because X is my friend." If pressed, the response might produce: "...because that is what friends are for." The circularity of such answers does not indicate any really mysterious quality about friendship. What it does suggest is that friendship moves beyond instrumental calculations in personal relationships. It can best be understood outside a model of utility maximization, even outside a model of duty. Perhaps friendship can best be understood in the context of a sense of grace. A secularization of this concept leaves a residue that makes an approriate analogy. Grace is a characterization of relationships of special decency, relationships that freely dispense kindness and affection. In functional terms the religious use of the concept is helpful. The emphasis upon its capacities for moral renewal or nurture do not contain the frightening overtones that characterize so much of post-liberal thought.

All this is not meant to romanticize friendship. Grace has of necessity an evanescent quality; it appears out of the ordinary character of everyday existence only to recede again. In endeavoring to "keep a friend" an instrumental cast of mind can develop. Friends can, and indeed do, drift apart. Many potential friendships do not quite complete their development. And who can deny that all social configurations have a base of coercion? In the context of friendship that base may be small, perhaps a gentle psychological tug, a fear of loss that is stronger in one party than in another.

Yet all of this discussion indicates that friendship may be a better model for a revised pluralism than the attempts of Dahl and Lowi. Dahl could not find a way to move beyond the utility maximizer. Lowi's objections to "interest group" liberalism were so intensely felt that he offered a liberal syndicalism. The concept of friendship as delicate as it is, is no less unstable than the elements of the pluralist vision now available. But most important, the concept introduces a social element to liberalism's utopianism without denying scientific premises.

However, it was stated that there were reservations, and it is in keeping with a limited sympathy with the post-liberals that this work should end with these considerations. There is the objection that the concept of friendship rests too squarely with a conventional liberal (or to state it harshly, bourgeois) view of reality. Friendship, after all, is a voluntary social relationship. It hopes to both "stand above" the social order and at the same surreptitiously partake of it. Its base as an organizing principle in society is limited, and perhaps it is as individually utopian as its precursors. The new liberal speaks of friendship as the old one did of rights. Meanwhile, people starve, are pushed around by corporations, and suffer from the thousand affronts that a racist and sexist society condones by its inaction. The issue here is not, however, whether friendship is a liberal principle. I admit to that. The issue is whether friendship can recapture liberalism's utopianism in a politically and socially meaningful fashion. The praxis is quite fragile but it does exist. Forster's contention that friendship is accidental is not totally correct. It is best to state the case in negative terms. Situations can be imagined in which a culture of self-absorption nearly wipes it out. Or, racism can so infect social relationships that friendship is very limited. Or, ideas of sexual inequality can be so severe as to prevent men and women from establishing friendships. Social policy in the service of the utopian premise can work to create conditions under which friendships would indeed be possible. Such effort would not be, I hope, in the manner of welfare liberalism which seeks stability through psychic equality and equality of condition but rather in the context of imaginative reform. There is a caveat, however, and a risk of the charge of conservatism in just mentioning it. Friendship indeed is a relationship not designed for a penciling in on the blueprints of the social engineer. An awareness of this truth need not be an invitation to complacency in regard to social problems but a caution, a limiting vision within the context of reform.

There remains a serious objection, one which conservatives have voiced since the inception of the liberal idea in history. Are there relationships that lie beneath friendships in society—firmer relationships which do not quite fit the model outlined—which may, in fact, silently sustain them? This discussion does not mention the family, let alone the religious question which Daniel Bell has raised. Let us just say that it does not seem impossible that liberalism is incapable of dealing with these concerns.

My final reservation takes the form of a query. Is the concept of friendship itself not really a resolution to the historical problems of liberalism but an ideological efflorescence, a tiny reformulation, the remains of a crystallization of the truly final "fag end" of liberalism?

NOTES

1. Isaiah Berlin, *Two Concepts of Liberty* (Oxford: Oxford University Press, 1958), p. 57.

2. Lionel Trilling, *E. M. Forster* (Norwalk, Conn.: New Directions Books, 1943), p. 13.

3. E. M. Forster, *Two Cheers for Democracy* (London: Edward Arnold, 1951), p. 67.

4. Ibid.

5. Ibid., p. 68.

6. E. M. Forster, *Abinger Harvest* (New York: Harcourt, Brace and World, 1936), pp. 23-24.

7. Ibid., p. 26.

8. Forster, *Two Cheers for Democracy*, p. 47.
9. Ibid., p. 68.
10. Ibid., p. 83.
11. Ibid., p. 79.
12. Ibid., p. 83-84.
13. Ibid., p. 84.
14. Leszek Kolakowski, *Toward a Marxist Humanism*, trans., Jane Zielenko Peel (New York: Grove Press, 1968), p. 174.
15. Ibid.
16. Ibid., pp. 183-84.
17. Ibid., p. 184.
18. Ibid.
19. Ibid., p. 182.
20. Ibid., p. 212.
21. Ibid.
22. Ibid., p. 213.
23. Ibid.
24. Ibid.

Bibliography

Adams, John. *The Works of John Adams.* Edited by Charles Francis Adams. New York: G. P. Putnam's Sons, 1907.

Aristotle. *The Politics of Aristotle.* Edited by Ernest Barker. New York: Oxford University Press, 1962.

Aron, Raymond. *An Essay on Freedom.* New York: World Publishing Co., Inc., 1970.

Austin, J. L. *Sense and Sensibilia.* New York: Oxford University Press, 1966.

Ayer, A. J. *The Problem of Knowledge.* New York: Penguin Books, Inc., 1955.

Bailyn, Bernard. *The Ideological Origins of the American Revolution.* Cambridge, Mass.: Harvard University Press, 1967.

Barber, Benjamin R. *Superman and Common Man.* New York: Praeger Pubs., 1971.

Barry, Brian. *The Liberal Theory of Justice.* Oxford: Oxford University Press, 1973.

Baskin, Darryl. *American Pluralist Democracy: A Critique.* New York: D. Van Nostrand Co., 1971.

Baier, Kurt. "The Justification of Government Authority." *Journal of Philosophy* 69 (1972): 700-16.

Bay, Christian. "Civil Disobedience: Prerequisite for Democracy in Mass Society." In *Political Theory and Social Change.* Edited by David Spitz, pp. 163-84. New York: Atherton Press, 1967.

———. "Needs, Wants and Political Legitimacy." *Canadian Journal of Political Science* 1 (1968): 240-59.

———. "Politics and Pseudo-Politics: A Critical Evaluation of ———. Some Behavioral Literature." *American Political Science Review 59* (1965): 39-51.

Bell, Daniel. *The Cultural Contradictions of Capitalism.* New York: Basic Books, Inc., 1976.

______."The Public Household." *Public Interest* 37 (1974): 29-68.

______."Meritocracy and Equality." *Public Interest* 41 (1972): 58-59.

Berlin, Isaiah. *Four Essays on Liberty.* Oxford: Oxford University Press, 1969.

______.*Two Concepts of Liberty.* Oxford: Oxford University Press, 1958.

Berman, Marshall. *The Politics of Authenticity.* New York: Atheneum Pubs., 1972.

Bloom, Allan. "Leo Strauss: September 20, 1899–October 18, 1973." *Political Theory* 2 (1974): 372-92.

Boorstein, Daniel. *The Americans: The Democratic Experience.* New York: Random House, Inc., 1974.

Chapman, John W. "The Political Theory of Pluralism." In *Voluntary Associations.* Edited by J. Roland Pennock and John W. Chapman, pp. 87-118. New York: Atherton Press, 1969.

Clor, Harry M. "American Democracy and the Challenge of Radical Democracy." In *How Democratic Is America?* Edited by Robert A. Goldwin, pp. 77-108. Chicago: Rand McNally & Co., 1969.

Coleman, Frank M. *Hobbes in America.* Toronto: University of Toronto Press, 1977.

Conolly, William. *The Bias of Pluralism.* New York: Atherton Press, 1969.

Coser, Lewis. "Greedy Organizations." *European Journal of Sociology* 8 (1967): 146-215.

______ and Howe, Irving. *The New Conservatives: A Critique from the Left.* New York: Quadrangle, 1973.

Dahl, Robert. *After the Revolution: Authority in the Good Society.* New Haven: Yale University Press, 1970.

______.*A Preface to Democratic Theory.* Chicago: University of Chicago Press, 1956.

______.*Who Governs?* New Haven: Yale University Press, 1961.

Devoly, John. *Liberalism and Social Action.* New York: Capricorn Books, 1963.

Douglass, Frederick. *The Life and Writings of Frederick Douglass.* Edited by Philip Foner. New York: International Pubs. Co., 1950.

Dunn, John. "The Politics of Locke in England and America in the Eighteenth Century." In *John Locke: Problems and Prospects.* Edited by John W. Yolton. Cambridge: Cambridge University Press, 1969.

Eckstein, Harry. *Division and Cohesion in Democracy: A Study of Norway.* Princeton, N.J.: Princeton University Press, 1966.

Edelstein, Joel C. "Mobilization, Immobilization and Spontaneous Forms of Fascism." *Politics and Society* 2 (1972): 263-75.

Elkins, Stanley, and McKitrick, Eric. "The Founding Fathers: Young Men of the Revolution." *Political Science Quarterly* 76 (1961): 181-216.

Engels, Frederick. *The Origin of the Family, Private Property and the State.* New York: International Pubs. Co., 1972.

Euben, J. Peter. "Political Science and Political Silence." In *Power and Community: Dissenting Essays in Political Science.* Edited by Philip Green and Sanford Levinson, pp. 3-58. New York: Random House, Inc., 1969.

Forster, E. M. *Abinger Harvest.* New York: Harcourt, Brace and World, 1936.

______. *Two Cheers for Democracy.* London: Edward Arnold, 1951.

Fox, Alan. "Is Equality a Necessity?" *Dissent* 1 (1975): 50-62.

Frankfurt, Harry G. "The Anarchism of Robert Paul Wolff." *Political Theory* 1 (1973): 405-14.

Friedman, Richard. "On the Concept of Authority in Political Philosophy." In *Concept in Social and Political Philosophy.* Edited by Richard E. Flathman, pp. 121-145. New York: Macmillan Publishing Co., Inc., 1973.

Fuller, R. Buckminster. *Operating Manual for Spaceship Earth.* New York: Pocket Books, 1970.

Galbraith, John Kenneth. *Economics and the Public Purpose.* Boston: Houghton Mifflin, 1973.

Girvetz, Harry. *The Evolution of Liberalism.* New York: Collier Books, 1963.

Gouldner, Alvin. *The Coming Crisis of Western Sociology.* New York: Avon Books, 1970.

Green, T. H. *Lectures on the Principles of Political Obligation.* Ann Arbor: University of Michigan Press, 1967.

Gregor, James A. *The Fascist Persuasion in Radical Politics.* Princeton, N.J.: Princeton University Press, 1974.

Hartz, Louis. *The Liberal Tradition in America.* New York: Harcourt, Brace and World, 1955.

Hayden, Tom. "Welfare Liberalism and Social Change." *Dissent* (1966): 75-87.

Himmelfarb, Gertrude. *On Liberty and Liberalism.* New York: Knopf, Inc., 1974.

Hobbes, Thomas. *Leviathan.* Edited by C. B. Macpherson. New York: Penguin, 1968.

Hobhouse, C. T. *Liberalism.* Oxford: Oxford University Press, 1971.

Hofstadter, Richard. *The American Political Tradition and the Men Who Made It.* New York: Vintage Books, 1953.

Hondrich, Ted. "The Use of the Basic Proposition of *A Theory of Justice.*" *Mind* 84 (1975): 63-78.

Jefferson, Thomas. *Notes on the State of Virginia.* Edited by William Peden. Chapel Hill: University of North Carolina Press, 1965.

Jouvenal, Bertrand de. *Sovereignty.* Chicago: University of Chicago Press, 1957.

Kant, Immanuel. *Foundations of the Metaphysics of Morals.* Translated by Lewis White Beck. Indianapolis: Library of Liberal Arts, 1959.

Kariel, Henry. "Making Scenes in a Liberal Society." *Massachusetts Review* 2 (1970): 223-55.

______.*Open Systems: Arenas for Political Action.* Itasca, Ill.: F. E. Peacock Pubs., Inc., 1969.

______.*The Promise of Politics.* Englewood Cliffs, N.J.: Prentice-Hall, Inc., 1971.

Kaufman, Arnold. *The Radical Liberal.* New York: Simon and Schuster, Inc., 1968.

Kolakowski, Leszek. *Toward a Marxist Humanism.* Translated by Jane Zielenko Peel. New York: Grove Press, 1968.

Kornhauser, William. *The Politics of Mass Society.* Glencoe, Ill.: Free Press, 1959.

Kristol, Irving. "About Equality." *Commentary* 54 (1972): 41-59.

______."Comment: New Right, New Left." *Public Interest* 30 (1966): 3-7.

______."Corporate Capitalism in America." *Public Interest* 41 (1975): 124-41.

______.*The Democratic Idea in America.* New York: Harper & Row Publishers, Inc., 1972.

______."'When virtue loses all her loveliness'—Some Reflections on Capitalism and the Free Society." *Public Interest* 21 (1970): 3-15.

Lawson, Alan R. *The Failure of Independent Liberalism.* New York: Capricorn Books. 1971.

Lenin, V. I. "The Immediate Tasks of the Soviet Government." In *The Lenin Anthology.* Edited by Robert C. Tucker. New York: Norton and Co., Inc., 1975.

Letwin, Shirley Robin. *The Pursuit of Certainty.* Cambridge: Cambridge University Press, 1965.

Locke, John. *Two Treatises of Government.* Edited by Peter Laslett. New York: Mentor, 1960.

Lowi, Theodore J. *American Government: Incomplete Conquest.* Hinsdale, Ill.: Dryden Press, 1976.

______.*The Politics of Disorder.* New York: Norton and Co., Inc., 1971.

Macdonald, Margaret. "The Language of Political Theory." In *Logic and Language.* First and Second Series. Edited by Antony Flew, pp. 174-93. Garden City, New York: Doubleday & Co., Inc., 1965.

Macpherson, C. B. *Democratic Theory: Essays in Retrival.* Oxford: Oxford University Press, 1973.

Marcel, Gabriel. *The Decline of Wisdom.* London: Harvill, 1959.

Marcuse, Herbert. *An Essay on Liberation.* Boston: Beacon Press, 1969.

______, Wolff, Robert Paul, and Moore, Barrington. *Critique of Pure Tolerance.* Boston: Beacon Press, 1963.

Marx, Karl. *Capital.* Edited by Lewis S. Feuer. Garden City, N.Y.: Doubleday & Co., Inc., 1959.

Mason, Gene. "1984 Revisited." In *1984 Revisited: Prospects for American Politics.* Edited by Robert Paul Wolff. New York: Knopf, Inc., 1973.

McWilliams, Wilson Carey. *The Idea of Fraternity in America.* Berkeley: University of California Press, 1973.

Mill, John Stuart. *On Liberty.* Edited by Gertrude Himmelfarb. New York: Penguin, 1976.

______, and Taylor, Harriet. *Essays on Sex Equality.* Edited by Alice S. Rossi. Chicago: University of Chicago Press, 1970.

Moore, G. E. *Principia Ethica.* Cambridge: Cambridge University Press, 1966.

Morgan, Edmund S., ed. *Puritan Political Ideas.* Indianapolis: Bobbs-Merrill Co., Inc., 1965.

Nisbet, Robert. *Community and Power.* New York: Oxford University Press, 1962.

______."The Pursuit of Equality." *Public Interest* 35 (1974): 103-20.

______.*Twilight of Authority.* New York: Oxford University Press, 1975.

Paine, Thomas. *The Essential Thomas Paine.* Edited by Sidney Hook. New York: New American Library, 1969.

Parsons, J. E. Jr. "J. S. Mill's Conditional Liberalism in Perspective." *Polity 5 (1972): 147-68.*

Pocock, J. G. A. *Politics, Language and Time.* New York: Atheneum Pubs., 1973.

Pranger, Robert J. *The Eclipse of Citizenship.* New York: Holt, Rinehart & Winston, Inc., 1968.

Rawls, John. *A Theory of Justice.* Cambridge, Mass.: Harvard University Press, 1971.

Reiman, Jeffrey H. *In Defense of Political Philosophy.* New York: Harper & Row Publishers, Inc., 1972.

Robbins, Caroline. "Algernon Sidney's Discourses." *William and Mary Quarterly* Third Series (1947): 267-92.

______.*The Eighteenth Century Commonwealthman.* Cambridge, Mass.: Harvard University Press, 1959.

Rogin, Michael Paul. *The Intellectuals and McCarthy.* Cambridge, Mass.: M.I.T. Press, 1967.

Rossiter, Clinton. *Conservatism in America.* New York: Macmillan Publishing Co., 1955.

______.Ed. *Federalist Papers.* New York: Mentor, 1961.

Rousseau, Jean Jacques. *The First and Second Discourses.* Edited by Roger D. Masters. New York: St. Martin's Press, Inc. 1969.

Sabine, George. "The Two Democratic Traditions." *Philosophical Review* 61 (1952): 451-74.

Santayana, George. *Dominations and Powers.* New York: Scribner's Sons, 1951.

Schaar, John H. "The Case for Patriotism." *New American Review* 17 (1973): 59-99.

______and Francis M. Carney, "The Circles of Watergate Hell." *New American Review* 21 (1974): 1-41.

______."Legitimacy in the Modern State." In *Power and Community.* Edited by Philip Green and Sanford Levinson, pp. 276-327. New York: Vintage, 1970.

______."Power and Purity." *New American Review* 19 (1974): 152-79.

Seidler, Murray. "The Socialist Party and American Unionism." *Midwest Journal of Political Science* 3 (1961): 207-36.

Skinner, B. F. *Beyond Freedom and Dignity.* New York: Bantam Books, Inc., 1972.

Strauss, Leo. *Liberalism Ancient and Modern.* New York: Basic Books, Inc., 1968.

Sumner, William Graham. *The Conquest of Spain and Other Essays.* Edited by Murray Polner. Chicago: Henry Regnery Co., 1965.

______.*The Essays of William Graham Sumner.* Edited by Albert Galloway Keller and Maurice R. Davie. New Haven: Yale University Press, 1934.

Talmon, J. L. *The Rise of Totalitarian Democracy.* Boston: Beacon Press, 1952.

Thomas, John L. "Romantic Reform in America, 1815–1865." *American Quarterly* 17 (1965): 656-81.

Tocqueville, Alexis de. *The Old Regime and the French Revolution.* Translated by Stuart Gilbert. Garden City, New York: Doubleday & Co., Inc., 1955.

Trilling, Lionel. *E. M. Forster.* Norfolk, Conn.: New Direction Books, 1943.

Truman, David. "The American System in Criris." *Political Science Quarterly* 74 (1959): 481-97.

Turnbull, Colin. *The Mountain People.* New York: Simon & Schuster, Inc., 1972.

Walzer, Michael. "Politics in the Welfare State." In *Essential Works of Socialism.* Edited by Irving Howe, pp. 809-34. New York: Bantam Books, Inc., 1971.

Wolfe, Alan. "Conditions for Community: The Case of Old Westbury College." In *Power and Community.* Edited by Philip Green and Sanford Levinson, pp. 195-222. New York: Vintage, 1970.

______."New Directions in the Marxist Theory of Politics." *Politics and Society* 4 (1974): 131-60.

Wolff, Robert Paul. *The Autonomy of Reason.* New York: Harper & Row Publishers, Inc., 1973.

______.*In Defense of Anarchism.* New York: Harper & Row Publishers, Inc., 1970.

______.*The Poverty of Liberalism.* Boston: Beacon Press, 1968.

______."There's Nobody Here But Us Persons." *Philosophical Quarterly 5 (1973-1974): 125-41.*

Wolin, Sheldon. "Paradigms and Political Theories." In *Politics and Experience.* Edited by Preston King and B. C. Parekh, pp. 125-52. Cambridge: Cambridge University Press, 1968.

______.*Politics and Vision.* Boston: Little Brown & Co., 1960.

Wood, Gordon S. *The Creation of the American Republic, 1776-1787.* Chapel Hill: University of North Carolina Press, 1969.

Woodward, C. Vann *Tom Watson: Agrarian Rebel.* New York: Macmillan Publishing Co., Inc., 1938.

Zolberg, Aristide. "Moments of Madness." In *The Politics and Society Reader.* Edited by Ira Katznelson, pp. 232-56. New York: McKay, 1974.

Index

Adams, John, 221, 223, 229
Adams, Samuel, 222
After the Revolution (Dahl), 94
Anarchy, State and Utopia (Nozick), 56, 66
Aquinas, Saint Thomas, 110, 195
Arendt, Hannah, 156-57, 195
Aristotle, 6, 40-43, 90, 195, 200, 205
Austin, J.L., 186
Autonomy of Reason (Wolff), 164, 176-80
Ayer, A.J., 110-11, 177

Bachrach, Peter, 209
Bailyn, Bernard, 222
Bay, Christian, 209
Bell, Daniel, 4, 6, 251; on individualism, 237-239; on religion, 251; as Whig, 8-9, 126-27
Bentham, Jeremy, 12, 72-73; on reform, 141, 143; and scientific liberalism, 21-22, 56, 111-13, 247; on utilitarianism, 165-166, 178-80
Berlin, Isaiah, 76-78, 205, 240
Bernstein, Eduard, 112
Burke, Edmund, 56, 90, 205, 213, 239; *Reflection on the French Revolution*, 56

Calhoun, John C., 92-93
Calvin, John, 185, 200
Capitalism, 13, 179, 213; justifications of, 129-130, 133, 142, 240; and scientific liberalism, 114, 119, 121-23
Chase, Stuart, 5
Citizenship, 36-37, 205-07, 244, 247-49
Community, 172-73, 198, 208-10, 237-38
Coser, Lewis, 144

Dahl, Robert, 4-12 passim; on citizenship, 206, 231; on equality, 97-99; as pluralist liberal, 23, 92-102, 106, 125, 173. Works: *After the Revolution*, 94; *Preface to Democratic Theory A*, 94
Das Kapital (Marx), 16
Dewey, John, 5, 12-13, 19, 50-51, 168
Discourses Concerning Government (Sidney), 222-23
Discourses, The (Machiavelli), 224
Douglass, Frederick, 219-20

Eclipse of Citizenship, The (Pranger), 208
Eighteen Forty Four Manuscripts (Marx), 146
Eighteenth Brumaire (Marx), 146
End of Liberalism, The (Lowi), 101-2
Engels, Frederick, 74-145, 149, 197

Equality: in Dahl, 97-99; in Kristol, 133-35; in Rawls, 32-34; 45
Evolution of Liberalism (Girvetz), 12

Fanon, Frantz, 4
Forster, E.M., 216, 241-44, 248-50
Fourier, Charles, 4, 144-45, 148, 153, 237
Fraternity, 185-92, 196, 198, 244-46
Freud, Sigmund, 7, 195
Friedman, Richard, 142, 164, 198-99, 211
Friendship, 216, 245-46, 249-51
Fuller, Buckminster, 124

Galbraith, John Kenneth, 216
Girvetz, Harry, 12-13
Gratitude, 217-20
Green, T.H., 19, 50, 68
Gross, Bertram, 120
Ground of the Metaphysic of Morals (Kant), 176

Harrington, Michael, 120-21
Hart, H.L.A., 159
Hartz, Louis, 3, 7, 23, 58, 93, 122, 126-27
Hayden, Tom, 209
Hayek, Frederick, 123, 129
Hegel, G.F.W., 4, 195
Heinlein, Robert, 239-40
History of European Models, The (Lecky), 236
Hobbes, Thomas, 12, 24, 30, 172, 186, 193, 199, 238; on contract, 58-59, 180-81; on gratitude, 215-16; on social conflict, 20-21
Hobhouse, L.T., 11, 19, 49-50
Hofstadter, Richard, 21
Hoover, Herbert, 128
Hume, David, 30, 125

Idea of Fraternity in America, The (McWilliams), 184-203, 211
In Defense of Anarchism (Wolff), 163-64, 172-74, 178
Individualism, 11-12, 15, 21, 24, 54, 118, 164-65, 174-75; in Tocqueville, 101

Jefferson, Thomas, 15, 23, 223, 227, 228-29
Jouvenal, Bertrand de, 105

Kant, Immanuel, 15, 24, 164, 176-177, 178; *Ground of the Metaphysic of Morals*, 176
Kariel, Henry, 4-11 passim; on citizenship, 210; on pluralism, 24; as utopian liberal, 144-47, 151-55, 158
Kaufman, Arnold, 142
Kohlberg, Lawrence, 42
Kolakowski, Leszek, 246-48
Kornhauser, William, 103-4
Kristol, Irving, 4-12 passim, 113, 126-37, 237, 239; equality in 133-35

Lawson, R. Allan, 5-6
Lecky, W.E.H., 236-37
Lenin, V.I., 79-80
Liberalism: form of General Will in, 46-48, 50-51; pluralist liberalism, 22-23, 86-94, 101, 104-6, 125, 131-33, 237; scientific liberalism, 20, 112-14, 122-25, 237; utopian liberalism, 23-25, 150, 158-59, 163-64, 184, 237; varieties of, 18-25; welfare liberalism, 18-20, 45-51, 237
Lincoln, Abraham, 214-15, 217, 225-27, 230
Lipset, Seymour, 125

Locke, John, 13, 41, 57, 61, 72, 113, 134, 144, 197, 220, 229, 240; citizenship in, 205; civil society, origin of, 141; on contract, 178; on natural law, 195; philosophy, task of, 110; utopian premise in; 14-15
Lowi, Theodore, 5, 23, 101-106, 237-238, 250. Works: *The End of Liberalism* 101-02; *Politics of Disorder*, 102-6

MacDonald, Margaret, 110
Machiavelli, Niccolo, 224
Macpherson, C.B., 4, 10, 58, 239; classification of liberalism, 17-18, 68-69; on freedom, 72-82
McWilliams, Wilson Carey, 4-12 passim, 213, 184-203, 211. *The Idea of Fraternity in America*, 184-203, 211
Madison, James, 14, 23, 29, 92, 102, 125, 156, 229, 231, 238
Malcolm X, 227, 228
Marcel, Gabriel, 217-18
Marcuse, Herbert 4-12 passim, 56, 112, 237; *critique of liberalism of* 147-53
Marx, Karl, 4, 6, 10, 21, 93, 123, 153, 179-80, 237, 240, 247; on class, 105; on classification of liberalism, 16-18; critique of utopian socialists and, 74; revolution and, 145-46, 149-50; on science, 110-13
Marxism, 16, 83, 125, 131, 137, 142, 150, 179, 246; on General Will, 47; patriotism and, 211-12, 221; Stalinism and, 246-47
Mill, James, 12, 14-15, 21-22, 72, 111
Mill, John Stuart, 56, 72-73, 112, 175, 247; critique by Macpherson of, 17, 68; critique by Wolff of, 166-70; utopian premise of, 15, 143-44, 240; on virtue and excellence, 40-42; and welfare liberalism, 18-19, 51
Mills, C.W., 240-41
Milton, John, 24, 56, 143, 240
Moore, G.E., 193
Mumford, Lewis, 5

Nietzsche, Frederick, 153-55, 159, 176, 237
Nisbet, Robert, 86-87, 207-8, 237
Nozick, Robert, 4-12 passim, 144, 184 *Anarchy, State and Utopia*, 56, 66; on individualism, 97-98, 123, 237-38; and scientific liberalism, 22, 55-82, 113.

Old Regime and the French Revolution (Tocqueville), 87-93
O'Connor, Flannery, 245
On Liberty (Mill, J.S.), 24

Paine, Thomas, 23, 222-24, 229, 230
Passage to India (Forster), 242-43
Patriotism, 211-15
Politics of Disorder (Lowi), 102-6
Pluralist liberalism, 22-24, 86-94; critiques of, 91, 125, 131-33, 237; group formation in, 104-6
Political Man (Lipset), 125
Poverty of Liberalism, The (Wolff), 164-165, 171, 173, 178-79
Plato, 110, 195, 199, 200, 237
Populist Democracy, 94, 133
Pranger, Robert J., 208
Preface to Democratic Theory, A (Dahl), 94

Prince, The (Machiavelli), 224
Proudhon, Pierre-Joseph, 43, 103

Rawls, John, 4-12 passim, 20, 28-52, 55, 68, 97, 184, 211, 216, 237-38; envy in, 44-45; on equality, 32-34; virtue and equality in, 40-43
Reflection on the French Revolution (Burke), 56
Rogin, Michael Paul, 93
Roosevelt, Franklin D., 4, 127-28, 217
Rossiter, Clinton, 113
Rousseau, Jean Jacques, 4, 110-11, 184, 237, 239, 240; on community, 95, 96, 99; on contract, 178; citizenship in, 205, 213; on General Will, 47-48

Santayana, George, 47, 55, 185
Sartre, Jean Paul, 4, 153
Schaar, John, 4-12 passim, 244; individualism in, 55, 112; patriotism, 205-31, 239, 241, 244
Schumpeter, Joseph, 6, 69, 123, 131
Scientific liberalism, 20-22, 112-14
Sidney, Algernon, 222-23
Skinner, B.F., 112, 124, 143, 171, 178
Smith, Adam, 41, 56, 111, 113; on capitalism, 122, 131, 143; on conflict, 14
Social Darwinism, 22, 63-64, 73, 111, 113, 121, 124
Sontag, Susan, 152
Sorel, Georges, 5, 158, 215
Spencer, Herbert, 143, 216, 240; as scientific liberal, 21, 122-23; utopianism in, 63, 73
Stalin, Josef, 80-81, 98, 113
Stern, Fritz, 4-5
Strauss, Leo, 195, 206-7
Subjection of Women The (Mill, J.S.), 19
Sumner, William Graham, 21, 63, 113-23, 127-29, 135

Theory of Democratic Elitism, The (Bachrach), 209
Theory of Justice, A (Rawls), 20, 28-52
Thomas, John L., 74-75
Tocqueville, Alexis de, 56, 98, 102, 125; freedom in, 87-93; *Old Regime and The French Revolution,* 87-93; pluralism in, 72-73; on religion, 142; self-interest in, 98, 102, 238-39.
Trilling, Lionel, 14, 241-42
Truman, David, 102, 106
Turnbull, Colin, 60-62, 65
Two Concepts of Liberty (Berlin), 77

Utopia, 14-16, 66-71, 74, 76, 96, 120, 144; in Nozick, 58, 65-67; in Skinner, 124
Utopian liberalism, 23-25, 150, 158-59, 163-64, 237

Virtue, 220-23, 228-29; in Rawls, 40-43, 45

Walden II (Skinner), 124
Watson, Tom, 219-20, 228
Weber, Max, 101, 112-13, 131, 156, 239
Welfare liberalism, 11, 18-20, 45-51, 237
Whiggery, 237; in America, 122, 126-27, 130; as model of politics,

22-23, 224, 239; and neo-conservatives, 131, 134-37
White, Orion, 155-57
Williams, Roger, 24, 201-2
Wolfe, Alan, 46, 209
Wolff, Robert Paul, 124, 184; and critique of liberalism, 163-81; as utopian liberal, 4, 6, 25, 237-38. Works: *Autonomy of Reason,* 164, 176-80, *In Defense of Anarchism*, 163-64, 172-74, 178, *The Poverty of Liberalism*, 164-65, 171, 173, 178-79
Wolin, Sheldon, 14, 111, 208

Zolberg, Aristide, 4-12 passim, 147-49, 152-53